Beginning UNIX™
Second Edition

Tutorial Guides in Computing and Information Systems

Series Editors
Professor David Howe, De Montfort University
Dr Martin Campbell-Kelly, University of Warwick

Other Titles in the Series

Software Project Planning
M. Cotterell and B. Hughes

Introduction to C++
D. Dench and B. Prior

Human Computer Interaction for Software Designers
Linda Macaulay

Information Systems: Strategy and Design
Chris Clare and Gordon Stuteley

Knowledge Engineering
P. Smith

Foundation Discrete Mathematics for Computing
D. J. Booth

Systems Analysis Techniques
Mary Prior and Barbara Robinson

Programming in C
J. R. Gray and B. Wendl

Beginning UNIX™
Second Edition

Mike Joy
Department of Computer Science
The University of Warwick
UK

INTERNATIONAL THOMSON COMPUTER PRESS
I(T)P™ An International Thomson Publishing Company

London • Bonn • Boston • Johannesburg • Madrid • Melbourne • Mexico City • New York • Paris
Singapore • Tokyo • Toronto • Albany, NY • Belmont, CA • Cincinnati, OH • Detroit, MI

Beginning UNIX™
Second Edition

Copyright © 1997 Mike Joy

I ⓉP A division of International Thomson Publishing Inc.
The ITP logo is a trademark under licence.

For more information, contact:

International Thomson Computer Press   International Thomson Computer Press
Berkshire House   20 Park Plaza
168-173 High Holborn   Suite 1001
London WC1V 7AA   Boston, MA 02116
UK   US

Imprints of International Thomson Publishing

International Thomson Publishing GmbH   International Thomson Publishing Asia
Königswinterer Straße 418   60 Albert Street #15-01
53227 Bonn   Albert Complex
Germany   Singapore 189969

Thomas Nelson Australia   International Thomson Publishing Japan
102 Dodds Street   Hirakawacho Kyowa Building, 3F
South Melbourne, 3205   2-2-1 Hirakawacho
Victoria   Chiyoda-ku, 102 Tokyo
Australia   Japan

Nelson Canada   International Thomson Editores
1120 Birchmount Road   Seneca, 53
Scarborough, Ontario   Colonia Polanco
Canada M1K 5G4   11560 Mexico D. F. Mexico

International Thomson Publishing South Africa International Thomson Publishing France
PO Box 2459   Tours Maine-Montparnasse
Halfway House   33 Avenue du Maine
1685 South Africa   75755 Paris Cedex 15
                                             France

British Library Cataloguing-in-Publication Data
A catalogue record for this book is available from the British Library

Library of Congress Cataloging-in-Publication Data
A catalog record for this book is available from the Library of Congress

First Printed 1997

ISBN 1-85032-263-5

Cover Designed by Crispin Goodall Design
Printed in the UK by Clays Ltd, St Ives plc

Contents

Preface   **x**

1 Introduction   **1**
   Screens and terminals   1
   Hardware and software   3
   Kernel and shell   4
   Files   5
   Bits, bytes, words and characters   6
   Input and output   7
   Networks   8
   Your local system   10
   History of UNIX   10
   Open systems   12
   Getting UNIX for free!   12
   Conventions used in this book   13

2 Getting started   **14**
   Usernames   14
   Logging in   15
   Typing in commands   15
   Finishing your session   16
   Commands and options   16
   Files   18
   The editor 'vi'   18
   Other editors   21
   Input and output streams   21
   Emergencies   28
   Pagers   28
   Electronic mail   29
   Communication with other users   30
   Pipes   31
   Scripts   32
   Here-documents   33
   Making copies of input and output   34
   Getting help   35
   Summary of utilities   37
   Problems   37

3 Files   **39**

The UNIX directory hierarchy 39

Filesystems 42

Manipulating files 43

'Dot' files 46

Groups 46

File access control 47

File contents 51

Text files 52

Printing files 58

File archives and file compression 59

Other relevant commands 60

Summary of utilities 62

Problems 63

4 Processes and devices   **64**

Processes 64

Foreground and background 66

Process control 66

Signals 67

Job control 67

Command history list 70

Running a job at a specific time 71

Running programs periodically 73

Big programs 74

Timing a program 74

Running programs in order 75

Environment 76

Global and local variables 78

Executable scripts 81

Quotes and escapes 83

Devices 84

Backquotes 86

Summary of utilities 87

Problems 88

5 Introduction to shells   **89**

Why do we need a shell? 89

Shell syntax 90

Types of shell command 91

Simple commands 92

Pipelines 92

Exit status 93

List commands 94

Arithmetic 95

Making decisions 98
Grouping commands 101
The 'if' statement 103
'For' loops 104
'While' and 'until' loops 105
Searching for files 107
Formatted output 109
Scripts which take arguments 111
Parameter expansion 113
Summary of utilities 117
Problems 117

6 **More on shells**												**118**
Simple arithmetic 118
Pattern matching 121
The 'case' statement 124
Entering and leaving the shell 126
More about writing scripts which require options 129
Symbolic links 131
Setting up terminals 132
Conventions used in UNIX file systems 134
Summary of utilities 136
Problems 136

7 **Advanced shell programming**										**138**
Sending and trapping signals 138
Functions 140
Aliases 142
The 'exec' mechanism 142
The 'eval' mechanism 143
Sending data across networks 144
Makefiles 147
Safe programming 149
Setting up a terminal 150
More on files 151
Miscellaneous utilities 153
Summary of utilities 155
Problems 155

8 **Regular expressions and filters**									**157**
Using filters 157
Collating sequence 158
Character-to-character transformation 158
Basic regular expressions 161
Extended regular expressions 163
Selecting lines according to their content 163

Stream editor 165
Choosing between these three filters 168
Splitting a file according to context 168
More on 'vi' 172
Summary of utilities 173
Problems 174

9   Awk   175
What is 'awk'? 175
Invoking 'awk' 176
Naming the fields 177
Formatted output 177
Patterns 181
Variables 182
Special variables 183
Arguments to 'awk' scripts 185
Arrays 187
Field and record separators 189
Functions 192
Perl 195
Problems 195

10 Internet and multimedia   198
Networks 198
Internet 200
World-Wide Web 202
Usenet news 202
Encryption and data security 203
FTP 204
Web browsers 206
HTML 206
Java 208
Other information services 208
X and GUIs 208
Locales and extended character sets 210
Text formatting and wordprocessing 210
Images 213
Audio 214
MIME 214
Legal issues 214

Answers to problems   217
Chapter 2 217
Chapter 3 218
Chapter 4 219
Chapter 5 219

Chapter 6 221
Chapter 7 224
Chapter 8 225
Chapter 9 225

Appendix – summary of utilities   **227**

Index   **231**

Preface

UNIX is an operating system which has seen dramatic growth in its popularity over the last few years, and is used by many universities and colleges, as well as in industry. This book is a *beginner's* guide to UNIX for students who have to *use* UNIX. No prior knowledge of programming is assumed, nor is any experience of using computers. We do, however, expect our audience to have a serious interest in computing, and a typical reader might be a student in the first year of a degree or HND course.

UNIX is more than just a computer operating system, it is a philosophy of programming. Learning UNIX involves becoming familiar not only with the commands it affords the user, but also with the methodology it employs. It is a very powerful tool in the hands of an experienced practitioner, but it can also be daunting for the novice. We introduce enough detail for the reader to be able to utilise the facilities in UNIX, but no more.

In 1993 an International Standard was published, known as 'POSIX.2', which specifies the constructs and commands which a UNIX system should have available to its users. This book follows that standard. Before 1993 several 'dialects' of UNIX grew up, and the new standard will not be available quickly on all systems – we indicate, where appropriate, the major differences between the standard and the older versions.

We discuss in this book *all* the basic constructs and commands of UNIX (as defined in POSIX.2), sufficient for the reader to be able to use each of them. We do not delve into any in fine detail – part of the UNIX philosophy is that such information is available 'online'. The reader who requires more sophisticated use of UNIX after reading this book will know how and where to find the extra information they need.

The recent rapid growth of networked communication and information services via the Internet has begun to revolutionise the way in which we use computers, and the accompanying technological advances have been immense. This new edition has been updated to take account of the many developments in computing and in information technology which have implications for a UNIX user.

To get the most from this book, you should have access to a UNIX computer system (or a PC running UNIX), as much of the text relies on you being able to try out examples.

Acknowledgements

Grateful thanks are due to several colleagues for commenting on draft versions of this book. In alphabetical order they are: Franc Buxton, Martin Campbell-Kelly, Jean Flower, Neil Fowler Wright, Matt Gibson, Ken Gowers, Steven Haeck, Jason Holloway, Nick Holloway, Michael Luck, Steve Matthews, Rod Moore, Roy Simmonds and Simon Stirley.

Changes incorporated in the second edition

This second edition of the book has been updated with extra examples and Chapter 1 has been brought up-to-date. Chapter 10 has been substantially re-written to reflect the tremendous impact the Internet has had on computing in the last couple of years. There are numerous minor changes and additions throughout the text.

Chapter 1

Introduction

OBJECTIVES

In this chapter you will learn:

- □ what UNIX is;

- □ basic computer concepts and terminology;

- □ the meanings of 'shell' and 'kernel';

- □ how UNIX and the POSIX standards evolved.

In the early 1950s, computers represented a technological breakthrough. Since then, computers have become a part of all our lives, and are present wherever we look. All these computers must be designed and programmed. To the student beginning his or her study of computers, this multitude of machines must be daunting.

In the last few years, however, one particular type of computer system has arisen which holds out the promise of a clear path through this maze. The name is UNIX. Since 1969 UNIX has grown from a research project to the fastest-growing system for medium and large machines. In the early days of UNIX, however, several 'dialects' arose; these are now being brought together under **POSIX**, a standard initiated by the **IEEE** and becoming a world standard.

Institute of Electrical and Electronics Engineers

POSIX consists of a number of interrelated standards, covering various aspects of UNIX systems. One of these, called **POSIX.2**, deals with the interface between the computer user and the UNIX system, that is the commands that users have available. This book is based around POSIX.2, and unless otherwise stated, everything which is introduced has been defined in that standard.

POSIX = 'Portable Operating System Interface'

UNIX has a reputation for being at times somewhat terse and unfriendly – this is true. Do not be put off – once you have mastered simple use of UNIX, you will find it a powerful tool well worth the initial effort.

Screens and terminals

In order to instruct a computer to perform a task we require a way to **input** that instruction. One way of doing this is to type the instructions on a typewriter-like **keyboard**. The computer will **output** messages on a television-like **screen** to tell you the results of those tasks. The word **terminal** is used for a piece of equipment which allows a computer user to communicate with a computer system, and includes a keyboard and a screen. There are two principal types of terminal in use today.

First are the so-called **dumb terminals** which still account for many such devices. A dumb terminal consists of a keyboard (of the 'QWERTY' variety, similar to a typewriter) and a screen. Sometimes called a **VDU**, a dumb terminal can display only the same sort of text and simple characters that a typewriter can. On the screen of this type of terminal will be a **cursor**, which will either be a block (a filled rectangle the size of a letter) or an underscore, which marks the point on the screen where anything you type will appear, and where any message the computer writes will begin.

VDU = 'Visual Display Unit'

Perhaps with a few extra capabilities, such as blinking and underlining

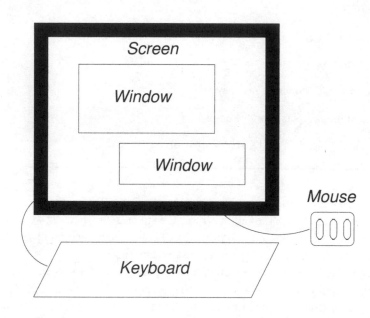

Figure 1.1   *A typical graphics terminal.*

The second type, which now represents a majority of terminals in use, comprises **graphics terminals** capable of more sophisticated output. These also have a keyboard and a screen, but the screen is a high-resolution display (usually colour), allowing lines and shading to be drawn as well as simple characters. A graphics terminal will also have a device, such as a **mouse**, whose purpose is to allow you to select and move items displayed on the screen. Usually a system is employed where the screen is divided up into rectangular areas called **windows**, with which you can communicate individually (see Figure 1.1). The terminal itself may be a **workstation** or a **PC**. In this book we will assume that you are using a dumb terminal – POSIX.2 does not address any issues related to graphics terminals. If you are using a graphics terminal, you can create a window which behaves as if it were itself a dumb terminal, having its own cursor. A graphics terminal will have a **global cursor** which moves each time you move the mouse; you can select which window the keyboard will communicate with by moving the global cursor so that it is within the chosen window. The windowing system most commonly used with UNIX machines is called **X**, and you may encounter terminals which use X, the most basic of these terminals is called an **X terminal**.

PC = 'Personal Computer'

The global cursor is often a cross or a small arrow

X is discussed in detail in Chapter 10

Figure 1.2   *A UNIX workstation screen using the 'Fvwm' window manager.*

The 'look and feel' of graphics terminals can vary enormously, as can the manner in which windows on a screen are manipulated. The software which controls the windows on a screen is called either a **window manager** or a **desktop manager**. The distinction between the two is somewhat blurred, but you would expect a desktop manager to have more features and capabilities than a window manager. Figures 1.2 and 1.3 are pictures of two real UNIX screens. For the moment, notice the *similarities*. Each has several windows, decorated with a **border** containing **buttons** which with the aid of the global cursor can be used to move the window on the screen, change its size, or destroy it. Each screen also contains other areas, including **icons** and buttons, some of which have borders similar to the windows.

These pictures are known as **screendumps**

Hardware and software

The **hardware** includes the terminal you are using to communicate with the system and the computers that make up that system. Connected to a computer system will be **devices** which are ancillary pieces of equipment over and above the computational electronics. Devices are usually pieces of communications equipment which allow a computer system to communicate with the rest of the world. The most obvious devices are terminals and printers.

The processing units inside a computer understand a language called **machine code**, and all the calculations a computer performs use machine code. A machine code, which is a **low-level** language, is specific to the particular make and model of computer on which it runs, and it is not designed to be read by humans. Any instruction given to a computer must be translated (somehow) to machine code before the computer will understand it. It

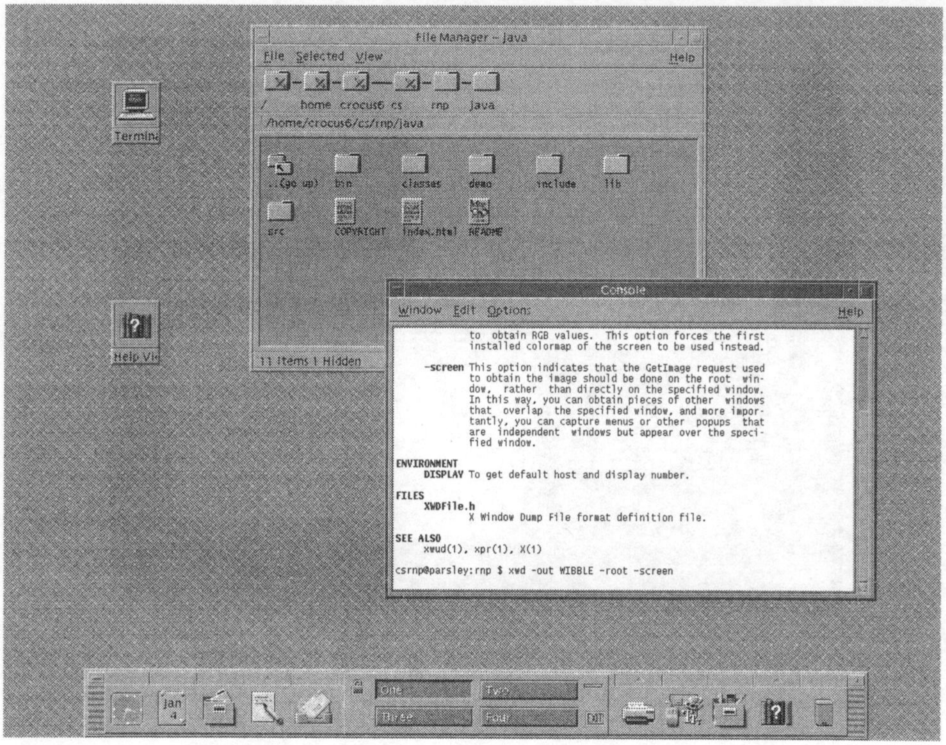

Figure 1.3   *A UNIX workstation screen using the 'CDE' desktop manager.*

is unlikely you will ever need to come into direct contact with machine code.

Such as Ada, Pascal, C, C++, BASIC, FORTRAN, Java, ...

A **program** will be written (usually) in a **high-level language** which is easily readable by humans. Such a program will need to be translated to machine code before a computer can understand it, and computer systems provide **compilers** and **interpreters** which perform this translation.

Kernel and shell

In order for a computer to do any useful work, it also has to perform 'housekeeping'. It has to understand that it has terminals and printers connected to it, and it has to know when a user wants to run a program. These tasks, together with many others which are required for the computer to work but are not of interest to the user, are performed by an **operating system**. An operating system is a program, or collection of programs, which is running whenever the computer is switched on. It controls your terminal, allows you to type in instructions to the computer, and performs many other necessary functions. UNIX is an operating system.

The tasks which the kernel should perform, and how a programmer can communicate with the kernel, are described in the standard called POSIX.1

A UNIX system can be split into two parts. While the system is operational, a program, called the **kernel**, is constantly running. This is what forms the core of the operating system and is central to UNIX. You do not need to know how the kernel functions.

The other part is a **shell**, which is the interface between a user and a UNIX system. It allows you to instruct the machine and to run programs. A shell communicates with the kernel, but keeps you at arm's length from it (see Figure 1.4). In order to use a UNIX system, it is sufficient to understand a shell; the kernel can remain hidden from you.

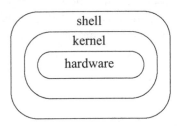

Figure 1.4   *The UNIX kernel and shell.*

The kernel is always present, but the shell is only active when someone is actually using the UNIX system. Since the shell enables the user to instruct the system to perform tasks, the instructions which can be given to the shell must be easy for a person to understand. Different people have had different ideas about exactly how a shell should be, and a number of different shells have been devised in the past. They are all similar to each other, but differ in details. The first shell, historically, is called the **Bourne shell**, known as sh and named after its creator. This shell is still used today, although newer shells with more powerful features have been created which are effectively extensions of the Bourne shell. These include the **Korn shell** ksh, the **Z shell** zsh, and bash. A programmer familiar with the Bourne shell would have no trouble using any of these three other shells. Indeed, if such a programmer were not using the extra features provided by these shells, he or she would be unaware that the shell was not the Bourne shell.

> S.R. Bourne

> bash = 'Bourne Again SHell'

The **C shell**, known as csh, has a syntax which resembles that of the programming language C, and is markedly different to any of the shells based on the Bourne shell. A programmer familiar with the Bourne shell would not be able to use the C shell without learning the differences between it and the Bourne shell. Just as there are shells which are extensions of the Bourne shell, so the C shell itself has been developed into shells with extra facilities. The most common of these is the the **T shell** tcsh.

> csh is pronounced 'seesh'

> tcsh is usually pronounced 'teesh'

POSIX.2 is the 'standard' shell, and is modelled principally on the Bourne shell. The POSIX.2 shell contains features that have been added to the Bourne shell in the light of experience gained with other shells. Much of what is mentioned in this book will thus be true for the Bourne shell. It is likely that as existing shells derived from the Bourne shell, such as ksh and zsh, are developed, each will be amended so that its specification conforms to POSIX.2.

Files

On a machine there will be a vast amount of information (**data**) which has to be stored, including programs, text, and the UNIX operating system itself. Each 'unit' of data – which may be small (for instance, a few words of text) or large (like parts of the UNIX operating

Compact Disk Read-Only Memory

system itself) – is stored in a **file**. A file is a sequence of bytes, stored somewhere on the system, perhaps on a **magnetic disk** or **tape**, a **CD-ROM**, or other storage device. We are not interested exactly where the file is stored, merely in the bytes which are its contents.

Each file has a **name**, which should consist of any letter, digit, or one of the characters . (**period**), - (**minus sign**), or _ (**underscore**). Other characters are also acceptable in a filename, but are discouraged in order to promote clarity. When we use files, we will normally refer to them by name. Some examples are:

A period is usually described as a 'dot'

```
test  11a  My_File  prog.c  p-1
```

Bits, bytes, words and characters

'Bit' is a contraction of bin-ary digit; the word was invented by John W. Tukey in 1947

'Byte' was first used with the IBM STRETCH computer, ca. 1956

Data inside a computer is stored as a sequence of binary digits. Each such digit is called a **bit**. Exactly *how* bits are stored does not concern us here, but several different methods can be used depending where on the computer system the data is required. Bits are grouped together in groups of (usually) 8 to form a **byte**. Bytes are then grouped in 2's, 4's or 8's to form **words**, the number of bytes in a word depending on the machine being used (see Figure 1.5).

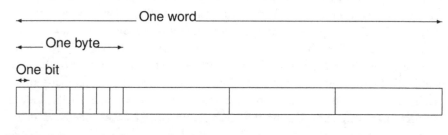

Figure 1.5   *A 4-byte word.*

It is rarely necessary to enquire what individual bits are stored on a computer. Normally you will regard the byte as the most 'basic' unit of storage on a machine. Since a byte contains 256 ($= 2^8$) permutations of eight binary digits, a byte can represent any number between 0 and 255 inclusive.

Just as with a typewriter you communicate character-by-character, so for UNIX. Unless you are dealing bit-by-bit with the data stored in the system's memory, it is helpful to think of each byte representing a **character**, such as the letter 'A' or the symbol '@'. There is a correspondence between characters and the numerical codes (between 0 and 255) which can be stored in a byte. The coding normally used is called **ASCII**. The codes in ASCII for the upper-case letters 'A' to 'Z' are 65 to 90, for lower-case letters 'a' to 'z' they are 97 to 122, and for the digits '0' to '9' they are 48 to 57. The codings for the other characters which a typewriter might use are known as **printing characters** or **graphics characters**. These include such characters as punctuation marks, and are presented in Figure 1.6.

ASCII = 'American Standard Code for Information Interchange'

In the earlier days of computing, the electronic components were often unreliable, and the final bit in a byte was used as a **checkdigit**, whose value is determined by a simple calculation from the other seven bits. If one of the other seven bits is changed, the value

Code	Key	Description	Code	Key	Description
32		space	58	:	colon
33	!	exclamation mark	59	;	semicolon
34	"	double quote	60	<	less than
35	#	number sign ('hash')	61	=	equals
36	$	dollar	62	>	greater than
37	%	percent	63	?	question mark
38	&	ampersand	64	@	commercial 'at'
39	'	apostrophe ('quote')	91	[	opening bracket
40	(	opening parenthesis	92	\	reverse slant
41	)	closing parenthesis	93	]	closing bracket
42	*	asterisk	94	^	circumflex ('caret')
43	+	plus	95	_	underline
44	,	comma	96	`	grave accent ('backquote')
45	-	minus	123	{	opening brace
46	.	period ('dot')	124	|	vertical line
47	/	slant ('slash')	125	}	closing brace
			126	~	tilde

Figure 1.6   *ASCII graphics characters.*

of the eighth, which is referred to as a **parity bit**, is also changed. This **parity check** can then be used to identify bytes whose contents have been accidentally altered.

Parity checking is an unsophisticated form of error detection, and modern equipment seldom uses it, so allowing 256 character codes to be stored in a single 8-bit byte, rather than just 128. Usually the first 128 match the ASCII character set, and the remaining characters are used for extra symbols, such as currency symbols and accented letters used by languages other than English. One such code is known as **LATIN-1**. For the symbols used in this book these two codings are identical. Other codings do exist, perhaps the most well-known being **EBCDIC** and the 16-bit **Unicode**, but we shall assume ASCII is being used.

LATIN-1 is discussed in Chapter 10

EBCDIC = 'Extended Binary Coded Decimal Interchange Code'

Note that if you total the number of letters, digits, punctuation marks and other graphics symbols, there are nowhere near 256 of them – some codes relate to **non-printing characters**. These are characters which rather than representing a symbol that can be printed on a computer screen, denote other actions that the computer can perform.

Input and output

When communicating with UNIX, the user will send to the system a stream of characters. Each time a key on the keyboard is pressed a character is sent to the machine. Normally the computer **echoes** the character, that is, the computer displays it on the terminal screen. When the system wishes to send the user a message, a stream of characters is sent to the user's terminal, which is able to interpret the ASCII coding and displays the characters on the screen accordingly.

While interacting with the system, the user types in lines of text from the keyboard, terminating each line by pressing the *RETURN* key. These lines are interpreted as instructions to UNIX, which then responds accordingly, and displays messages on the screen. On a graphics terminal, this dialogue is between the keyboard and a specific window (normally the window over which the global cursor has been placed). On a windowed terminal, manipulation of other devices such as a mouse also results in the transmission of characters to the UNIX machine. However, these are interpreted as relating to the management and display of the windows, and are not sent to the shell. We shall see later that the shell is just one example of a program that can run on a UNIX system, but is special since it is the principal interface between a user and the kernel.

Most characters that we shall use are the **printing** characters. These, which include letters, digits, punctuation marks and the other symbols marked on the keyboard, will be displayed in the obvious way. There are other characters which may be required by a UNIX system. These are known as **control characters** and are listed in Figure 1.7. For instance, the character whose code is 7 and is sometimes referred to as '**bell**', if printed on your terminal, will normally cause it to make a noise (typically a 'beep'). The bell character was used on 'teletype' terminals to attract the attention of the user in the days of the telegraph. Each control character has a name, which is typically an acronym of its description. For character number 7 this is 'BEL', short for 'bell'. Each control character can be input by pressing one of the keys while keeping the **CTRL** key held down. For BEL this key is G, and for this reason BEL is often called **ctrl-G** or ^G. Most control characters will not concern us here.

The control characters have purposes which for the most part are obscure. Many of them are used by operating systems (not necessarily UNIX) to structure data, and have meanings which have historical relevance only. Some of them are useful, and these include the following:

- The character **TAB** has the effect when sent to the screen of moving the position of the cursor to the next **tab position** (usually columns 8, 16, 24, 32, etc.). The key marked *TAB* or → when pressed will transmit a *TAB* character to the computer.

- The character **NEWLINE** causes the cursor to move down to the left-hand side of the next row on the screen. This character is input to the machine whenever the key marked **RETURN** is pressed.

- The **escape character**, which would not normally be displayed on a screen at all, is sometimes required when typing in data. There should be a key on your keyboard marked **ESC** or **ESCAPE**.

Networks

A computer system will contain at least one computer. It is becoming increasingly difficult to define what is meant by 'a computer' – until a few years ago, a computer would have had a single piece of electronics called a **CPU** which would perform all the computational tasks.

Sometimes marked ↩ or ENTER

Pronounced 'control Gee'

CPU = 'Central Processing Unit'

Code	Ctrl-key	Name	Description
0	^@	NUL	null
1	^A	SOH	start of heading
2	^B	STX	start of text
3	^C	ETX	end of text
4	^D	EOT	end of transmission
5	^E	ENQ	enquiry
6	^F	ACK	acknowledge
7	^G	BEL	bell
8	^H	BS	backspace
9	^I	HT	horizontal tab
10	^J	NL	newline (linefeed)
11	^K	VT	vertical tab
12	^L	NP	new page (formfeed)
13	^M	CR	carriage return
14	^N	SO	shift out
15	^O	SI	shift in
16	^P	DLE	data link escape
17	^Q	DC1	device control 1
18	^R	DC2	device control 2
19	^S	DC3	device control 3
20	^T	DC4	device control 4
21	^U	NAK	negative acknowledgement
22	^V	SYN	synchronous idle
23	^W	ETB	end of transmission block
24	^X	CAN	cancel
25	^Y	EM	end of medium
26	^Z	SUB	substitute
27	^[	ESC	escape
28	^\	FS	file separator
29	^]	GS	group separator
30	^^	RS	record separator
31	^_	US	unit separator
127		DEL	delete

Figure 1.7   *ASCII control characters.*

Nowadays, a computer may contain several processing units around which the workload will be distributed. In addition, several computers may be connected together in a **network**, where each constituent computer can communicate with others in the network.

In some cases, the computers in a network will be very intimately connected, and the network will appear to a user as a single but very large computer. We use the word **system** to mean either a computer or a network of computers which appear to the user as a single entity. A campus-wide UNIX network would be an example of such a system; a more loosely-connected network such as the Internet would not be. When using a terminal on a network, you will still be communicating with a *specific* machine. Each window allows a dialogue with a single UNIX machine, and it is that target UNIX machine with which we shall be concerned.

Your local system

POSIX compliant systems conform to the POSIX.1 and POSIX.2 standards

No UNIX system is likely to be **POSIX compliant** and have *only* the facilities which POSIX defines – many other tools and utilities will be included. This book covers those topics which will be relevant to any POSIX compliant system. If your system is not POSIX compliant – and some older UNIX systems will not be – then some of the commands discussed will either not exist, or will have different names or behaviour. The most common differences between POSIX and the older UNIX systems are mentioned.

If you are using UNIX on your own personal computer, make sure you read the handbook supplied with the machine in conjunction with this book. If there are any differences, it will be an invaluable help. It is more likely, however, that you are using UNIX as part of a course, and you have been given access to a multi-user UNIX system. We assume this is the case. Someone, somewhere, will be in day-to-day charge of the system – we shall call this person the **System Administrator**. Should you have problems which neither you nor your Tutor is able to resolve, then the System Administrator will either be able to help, or at least point you in the direction of someone who can. Find out who your System Administrator is, and make sure that you are in possession of any documents that he or she wishes users of the system to have.

There is a user of the system who is called the **SuperUser**. He or she has special privileges on the system, and can do certain actions forbidden to ordinary users such as the unrestricted right to change and to delete files on the system. The SuperUser may or may not be the same person as the System Administrator, and the SuperUser will occasionally be mentioned.

History of UNIX

The first UNIX system was built at Bell Labs, the research division of the US telephone corporation AT&T, in 1969. Previous to that date, Bell (together with General Electric and

MIT = 'Massachusetts In-
stitute of Technology'

MIT) had been engaged in developing a large-scale operating system, known as 'Multics'. This collaboration between industry and the academic community had begun in 1964, but five years later it had become clear that the three participants had different goals for the project. By this time a vast amount of work had gone into Multics, but more needed to be done for it to fulfil the aspirations of any of the participants, and Bell Labs pulled out.

Faced without a state-of-the-art operating system with which to work, a number of researchers at Bell, led by Ken Thompson and Dennis Ritchie, decided to create a new operating system 'from scratch'. Multics had become complex, and it was felt that a much simpler system was needed — the name 'UNIX' arose to emphasise that difference between it and Multics. The experience gained during the development of Multics contributed much to the design of UNIX.

UNIX is not an acronym

A number of fundamental design decisions were taken which pervade the whole of UNIX. Programs written for UNIX should be simple, and should each do a single task well. This was different to the style adopted in some other operating systems, where large programs would be developed with many different capabilities, and which would be commensurately complex. Also, programs should be designed so that they could easily be linked together, the output from one becoming the input to another. Thus it would be possible to build more complex programs by joining simple ones together.

Part of the philosophy underlying the design of UNIX was that the kernel should be as small as possible, and only perform those functions which are absolutely necessary — all other tasks should be the responsibility of the shell. At the same time as UNIX was being written, the language C was being designed, and in 1973 a UNIX kernel was written using C. C is a high-level language, and as such is machine-independent, so the new (small) kernel and shell could be transferred to a different machine easily. This was found to work well, and Bell Labs were happy to let the source code for the kernel be distributed to universities.

For a PDP-11 computer

In the next few years, work on UNIX was carried on principally by Bell Labs and by the University of California at Berkeley. These two organisations, however, developed their own versions of UNIX, known respectively as **System V** and **BSD**. Industrial users have tended to use System V, whereas BSD UNIX was common in universities and colleges.

Known as UCB
V = 'five' (Roman numeral)

BSD = 'Berkeley Standard Distribution'

By the late 1980s UNIX had been implemented by many manufacturers, each of whom had developed versions which, although based either on System V or on BSD, had their own features. It became apparent that the popularity of UNIX, coupled with the proliferation of 'dialects', had resulted in a pressing need for a recognised standard for UNIX to be developed. This was taken on board by the IEEE under the name **POSIX**. POSIX consists of a number of interrelated standards (see Figure 1.8).

POSIX.n	Description	IEEE Standard
POSIX.1	The library functions defining the kernel	P1003.1
POSIX.2	The shell and 'standard' utilities	P1003.2
POSIX.3	Test methods and conformance	P2003 and P2003.1
POSIX.4	Real-time extensions	P1003.4
POSIX.5	ADA language bindings	P1003.5
POSIX.6	Security	P1003.1e and P1002.2c (draft)
POSIX.7	System administration	
POSIX.8	Transparent file access	
POSIX.9	FORTRAN language bindings	P1003.9

Figure 1.8   *The family of POSIX standards.*

PASC = 'Portable Applica-
tions Standards Commit-
tee'

Now part of the **PASC** project, there are more than 9 proposed POSIX standards, but only the first few are near completion. The nomenclature has changed somewhat, and several of the standards have IEEE codes which appear to be out of step with the original POSIX numbering scheme. In this book we only deal with POSIX.2 since the other standards are not necessary for understanding the shell.

Open systems

Specifying a standard for an operating system does not, of course, specify a whole computer system. There are many hardware issues which will determine what a computer is capable of doing, and what equipment can be connected to it. There is also the issue of software which will be used on the system – the fact that a program works running under UNIX on system A is no guarantee that it will work on system B, if A and B are manufactured by different companies. This is where the concept of **open systems** comes in. In an ideal UNIX world it would be possible to purchase a computer from company A and a program from company B and expect that program to work on that computer. Software written for a specific computer system will often be written so as to take account of the special features of that system. In practice, this is a minor problem, since the POSIX (and related) standards are wide-ranging, and only software which is hardware-specific is likely not to be portable. In order for incompatibilities between products not to arise, the vendors of hardware and software must make a conscious decision to create products which will work together. In an open system, you would be able to purchase any piece of equipment from any manufacturer, together with any software, and – within reason – expect to be able to plug in the equipment and run the software without any significant effort.

OSF = 'Open Software
Foundation'

A number of organisations have been formed to promote open systems. At the time of writing, **OSF** and **X/Open** are the two major consortia of manufacturers and vendors. OSF, founded in 1988, is involved principally in promoting technological innovations and ensuring their portability and interoperability. The X/Open Company, which was founded in 1984, concentrates its activities on standards, and is instrumental in defining and promoting new open standards prior to their adoption by bodies such as the IEEE and the ISO. X/Open bought the UNIX trademark in 1994, and thus has effective control over the future development of UNIX. In 1996 OSF and X/Open joined forces to create **The Open Group**, a single umbrella organisation to coordinate the development of open systems.

API = 'Application Programming Interface'

Under the umbrella of X/Open, specifications for open systems are being promoted, which include the **Single UNIX Specification**. Commencing as the **Common API Specification** this standard initially became known as **SPEC 1170** in 1993, as it specified 1170 **API**s, chosen to cover 50 successful applications programs such as wordprocessors, spreadsheets and databases. The Single UNIX Specification includes POSIX.1, POSIX.2 and the **ISO C** standard (still often referred to as '**ANSI C**').

Getting UNIX for free!

If you are reading this book, you probably have access to a UNIX system via your university or college. If you don't, or you would like to use UNIX on your PC at home, you can.

For many years there has been a tradition in universities of freedom of information, and results of research are published. Furthermore, software created during that research is often made available free-of-charge, either as **public-domain** (where copyright no longer applies) or as **shareware** (where although copyright still applies, the copyright-owner permits copying).

When UNIX was being developed, and before UNIX systems were marketed by the major software companies, much of the operating system had been developed by people who wanted it to be disseminated as widely as possible. As a result, a version of UNIX, known as **Linux** has been written independently.

You can copy Linux from FTP site `sunsite.unc.edu`, or from many other sites across the world. Alternatively, you can purchase books on Linux which include CD-ROMs containing the software you need.

FTP is discussed in Chapter 10

Conventions used in this book

Several different fonts are used in this book. **Bold face** is used when names or concepts are first introduced, and occasionally for emphasis. When dialogue with a machine is displayed, `courier font` is used for messages the UNIX system prints, and `bold courier font` for instructions typed by a user. If a word appears in the text which would normally appear in such a dialogue, `courier font` is again used.

Chapter 2

Getting started

OBJECTIVES

In this chapter you will learn about:

☐ conducting a simple dialogue with a UNIX machine;

☐ simple use of the text editor vi;

☐ getting help via the command man;

☐ using electronic mail;

☐ input and output streams;

☐ input and output redirection and pipes.

This chapter describes how you start (and finish) a session at a UNIX terminal, together with some of the basic commands which you can use.

Usernames

In order to use your site's UNIX system you will need a **username** and a **password**. The username is a code which will allow you to access the system, and to distinguish you from any other users. For the rest of this book, we shall assume you have been given the username chris. The password is to verify that you are in fact the person allowed to use that username, and is similar to the PIN of an ATM but longer and more secure. You should already have been told what arrangements have been made for allocating you a username. If not, you must ask your System Administrator.

PIN = 'Personal Identifica-tion Number'

ATM = 'Automatic Teller Machine' — a bank cash dispenser

You will either be asked to choose a password, or you will initially be allocated one, in which case you will have the opportunity to change your password at a later time. When choosing a password, which can normally be up to eight characters long, bear in mind that you don't want anyone else to guess what it is. Some simple rules will help you. *Always* use a mixture of upper- and lower-case letters, together with digits or other symbols. *Always* choose passwords which are eight characters long. *Never* choose as password a word which would occur in a dictionary, or is the name of a person. If you ever think that someone has discovered your password, *change it immediately and tell your System Administrator*. It is also good practice to get into the habit of changing your password every few weeks as a matter of routine.

Logging in

Having found a terminal, you are now in a position to use the UNIX system. Sit down *and make yourself comfortable.* Make sure you can see the screen clearly and that you can reach the keyboard easily. Not only can an awkward body posture be uncomfortable, it can be dangerous, contributing to **RSI**, if held for more than short periods of time.

RSI = 'Repetitive Strain Injury'

Check that your terminal is turned on – you may need to press the *RETURN* key since some terminals darken their screens after a period of inactivity. Adjust the screen's brightness so that it is at a comfortable level. Somewhere on the screen you will see the line

```
login:
```

If your terminal is a graphics terminal with windows, use the mouse to ensure that the cursor is within the window containing the `login:` message. Now type in your username followed by *RETURN*. The computer will then print on the screen the message

This process is known as 'logging in'

```
Password:
```

and you should then type in your password. *What you type in as the password will not appear on the screen*, for obvious security reasons. If there are other people in the same room as you, be discrete when typing in the password, and make sure no-one is standing looking over your shoulder. If you make a mistake typing in your username or password, don't worry – you'll be given another chance. If you forget your password, your System Administrator can allocate you a new one.

Be careful when you type that you distinguish between upper-case and lower-case letters – UNIX treats them as different. If your username is `chris`, and you enter **Chris** at the `login:` prompt, the system will not allow you to login.

Most UNIX systems appear different to their users in many superficial ways. For instance, types of computer terminal will vary. The messages displayed on the screen when you login to the system will probably be tailored to the needs of the site. It is likely that a document is produced by your site to explain how to use the UNIX machines, and *you should consult that document*. It will clarify differences (if any) between your UNIX system and the standard version described here.

Typing in commands

After you have logged in, the system will **prompt** you to type in a command. The prompt is usually $ (**dollar**), though many systems will change this, and you will yourself be able to alter it.

Beware, however, if you get a prompt which terminates in % (percent) – this is usually an indication that the shell you will talk to is either the C shell or a derivative of it, and not a POSIX shell. Although most of the next couple of chapters will still be valid for such a shell, there are significant incompatibilities, and much of Chapters 5–7 will not be correct. In such a circumstance, it may be possible for your login shell to be changed to a POSIX shell. Again, consult your System Administrator. Try now typing **date** (remembering to

Such as bash

press the *RETURN* key at the end). You should see on the screen something like

```
$ date
Wed Aug 6 15:51:21 BST 1997
$
```

By typing **date** you have instructed the machine to obey the command called date; it has executed the command and has printed on your terminal a message (as instructed by the command date). When that command completes, you are then given another prompt. Try now typing nonsense – you should get something like

```
$ qwerty
qwerty: command not found
$
```

telling you that it doesn't understand what you've typed in.

The command date is the name of a program – it's written in machine code, and you don't need to know the details of *how* it works, just *what* it does. To describe a program such as date being obeyed, we use the words **running** or **executing**.

You will have been notified of the command you must type for changing your password; this is usually passwd, although some System Administrators prefer to install their own command. On some systems passwd can work very slowly, and your new password may not take effect until a few minutes after you have entered it, especially if your UNIX system is a network of machines rather than a single computer.

passwd is not POSIX

Finishing your session

Sometimes the system will be set up so that ctrl-D fails to work, in which case you should type exit instead

When you wish to finish using UNIX – known as **logging out** – you should type **ctrl-D** on a line by itself. The machine will respond by giving you the login: prompt so that the next user can log in. If you are using a graphics terminal with windows, you may also need to take further action – check your local documentation. **Logout** now and login again – with your new password if you changed it.

Commands and options

UNIX commands take the form of a name (such as date), possibly followed by **options**, and other **arguments** as required. An option is denoted by a hyphen (-) followed by a single character (itself possibly followed by arguments). For example, the command date can take only one possible option, namely -u. Without this option, the date and time are printed for the local timezone; with option -u the time is converted to **UTC** thus

UTC = 'Universal Coordinated Time', which is GMT

```
$ date -u
Wed Aug 6 14:51:21 UTC 1997
```

Information about exactly what machine and operating system version is being used can be found by typing uname. This command will either give a brief (one word) description (typically the name of the operating system), or more detailed information. uname allows several options, including -a to display all information about the system. For instance,

```
$ uname
StarOS
$ uname -a
StarOS box 4.1 7 star4c
```

The output from uname indicates that the operating system has proprietary brand name StarOS, its **release** is 4.1, **version** 7, and the name of the machine you are using is box. The hardware being used (i.e. the type of physical machine, as opposed to the operating system, which is software), is a star4c.

Options -m (machine), -n (nodename), -r (release), -s (system name) or -v (version) can be used to print out *part* of the information that -a (all) supplies. With no argument, -s is assumed by default. You can combine options, for instance to print out the release *and* version of your system, you can combine the options in one of four ways:

```
$ uname -r -v
4.1 7
$ uname -v -r
4.1 7
$ uname -rv
4.1 7
$ uname -vr
4.1 7
```

Try entering uname with the various options.

You will be communicating with the machine from a **terminal**. The command tty will display the name of the terminal you are currently using. If you are using a windowed terminal, UNIX treats each **window** as a separate terminal with its own name.

What is the name of the terminal or window you are using?
Solution: Use **tty**:

```
$ tty
ttyr1
```

and the name is ttyr1 (or whatever is printed on the screen by tty).

---

uname = 'UNIX name'

a = 'all'

A company which writes a UNIX operating system will have its own name for it, and will update it periodically; major updates are called releases, minor updates are versions

tty = 'teletype'

Worked example 2.1

Some systems, including Sun's 'Solaris', have more complex names, such as /dev/pts/1

Another command you can try now is who:

```
$ who
chris      ttyr1      Aug 3 14:23
sam        ttyp2      Aug 3 08:38
jo         ttyr4      Aug 3 13:58
```

On some systems who will also display extra information

u = 'unused'

This command lists those people currently logged in to the machine by **username**, together with the terminal they are using and the date and time they last logged in. So chris in the above example logged in at 2.23 pm on Aug 3 to a terminal known as ttyr1. This command allows several options, including -u; try typing the command who -u. The output you will get is similar to that for who on its own, except that an extra column of information is given, perhaps:

```
$ who -u
chris      ttyr1      Aug 3 14:23
sam        ttyp2      Aug 3 08:38 01:03
jo         ttyr4      Aug 3 13:58 00:02
```

This extra column indicates **idle time** – the amount of time a user has not touched the keyboard. So chris is active at the present moment (a dot is used in place of a time if the user has actually used the system in the previous few seconds). However sam has been idle for 1 hour and 3 minutes (perhaps sam has forgotten to logout?), and jo has been idle for only two minutes (perhaps thinking about what to do next).

Files

ls = 'list'

There may also be 'hidden' files, which we will discuss later

You will be able to create, delete and edit files; but before attempting to perform such operations on your files, you will need to be able to check which files you have at the moment. The command for this is ls.

If you have only just started to use the UNIX system, you should not have created any files. Type ls on its own, and this should be confirmed when it prints nothing in response, so:

```
$ ls
$
```

The editor 'vi'

Pronounced 'vee-eye'

vi = 'visual editor'
If you have already created a file called myfile then choose a filename which you do not have

You will need to create and update files containing text (for example, programs written in Pascal or C, or word-processed reports). The command vi invokes the standard screen editor, which has many powerful facilities to enter text into a file and to change text already there. In this section we discuss only a small proportion of those facilities, enough to allow you to create and edit files for the rest of this book. To edit the file myfile (say), type vi followed by the name of the file; so:

```
$ vi myfile
```

Your screen (or window) will be cleared, and the cursor will appear in the top-left corner of the screen. Along the left-hand side of the screen will be a column of ˜, indicating that those lines on the screen are not (yet) being used by vi. Additionally, a message may appear on the bottom line of the screen.

˜ = tilde

Now type the letter a and type in several lines of text – the *RETURN* key will terminate each line – followed by *ESC*. Then press h, j, k, l, and see the cursor moving around the screen one square at a time.

a = 'append text'

As pictured in Figure 2.1

Figure 2.1   *Cursor movement in* vi.

You won't be allowed to move the cursor anywhere which does not contain text. Position the cursor near the centre of your text and press a again. Type in more text – it will appear after the cursor position. As before, *ESC* will terminate the input. If you're not sure whether or not you have typed *ESC*, then type it again – if you type too many the extra ones will be ignored and will do no harm. Move the cursor to the centre again and type i, and repeat what you did for a – you will see that text is inserted, but this time *before* the cursor position.

i = 'insert text'

To delete text, you can remove one character at a time by placing the cursor on it and typing x. To remove a whole line, place the cursor on the line and type dd. To remove part of the line from the cursor to the end of the line type D. Try these commands now.

When you have finished making all the changes you desire, type ZZ and the contents of the file will be stored on disk and you will be returned to the shell.

Use capital letters for ZZ

There are three 'modes' which vi may be in. There is **command mode**, during which you can move the cursor around the screen, and generally move from one part of the file to another, deleting and altering text where you place your cursor. When you enter vi you always start in command-mode. Secondly, there is **colon-mode**. This is necessary when you wish to perform more complicated operations on your file which cannot (easily) be done with simple keystrokes. Third, there is **input mode** during which you can enter text.

To enter colon-mode, you must be in command-mode, so make sure you are not entering text (type *ESC* if necessary). Then type a colon (:) (not followed by *RETURN*). The cursor will immediately move to the bottom line of your screen and will be preceded by a colon. At this stage, there are a few colon-mode commands that you must know. If you make a mistake while typing, then the command u, either in colon-mode or in command-mode, will correct it. If you accidentally type a colon, you can return to command-mode by just pressing *RETURN*. In the following discussion we assume that you are in command-mode unless otherwise stated.

u = 'undo'

Try using `vi` to create in file `myfile` just two lines:

```
hello
there
```

After you have done this, and left `vi` by typing `ZZ`, use the command `ls` to check which files you now have. You should find:

```
$ ls
myfile
```

Now edit the file `myfile` again and remove the two lines by typing `dd` twice to delete each one in turn. Choose another document, such as a book or a newspaper, and copy a couple of paragraphs into the file. Make sure that you enter them correctly, using the `vi` commands we have just discussed to make any corrections. If the file fills more than one screen you can 'scroll' backwards and forwards through the file by typing **ctrl-U** and **ctrl-D** respectively.

Some other cursor-moving commands are useful:

^ = caret

$ = dollar

- ^ moves the cursor to the start of the current line,

- $ moves the cursor to the end of the current line.

The file will contain words, which just as in English are sequences of letters and/or digits:

- w moves forward through the file to the *start* of the next word,

- e moves forward through the file to the next *end* of a word,

- b moves *backwards* to the *start* of a word.

If you know that there's a word, or sequence of characters, in the file that you wish to find, then `vi` will search for that string:

- typing / followed by the string you are looking for, followed by *RETURN*, will look *forwards* in the file for the string, and

- typing ?, rather than /, searches for a *previous* occurrence of a string.

So in order to search for the next occurrence of `hello`, you should type

```
/hello
```

followed by *RETURN*. If a line is too long, you can split it into two by positioning the cursor where you wish it to be split, and using `i` or `a` to insert a *NEWLINE* character. If you have two lines you wish to join to a single one, place the cursor on the first one and type `J`.

J = 'join'

There are also colon-mode commands for moving about the file. For each colon-mode command you must press *RETURN* at the end of the command:

- : 0 moves the cursor to the start of the file,   0 is digit zero

- : $ moves the cursor to the beginning of the last line of the file,

- : *n* moves the cursor to the beginning of line *n*.

Practise the other commands listed above and those in Figures 2.2 and 2.3, and get used to them. You will have to create many files, and it is worthwhile getting used to the editor at this stage. Some sites will support a command called `vilearn` which is a user-friendly   `vilearn` is not POSIX
program that teaches you how to use `vi`, and if it is available you may find it very helpful.
  At this point mention must be made of an editor called `ex`. Strictly speaking, `ex` and `vi` are the same animal — think of `vi` *permanently in colon-mode* so that after each colon-mode command the cursor is prompted on the bottom line by a colon, and you have `ex`. The command `visual` to `ex` will turn it into `vi`. If you are in `vi` and in command-mode the command `Q` will put you permanently in colon-mode, namely in `ex`.   Q = 'quit'

Other editors

At the time of writing, two principal text editors are in common use: `vi` and `emacs`. These   `emacs` is not POSIX
editors differ greatly in style, and being competent in using one will not necessarily help you when you use the other. If your System Administrator recommends another editor in place of `vi` you may wish to use that editor instead of `vi`, and you should refer to the relevant system documentation that you will have been provided with. The principal advantage of `vi` is that, being a 'standard' editor, you can rely on it being available on all UNIX systems. In common with many UNIX utilities, `vi` is somewhat terse, and some people simply don't like it. Advantages of `emacs` are that you can 'customise' its commands, and that it includes many powerful facilities not available in `vi`. However these are offset by the complexity of `emacs` for the novice user.
  Several other editors should be mentioned. The 'simplest' editor is `ed`, which looks to the   ed = 'edit'
user similar to `ex` in colon-mode. It is used where full-screen editing may be problematic, for instance if you are accessing the UNIX system via a slow communications link. If you   Such as a telephone line
can use `ex` then learning `ed` will present no major problems. Like `ex`, `ed` is a standard   and a modem
editor which you can expect to find on all UNIX systems. The commands available to `ed` are similar (though not all are identical) to those used by `ex`, but `ed` cannot be used as a full-screen editor. The machine can also edit files as well as the user; this can be done using `sed`, which we discuss in Chapter 8.
  If you are using a graphics terminal, you may have access to a window-based editor. Several of these have been written, but none can yet be identified as being very widely   Neither command is de-
available, although you may find either `xedit` or `axe` on your system.   fined in POSIX

Input and output streams

When you type in text at the terminal, the input is **buffered**; the characters you type in are not immediately transmitted to the shell. They are initially stored in a temporary area of

a	enter insert mode after cursor position
b	moves the cursor back to the previous start of a word
cw	change the word the cursor is on by deleting it and entering insert mode
D	delete rest of line after cursor position
dd	delete the line the cursor is on
dw	delete the word the cursor is on
e	moves the cursor to the next end of a word
i	enter insert mode before cursor position
J	join the line the cursor is on and the following line together
o	open a new line, position the cursor at the start of it and enter insert mode
w	moves the cursor to the start of the next word
x	delete the character at the cursor
ZZ	write all changes to the file, and quit vi
^	moves the cursor to the beginning of the current line
$	moves the cursor to the end of the current line
/word	search forward for the string word
?word	search backwards for the string word
ctrl-D	move down the file half a screen
ctrl-U	move back up the file half a screen

Figure 2.2   'Command-mode' commands in vi.

q	quit vi, provided you have not changed your file at all since you last saved it (if you have altered the file, vi will warn you and will not terminate)
q!	quit vi, and any changes you have made to the file will be discarded and the file left in its original state
w	writes all the changes to the file, but remain in vi
wq	equivalent to performing command w followed by command q; same as command-mode ZZ
0	moves the cursor to the beginning of the file
$	moves the cursor to the end of the file
number	moves the cursor to the start of line number

Figure 2.3   'Colon-mode' commands in vi.

the computer's memory called a **buffer**; the contents of the buffer are usually transmitted to the shell at the end of each line, when you press *RETURN*. A consequence of buffering is that if you make an error when typing in data on your terminal, you can correct it. Systems vary in the amount of 'line-editing' they allow, but you can expect at least the following:

DEL   deletes the most recent character typed in
ctrl-U   deletes the whole of the line currently being typed

Once you have typed in a command, and the command begins to be executed, you may be requested to type in data as **input** to the command, and it will send messages as **output**. Output consists of the stream of characters usually sent to the screen. The commands we have looked at already — ls, date and who — give output but require no input. Some commands — such as vi — will 'interact' with you, and need you to type in data while they are running. For simple commands which require input, the input is formed by the characters you type in on the keyboard. More complex commands (vi is in this category) may also have other input and output, but this description of how a command communicates with the system will serve us for the present.

Each command has associated with it three input and output **streams**, as shown in Figure 2.4. They are called **standard input**, **standard output** and **standard error** (often abbreviated to **stdin**, **stdout** and **stderr** respectively). Normally, standard input will be taken from the keyboard, and standard output and standard error will both be sent to the terminal screen. A command may in addition have other input and/or output streams. Each input/output stream is also given a number: 0 for standard input, 1 for standard output and 2 for standard error. Commands that require input will usually take it from standard input,

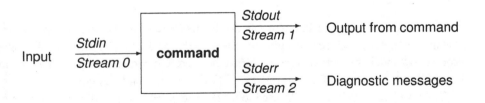

Figure 2.4   *Input to and output from a command.*

and the normal output of a command will go to standard output. Standard error is used for other messages, typically warning messages if the command could not be executed as intended (for instance, if you try to print a file which does not exist). Thus the output from a command and the diagnostics can be separated, as we shall discuss later. The messages sent to standard error are not always error messages, and will include general information of use to you which is not part of the usual output of a command — it's called 'standard error' simply because the majority of messages output on it tend to be error messages.

To terminate input to a command, type *ctrl-D* on a line by itself. When you login, each time you type in a command, that represents a new line of input to your login shell. A shell is simply a program that takes commands as its input. Terminating input to your login shell by typing *ctrl-D* causes that program to finish; that's all that logging out really is.

`cat` = 'catenate'

A useful command is `cat`, which takes names of zero or more files as argument and copies them, in order, to the standard output. We can use `cat` to display files that we have created. If `cat` has no arguments, the standard input is copied directly to the standard output. For instance, to display the file `myfile` which was created earlier using `vi`:

```
$ cat myfile
hello
there
```

`cat` echoes each line as soon as it has been typed in since input is buffered

With no arguments, `cat` will take its input from the standard input:

```
$ cat
abc          ← standard input
abc          ← standard output
def          ← standard input
def          ← standard output
ctrl-D
```

It is possible, indeed common, to **redirect** input and/or output. Instead of input coming from the keyboard, it can be the contents of a file or the output of another command. Similarly output from a command can be sent to a file or used as input to another command.

The symbol < indicates that standard input should come from a file, and the following will produce the same output as `cat myfile` (Figure 2.5):

```
$ cat <myfile
hello
there
```

You can skip this paragraph at first reading

So, having created file `myfile`, you can display its contents on the screen in two ways. In the first case, `cat` is given one argument, the filename `myfile`, the contents of which are copied to standard output; in the second, `cat` is given zero arguments and thus the standard input, which has been redirected from `myfile`, is sent to standard output.

The standard output can be directed to a file. The output from `date`, for example, can be sent to file `xyz` (Figure 2.6):

```
$ date >xyz
```

This is probably the simplest way to create a file without needing an editor

Now do `cat xyz` to examine the contents of file `xyz`. The symbol > indicates that the standard output from `date` is to be sent to a file, whose name immediately follows it. In the case of `cat`, we can do the same, but remember that `cat` also requires input from the standard input stream (Figure 2.7):

```
$ cat >xyz
have a nice  ← standard input
day          ← standard input
ctrl-D
```

You can copy several files to standard output:

```
$ cat myfile xyz
hello
there
have a nice
day
```

A command can redirect both its input and its output; the following will create a copy of file myfile called def (Figure 2.8):

In this example cat takes zero arguments

```
$ cat <myfile >def
```

The *effect* of this is the same as if you had *not* redirected standard input and had given cat a single argument myfile:

```
$ cat myfile >def
```

Beware that you do not take input from and send output to the *same* file — it won't work. The file you try to take the input from will be destroyed in preparation for receiving the output *before* anything is read from it.

WARNING!

A command which requires a filename as an argument can use the symbol - (hyphen) to denote standard input. The following dialogue illustrates this:

```
$ cat myfile -
hello          ← file myfile
there          ← file myfile
Mike           ← standard input
Mike           ← standard output
ctrl-D
```

Thus we can refer to the standard input in situations where simple redirection using < would be inappropriate. The hyphen can be used wherever the name of a file is used, so you can refer to standard input as a file (rather than using the notation for redirection).

Create a file called theusers containing a list of those users currently logged in.
Solution: The command who will send a list of users to standard output, so we need only redirect the standard output of who to the file:

Worked example 2.2

```
$ who >theusers
```

If you now type cat theusers a list of users who are logged-on will be displayed on the screen.

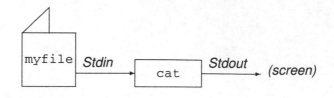

Figure 2.5   `cat <myfile.`

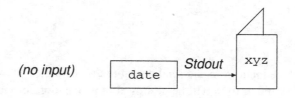

Figure 2.6   `date >xyz.`

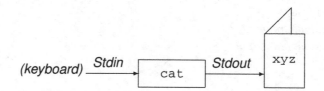

Figure 2.7   `cat >xyz.`

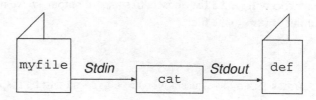

Figure 2.8   `cat <myfile >def.`

Having created files, you will from time to time wish to remove some of them. The command `rm` will delete a file. Take care, as it is very easy to delete a file accidentally — if you use `rm` with option `-i` it will ask you to confirm that you do in fact wish to delete the file:

`rm` = 'remove'
`i` = 'inquire'

```
$ rm -i theusers
rm: remove 'theusers'?  y
```

We can separate standard output and standard error. To illustrate this we set `cat` up so that it produces good output and an error message by asking it to copy two files, one of which (say `myfile`) exists, and the other (`qwerty`, for instance) does not. We send the standard output to file `output` and the standard error to file `error`:

```
$ cat myfile qwerty
hello
there
cat: qwerty: No such file or directory
$ cat myfile qwerty 2>error 1>output
$ cat output
hello
there
$ cat error
cat: qwerty: No such file or directory
```

By prepending the symbol > with the number of the output stream, that stream is redirected to the named file. When > is used alone, it is equivalent to 1>, so that the diagnostic messages are still sent to your terminal unless you explicitly request otherwise.

This notation will not work for the C shell and its derivatives

Although in normal use UNIX commands will have only one input stream, it is possible to write programs which have more than one such stream. In that case the same syntax applies as for output, namely that 0< denotes taking input stream number 0 from a file, and 0< is synonymous with <.

If a command redirects output, from whatever stream, to a file using >, then if that file does not exist it will be created. If the file does exist, then it will be overwritten and its previous contents will be lost. If you wish to **append** data to the end of a file, then replace > by >>. Consider the following dialogue:

Appending data to a file means adding it on at the end without affecting the data already stored in it

```
$ date >outfile
$ date >>outfile
$ cat outfile
Wed Aug 6 15:55:21 BST 1997
Wed Aug 6 15:55:25 BST 1997
```

The first time `date` is called, the standard output is sent to file `outfile`; the second time, the output has been added on to the end of that same file.

Emergencies

What happens if you type in a command which you realise you shouldn't have? It may be that UNIX will provide you with an error message indicating this; if, however, your command was a valid UNIX command that simply does something different from what you intended, then the situation becomes more complex.

The worst-case scenario is if your command runs and does damage, such as deleting a file which you did not wish to delete. In that case, you probably cannot recover from the error, and you quickly learn to be more careful in future! Fortunately such mistakes are infrequent, as there are few commands which will destroy data. More common is the following: you write a program, try to run it, and find that either it 'hangs' (it sits there apparently doing nothing) or begins to output incorrect results. You know something has gone wrong. The remedy is to 'interrupt' the command, which can be done by typing **ctrl-C**, which will cause the command to terminate immediately. This is not the same as *ctrl-D*, which simply indicates to the system that the standard input stream has been closed. Try this out – there should be a file called /usr/dict/words on your machine; try to print it on your screen using cat. It's a very big file, and will take perhaps a minute to fully appear, so you will have ample time to press *ctrl-C*.

The file /usr/dict/words simply contains a list of English words and abbreviations, one on each line. If your system does not have such a file, create a similar file yourself using vi, since /usr/dict/words is used for several examples later on. If you call this new file mydictionary, then you should substitute mydictionary whenever /usr/dict/words is mentioned in subsequent chapters. To indicate the words that might occur in the file, the following is a typical section of /usr/dict/words:

Neither ctrl-C nor ctrl-D will get you out of vi

The meaning of '/' is discussed in Chapter 3

```
O'Donnell
odorous
O'Dwyer
Odysseus
Odyssey
Oedipal
Oedipus
o'er
oersted
of
off
offal
```

Pagers

A **pager** is a program which will allow you to browse through a file 'one page at a time', moving backwards and forwards through the file with the minimum of keystrokes. The standard pager is more, although others may be available on your machine (two other commonly encountered pagers are pg and less). To invoke more, type more followed by the name of the file you wish to examine. For example, to view the file called /usr/dict/words:

pg = 'page'

```
$ more /usr/dict/words
```

The following keystrokes will be useful:

SPACE	view next page
b	view previous page
RETURN	scroll forward one line
?	print a page of help on your terminal
q	quit

The commands that `more` understands are similar to `vi`, and you can for instance type `/hello` to move to an instance of the string `hello` in the file. The command `cat`, which was discussed earlier, is fine for viewing small files, but should not be used as a substitute for a good pager for general viewing of text files.

Electronic mail

A big advantage of modern computer networks is that messages may be sent between users of machines on such a network, or people on the same machine, electronically. The standard command for sending such a message is `mailx`. To make use of this, you need to know the username of the person you wish to send a message to. Type `mailx` followed by that username, and then type in the message terminated by *ctrl-D* on a line of its own. If option `-s` is given to `mailx`, the string following `-s` will be used to denote the *subject* of the message to the recipient. For example,

Generally referred to as 'email'

i.e. the message is the standard input for `mailx`

It is always good practice to give an email message a subject

```
$ mailx -s "Programming Assignment" sam
Hello Sam.
Have you finished the assignment yet?
ctrl-D
```

will send a message to user `sam`. If you have a tilde (the symbol ˜) as the first character on any line you type in, this will be interpreted by `mailx`. For instance, if you wish to edit a message half-way through typing it in, type ˜v and you will then be editing it using `vi`.

If the subject string contains spaces, then it must be enclosed in quotes

If you have a friend who is currently logged in, mail them a short message and ask them to mail you one. If not, mail one to yourself. In either case, the mail should take less than one minute to arrive.

In order to read mail that has been sent to you, just type `mailx` on its own. If you have mail which you have not read, it will print out a brief list of messages awaiting you, with the date they were received, the name of the sender, and the subject (if specified by the sender). For instance,

```
$ mailx
>N  1 sam Wed Jul 27 15:28   16/465    Programming Assignment
 N  2 jo  Thu Jul 28 19:33   77/1220
```

In this example, you have two messages (each message is given a number), the first from user `sam`, the second from user `jo`. The mail from `sam` has subject `Programming Assignment`, is 16 lines long and contains 465 characters; that from `jo` was sent without a subject specified, is 77 lines long, and contains 1220 characters. While you are reading your mail, at any particular moment one message is **current**, and may be read, deleted, saved in a file, or edited. The > symbol indicates that message number 1 is the current message. The command `p` will then display the current message on the screen. If you type `?` a screenful of 'help' messages will be printed indicating what other commands you can give to `mailx`.

`p` = 'print to screen'

Most UNIX systems are equipped with a collection of other programs for electronic mail, and `elm`, `mail`, `mush` and `xmail` come to mind. These commands are similar to `mailx`, but the sophistication and facilities vary. Check with your System Administrator which are the preferred mail programs on your machine, and if they differ from `mailx` for simple use.

Not POSIX

Most Web browsers include commands to let you send mail

Communication with other users

Electronic mail is useful for sending messages, but not for holding a 'conversation', nor for sending urgent messages (since the recipient may not read their mail very frequently). Two utilities are provided in UNIX to enable 'real-time' communication between logged-in users. The first is `write`: suppose user `sam` is logged on, and you wish to send them a (short) message; use `write sam` followed by the lines of the message then *ctrl-D*.

```
$ write sam
Hi Sam.
It's coffee time
```

The message will be sent across line-by-line. On Sam's screen will appear your message, preceded by a line telling them who's sending the message:

```
Message from chris@box on ttyp9 at 14:42 ...
Hi Sam.
It's coffee time
```

If `sam` were logged on at several terminals at once (possible if they have multiple windows on a graphics terminal), you could specify the terminal the message should appear on, so:

```
$ write sam ttyp7
```

Sam can reply to you with the command `write chris`. Whatever `sam` is doing, the lines you type will appear on their screen.

It could be that the recipient of your message does not want this to happen (perhaps they are doing a complicated operation and don't wish to be disturbed). They can prevent messages being displayed by means of `mesg`. To deny other users permission to write messages to your screen, type `mesg n`. To allow this permission, then `mesg y` will reverse the effect of `mesg n`. If you try to `write` to a user who has denied you permission, you will simply get an error message. You can use `write` in a script, and since the input is

`n` = 'no', `y` = 'yes'

standard input this can be redirected or piped (see below) just as with any other UNIX command.

The second communications mechanism is `talk`. Rather than sending lines of messages, `talk` is the nearest you will come to actually talking to another user. It sends messages character-by-character as you type them in, and will work over networks. To run `talk`, the syntax is just as for `write`. After you have typed `talk sam`, a message will appear on Sam's terminal:

See the discussion of audio files in Chapter 10

```
Message from chris@box
talk: connection requested by chris@box
talk: respond with: talk chris@box
```

When `sam` types `talk chris@box` (or whatever address `talk` specifies) both your screen and Sam's will be cleared, and divided into separate regions, one for each of you. When you press a key, it will appear in 'your' part of the screen, when Sam presses one it will appear in 'their' part. You can use the *DELETE* key if you press a key by mistake. Your conversation will be terminated when either of you presses *ctrl-C*. Standard input and standard output are not the mechanisms employed by `talk` and you cannot use `talk` in a pipe. Find a friend who is also logged in and experiment with `write` and `talk`.

Pipes

An extension of redirecting input and output to and from files is to redirect to and from other commands. The syntax for **pipes** is similar to that for file redirection, except that the symbol | is used instead of < and >. If we have a command X whose standard output is to be used as the standard input to a command Y, we could have

| is a vertical bar

```
$ X > tempfile
$ Y < tempfile
```

storing the output of X in a temporary file `tempfile`. However this is not elegant, and in some situations impossible (if you require Y to process the output of X as soon as it is produced). By means of a pipe we can join the two streams together, thus (Figure 2.9):

```
$ X | Y
```

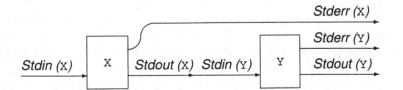

Figure 2.9   X | Y.

Worked example 2.3   Send an email message to user `sam` which will inform `sam` of the current time and date.
Solution: The command `date` sends to its standard output the time and date, and `mailx`
sends an email message from the standard input stream. Therefore we can pipe the output
of `date` to the input of `mailx`:

```
$ date | mailx -s "Today's time and date" sam
```

Using > or < different input or output streams can be specified, but pipes only connect
standard output to standard input, and cannot be used with the standard error stream.

Scripts

A method of performing several commands, one after the other, is to create a file containing
those commands, one per line, and then 'execute' that file. As an example, create a file,
using `vi`, called (say) whenandwho, and containing two lines:

```
date
who
```

Now, type

`sh` = 'shell'   **sh whenandwho**

and the commands `date` and `who` mentioned in the file whenandwho will be executed,
and you will get

```
$ sh whenandwho
Wed Aug 6 16:22:18 BST 1997
chris      ttyr1     Aug 3 07:21
sam        ttyp2     Aug 3 08:38
jo         ttyr4     Aug 3 14:58
```

'Script' for short   A file such as whenandwho, which contains commands, is called a **shell script**.
  At this stage it is important to understand how UNIX executes commands in a script.
When you are logged into your system, you will be communicating with it via a program
called a shell. The shell which is run from the moment you login to the end of your session
is your **login shell**. It is possible to run further copies of the shell by typing the command
`sh`. In order to execute a shell script, the program `sh` is run, but instead of taking standard
input from your terminal, the input comes from the file. Thus while the script is executing
there will be two copies of `sh` running. The login shell will be running one command,
namely `sh`, and this shell will execute the commands in the file.
  When writing scripts the command `echo` is very useful. This command takes arguments
and simply copies them to the standard output, thus:

```
$ echo Hello there
Hello there
```

Write a script called `niceday` which will output today's time and date together with a user-friendly message, thus:

```
$ sh niceday
The time and date are now:
Wed Aug 6 16:30:18 BST 1997
Have a nice day!
```

Solution: We can use `date` to output the date and time, and `echo` to output the messages on lines 1 and 3. To create the file `niceday`, use either `vi`, or if your typing is good, simply use `cat`:

```
$ cat >niceday
echo The time and date are now:
date
echo Have a nice day!
ctrl-D
```

A script may contain input and output redirection, and pipes.

In a script, mail `sam` a message which says `Running my script now.`

Solution: Using `vi`, create a file containing:

```
echo Running my script now | mailx -s "What I'm doing" sam
```

Here-documents

You will sometimes wish to give input to a command, where that input consists of a small number of lines – for example, if you wished to create a script which after it had executed its commands mailed `sam` a message, and that message was to be more than a single line.

One possibility would be to create a file for that message (`mymessage`, say), redirect the input for `mailx` to come from that file, and include the line

```
mailx sam <mymessage
```

as the last line of the script. This would work, but would involve creating two files (one for your script, and one for the message) rather than just one. In large scripts it might become confusing if too many files had to be created. Note that this would not be a problem if `mailx` was not in a script, as you could take the input to `mailx` from your terminal – but since the input to a script may be redirected from elsewhere this is not always possible.

A solution is known as a **here-document**. Following the symbol << comes a word, and all subsequent lines of standard input, whether they are typed in at the terminal or are subsequent lines in a script, are treated as the standard input for the command, up to (but not including) that word. For instance,

```
mailx sam <<END
```
line 1 of message
...
last line of message
END

The line that terminates the input need not be END — any word will do. Try mailing yourself a message using a here-document. Although here-documents work perfectly well interactively, their principle use is in scripts.

Making copies of input and output

Suppose you have a command which prints something on your screen, which you wish to save in a file. So far, we have discussed only how that output can be redirected to a file, so that in order to see it on the screen *and* save it in a file there are two possibilities. Firstly, you could run the command twice (the first time with no redirection, and then directed to a file). Secondly you initially run the command with output sent to a file and then view the file using a pager. Both methods involve duplicating the output to the command, firstly by producing it twice, and secondly by storing it and then copying the stored output.

The first method is no use if the command you run is *interactive*, conducting a dialogue with you while it is running. If you ran the command twice you might give it different input each time, so the two outputs would probably differ. If your command was time-sensitive, such as date, the second method would simply give you the wrong answer when you tried to view the output.

If you wished to make a copy in a file of the input to a command, there would also be a problem. If the command is interactive, so we cannot store the input in an intermediate file, we have not yet met any mechanism at all which will perform this task

Tee= ⌐→
        ↓

The solution is to use the command tee. which duplicates the standard input so:

tee will overwrite the file
copy_of_input

```
$ tee copy_of_input | command_name
```

This has the same effect as the command *command_name* on its own, except a copy of all the standard input to the command is sent to *copy_of_input*.

Worked example 2.6

Send user jo a message and keep a copy of the message in file jo_message.
Solution: mailx will read standard input as the message; use tee to copy it:

```
$ tee jo_message | mailx jo
```

To use tee to copy standard output, pipe the output of a command through tee.

Run the command `who`, but store a copy of the output in file `who_out`. **Worked example 2.7**
Solution:

```
$ who | tee who_out
```

Getting help

There is an on-line help facility available on UNIX systems. It goes under the name of **manual pages**, and the command to get help is `man` (followed by the topic you require assistance with). The manual pages give very detailed information about UNIX commands, and may appear intimidating at first – the manual 'page' for the C compiler `cc` often runs to 20 or more screens of text. As an example, suppose we require more information on the command `who`, we might get:

```
$ man who
WHO(1)                                          WHO(1)


NAME
        who - show who is logged on

SYNOPSIS
        who [-mTu]

DESCRIPTION
        If given no arguments, who prints the
        following information for each user currently
        logged on:


                login name
                terminal line
                login time


OPTIONS
...
```

The division of UNIX manual pages into volumes is not part of the POSIX standard, nor is the exact format of a manual page that we describe here

Do not panic! Although their format looks a bit strange, each manual page is structured in the same way. First of all, on the top line is the name of the command followed in parentheses by a number – the manual pages are divided into **volumes**, usually numbered 1 to 8 inclusive. We are concerned principally with commands in volume 1, which are commands you can type in to the shell. Other volumes give information on other UNIX utilities, such as libraries available to language compilers. The top line may also tell you who wrote the utility, and when it was last updated.

There then follows a sequence of headers (such as NAME) and information under that heading:

NAME	The name of the command, and a short description
SYNOPSIS	What arguments (if any) it expects
DESCRIPTION	A *detailed* description of the command
OPTIONS	A list of the possible options, and what they do
FILES	Which files are used by the command
SEE ALSO	Related topics or commands with manual pages
DIAGNOSTICS	What to do if the command fails
NOTES	Miscellaneous other useful information

Remember that UNIX commands are usually (though not always) lower-case, and that if you type them upper-case by mistake the machine will not understand you. In the example of who above, under the heading SYNOPSIS, we have:

```
who [ -mTu ]
```

The square brackets indicate that options -m, -T and -u are *optional* and can be typed in any order and combination. For the meanings of the options and arguments, you look further down the manual page.

Worked example 2.8

Find out how to print the current hardware type on which your system is running by using uname.

Solution: By typing **man uname** we get:

```
UNAME(1)                                                        UNAME(1)


NAME
        uname - print system information


SYNOPSIS
        uname [-amnrsv]


DESCRIPTION

                                    . . .

OPTIONS

                                    . . .

        -m              Print the name of the hardware type
                        on which the system is running.

                                    . . .
```

m = 'machine'

and thus the command you require is uname -m.

If you are unsure which (if any) command you can use to perform a particular task, type man -k followed by a keyword related to that task. You will be given a brief (1-line) description of all commands indexed by that keyword. You can then select which command you would like detailed information on. You can only give man one keyword at a time, so if the first keyword you try doesn't indicate a suitable command, try a couple of others.

You wish to find who else is logged in; which command can you use?

Solution: Use man -k; choose a single keyword relevant to the topic, say logged:

```
$ man -k logged
who (1)          - show who is logged on
```

So you should use command who.

Summary of utilities

cat	concatenate and print files to standard output
date	display current time and date
echo	write arguments to standard output
ed	basic text editor
ex	text editor (see vi)
logname	display your login user name
ls	list files (directory contents)
mailx	process electronic mail messages
man	display manual pages
mesg	allow or deny messages on your terminal
more	'pager'
rm	remove a file
sh	the shell
talk	talk to another user
tee	duplicate standard input
tty	display the terminal name
uname	display the system name
vi	full-screen text editor
who	list who is using the system
write	write a message on another user's terminal

Problems

2.1 Which command will print out just your login name? *Hint*: try keywords for man.

2.2 Using vi create a file called Parone which contains the first paragraph of Chapter 1. Make sure you correct any typing mistakes you make.

2.3 What argument would you give to date so that it would output today's date and time in the format:
```
11:22:35 PM on Wednesday 23 April 1997
```

2.4 Suppose you have a file called important; using a *single-line* command, make two copies, one in file backup1 and the other in file backup2. *Hint*: this can be done in several ways.

2.5 Write a script which will list the users currently logged in to the system preceded with a one-line message `The following are logged in:`

2.6 You are editing a file using `vi`. You realise that you have mis-spelled the word *vision* as *cision*. What keystrokes could you use to correct the mistake?

Chapter 3

Files

OBJECTIVES

In this chapter you will learn about UNIX files, including:

☐ the UNIX file structure;

☐ common commands which deal with files;

☐ the UNIX file access and security mechanisms.

This chapter concentrates on the basic information you need to know about UNIX files and the utilities which relate to them.

The UNIX directory hierarchy

A typical UNIX system will have many users and usernames. The machine will store large numbers of programs and datasets which are either 'system' files (required for the running of UNIX) or files for the benefit of the system's users (such as the UNIX commands we discuss in this book). In addition, each user will have their own collection of files. On a large UNIX system it would not be unreasonable to expect to find millions of files occupying hundreds of **gigabytes** of space.

If I choose to create a file called myfile (say), it is unlikely that I will be the only user on the machine to have chosen that particular name for a file. It would be unreasonable to expect me to choose a filename in lieu of myfile which was different to all files created by all the other users. Therefore UNIX must impose a structure on the filespace which will make it easy to manage a large number of files. The solution adopted is simple yet very powerful.

We can think of the available file storage for our machine as partitioned into separate **directories**. At any given time you can access files in one particular directory, which we can think of as the **current** directory. You can also 'move' between different directories and so change which is the current directory. A directory need not be a contiguous section of disk, and might be fragmented. That is, the various files contained within this storage area which we call a directory may in fact be physically located on different parts of a disk, or even on completely different disks or storage devices. This does not matter to the user – the logical structure of the machine's memory is important, not how it is physically implemented. In order for the machine to know how to find the data in these directories,

A gigabyte is a unit of storage equal to 1000 megabytes

. = 'period'

each has a file, called **dot** and referred to by the 'dot' symbol (.) which stores information about that directory (such as which files are stored within it, how big they are , and precisely where on disk they are stored). The word *directory* is also used to describe a file such as *dot* which contains the vital statistics for a directory storage area. Since the physical layout of a directory is not important to us, this dual meaning for the word presents us with no ambiguity.

Trees grow downwards ...

Pronounced 'root'

Within a directory are files, some of which may themselves be directories. Directories are organised in a **tree**-like structure. At the base of the tree is a directory whose UNIX name is '/'. So we might have the situation in Figure 3.1.

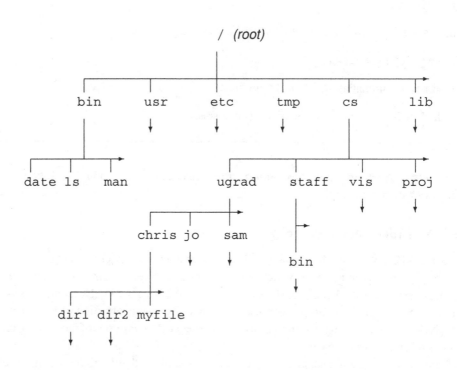

Figure 3.1   *A typical UNIX directory hierarchy.*

In each directory, in addition to the file dot, is a file called **dotdot**, referred to by the symbol '..', which is a synonym for the **parent** of that directory in the tree. Since a file *dot* and a file *dotdot* exist in each and every directory, we do not usually mention them when describing a UNIX directory hierarchy.

There are two means by which we may refer to the name of a file. Either we can name it **relative to** our current directory, in which case we need only use its simple name, such as myfile. Alternatively, we can use its **absolute** filename *relative to the root*. In this latter

/ = 'slash' or 'solidus'

case, its name commences with a /, followed by the intervening directories between the root and the file separated by /'s, and finally with the filename. Thus in the above tree, file myfile has absolute name /cs/ugrad/chris/myfile. If a filename commences with the character / then it is an *absolute* name, otherwise it is *relative*. Each file thus has a *unique* absolute filename. Moreover, since these filenames can be as long as required and the 'depth' of the tree can be as great as needed, we can cope with a UNIX system containing as many files as desired. Since the current directory has several names, there will be several names for an individual file; if the current directory is /cs/ugrad/chris then the following names are all of the same file:

Within reason — each system has a limit

```
/cs/ugrad/chris/myfile
myfile
./myfile
../chris/myfile
./././././myfile
../../../cs/ugrad/./chris/myfile
```

You can insert /. after any intermediate directory name without affecting the meaning

When logged in to the machine you are always in a current directory somewhere. When you initially login, you start in your **home directory** in which you can create your own files. This directory has a synonym, ˜, which you can use whenever you need to refer to your home directory. To find your current location within the file system use the command pwd. For example,

˜ = tilde

pwd = 'print working directory'

```
$ pwd
/cs/ugrad/chris
$
```

It is not always convenient to have your home directory as the current directory, since this might involve much typing of absolute filenames if you wish to access a file elsewhere. By means of the command cd you can move around the filesystem. By typing cd followed by the name of a directory, that will become the current directory (if it exists — if not, an error message will be output and your current directory will not change). For instance, to move to user sam's home directory, and thence to a non-existent directory called /squiggle:

cd = 'change directory'

```
$ cd /cs/ugrad/sam
$ cd /squiggle
/squiggle:  No such file or directory
```

You may also want to know what files exist on the machine. The command ls which we have already met will accomplish this. By default, ls will list the files in the current directory; if, however, you give ls one argument which is the name of a directory (either relative or absolute) the files *in that directory* will be listed. For instance:

ls = 'list'

```
$ ls /
bin etc tmp usr lib cs
$ cd /bin
$ pwd
/bin
$ ls
date ls man
```

```
$
```

Try this on your own machine. The output will not look exactly the same, and there will be many more files which are listed. If you give `ls` an argument which is an ordinary file, not a directory, just that filename will be displayed. Do not be afraid of 'getting lost' by changing to different directories — you can always return to your home directory by typing `cd` with no arguments (alternatively `cd ~`). Since ~ always refers to your home directory, you can always refer to files relative to that directory, so if ~ is `/cs/ugrad/chris`, then `/cs/ugrad/chris/myfile` could equally well be referred to as `~/myfile`

If you follow ~ by the name of the user, that user's home directory is referred to — so if you are `chris` then ~ is equivalent to `~chris`, and `sam` has home directory `~sam`.

Worked example 3.1   What files does `sam` have in their home directory?
Solution: Use `ls` followed by the name of `sam`'s home directory:

```
$ ls ~sam
```

Pronounced 'eye-node'   When a file is created, space to store it is found on the machine. That space is given a unique number, called an **inode**, which remains with that file until it is eventually deleted. At creation, the file is also given a **name**. The file is created in a directory, and at creation the directory is updated so that it contains the name of the file and the inode where that file is stored.

Filesystems

UNIX does not have the notion of 'a disk' which the programmer is allowed to work with. Not only is this concept somewhat vague, but developments in hardware and in storage devices may well mean that thinking in terms of disks might be inappropriate in the future. Instead, the concept exists of a **filesystem** within which inodes are unique, which is named and known by the machine, and which is associated with a specific directory in the file hierarchy. Each filesystem is set up with an allocated amount of storage space which the user cannot change.

When manipulating files, you will occasionally get error messages telling you that a filesystem is 'full'. In order to discover the amount of free disk space we can use the command `df`, which will also give information on which filesystems are set up for the system:

df = 'disk free'

```
$ df
Filesystem   1024-blocks    Used Available Capacity Mounted on
/dev/id000a        10637   10103      -529     106%  /
/dev/id001b       186723  155666     12385      93%  /usr
/dev/id000f        93033   42924     40806      51%  /export
/dev/id000d        46508   15384     26474      37%  /var
/dev/id001a       373463  266931     69186      79%  /usr
```

/dev/id001h	124263	93306	18531	83%	/usr/local
/dev/id001e	57802	39182	12840	75%	/var/tmp
/dev/id000g	747582	600260	72564	89%	/cs/staff
/dev/id001f	61803	50714	4909	91%	/cs/ugrad
/dev/sd8e	863422	700676	76404	90%	/cs/seng
/dev/id002h	560203	456846	47337	91%	/cs/res
/dev/sd8d	878162	562567	227779	71%	/cs/acad
/dev/id001d	186723	184473	2250	99%	/ex/swap2
/dev/id002f	524542	393609	130933	75%	/ex/swap
/dev/id000e	93033	80079	3651	96%	/ex/root

We see the storage for the machine divided into the filesystems, and their sizes are listed
together with how much of each is in use, and where within the directory hierarchy it is
placed. Notice that, in this example, /dev/id000a is more than 100% full – this is not
a printer's error! For each filesystem, normally only 90% of the physical space on that
device is available. This gives UNIX leeway to warn a user if they attempt to use more of a
filesystem than actually exists. Without this extra space, the kernel might find itself without
enough workspace to continue, and the system might crash. However, the SuperUser is
allowed to use the final 10% of a filesystem, and the capacity is measured relative to the
normally allowed 90% of the filesystem. Although most UNIX systems are set up in this
way, the 90% is not cast in stone, and the SuperUser may change it as local circumstances
dictate.

Manipulating files

There are lots of things you can do with a file. You can create, destroy, rename and copy it,
and you can protect it so that only certain users have access to its contents. These simple
actions have UNIX commands to effect them, which are generally simple commands.
Directories contain information about files other than themselves, unlike ordinary files,
and operations on them are in consequence more complex. We shall start by looking at
directories.

To create a new directory, the command mkdir, followed by the name you wish it to   mkdir = 'make directory'
have, will make a new directory with that name. For instance to create a file called dir1
in the current directory:

```
$ mkdir dir1
```

Conversely, to destroy a directory, use rmdir. Note that rmdir will only work if the   rmdir = 'remove direc-
directory you are trying to remove contains no user files. You should get used to structuring   tory'
your home directory so that it contains structured subdirectories. If you do not, and you
have more than a very small number of files, then you are likely to find difficulty keeping
track of which data you have stored where. A common way of organising your filespace
is to use the same conventions that are used on the system files. This involves creating
directories with 'standard' names, such as shown in Figure 3.2, for instance:

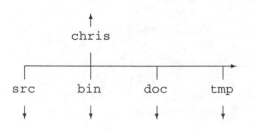

Figure 3.2   *A typical user's directory hierarchy.*

bin   commands you have written
src   source code for the commands you have written
doc   documentation
tmp   temporary files.

Worked example 3.2   Create a directory called tmp in your home directory.
Solution: Firstly, change your current directory to your home directory by typing cd; check that no file called tmp already exists by using ls; and then type mkdir tmp.

The first thing that must happen to a file before anything else is that it must come into existence. This may happen by design of another command (when you create it with an editor, for instance) or as a side-effect. You will frequently find that the current directory contains files you don't remember anything about! When the data held in a file are no longer required, you may wish to delete the file. Just as for file creation, this may be explicit or implicit (some automatically created files may disappear spontaneously).

cp = 'copy'   Suppose you have created a file called myfile. You can create another file with a copy of the contents of myfile using the command cp. If you decide the name of a file needs
mv = 'move'   to be changed, the command mv will do simply that. For instance:

```
$ ls
myfile
$ cp myfile foo
$ ls
foo myfile
$ mv myfile bar
$ ls
bar foo
```

When the command cp is called, a completely new file is created, *with a new inode*. The directory in which the new file is to be located is amended with the information about the new filename and the new inode. The data in the file being copied is not changed at all.

Sometimes it is useful to give a file several different names. This can often happen if you have data which needs to be accessed in several different directories, and any changes to it need to be made consistently. If you created several copies of the file, you would have to perform updates several times, once on each copy. This is inefficient, and errors might creep in. Also, storage space would be wasted – and if the files concerned are large data files this might well be an important consideration. We can use the concept of an inode to good effect here. Since a directory associates names with their storage locations via inodes, there is no reason why a particular file should not have several names, perhaps in different directories.

To create a second name for a file, which must already exist, we can create a **link** – sometimes called a **hard link** – to it using the command `ln`. With two arguments, which must be filenames, provided the first file does exist and the second does not, we can create a link from the first to the second. For instance, suppose user `sam` whose home directory is `/cs/ugrad/sam` has a file `datafile` which I wish to have in my own home directory under the name `samsdata`, then the command `ln` can be used to create a link between the two:

`ln = 'link'`

```
$ ln /cs/ugrad/sam/datafile samsdata
```

We say that `samsdata` has *two links*, and it has two names, one `samsdata`, the other `/cs/ugrad/sam/datafile`. The file has a single inode, however. When `samsdata` is amended, the contents of `/cs/ugrad/sam/datafile` are changed at exactly the same time (and vice versa). If we delete `/cs/ugrad/sam/datafile`, we actually delete that file*name*, and the file continues to exist, but with only one name (`samsdata`) and one link. The kernel will keep track of how many names (links) an inode has, and when this drops to zero the filespace allocated to that inode is released for use elsewhere. There is one important point to note here – inodes are unique only within a single filesystem, and therefore you can only link a file to another file within the same filesystem. We can check precisely which inodes are allocated to which files by using option `-i` to `ls`:

`i = 'inode'`

```
$ ls -i
total 561
241563 myfile    43532 dir1    86475 dir2
567721 prog.c   563341 foo     563341 bar
```

In this example, files `foo` and `bar` have the same inode, namely `563341`, and have therefore been linked. Note that two linked files do not necessarily have to be in the same directory.

At this point, it is worth discussing briefly what a directory actually is. If you type `ls` while in a particular directory, any directories contained within that directory (referred to as **subdirectories**) will appear as if they were files. In a sense, this is correct – every directory can be considered as a file, with its own inode. This 'file' contains – in a form which need not concern us – information as to where the files in that subdirectory are stored. By typing `cd` followed by the name of a directory, the file which is that directory is examined, the data in that file which indicates 'where it is stored' is retrieved, and that information is used to work out where the new current directory is stored.

Worked example 3.3

What is the inode of your home directory?

Solution: First of all, type `cd` to change to your home directory. If you then type `ls  -i`
the inodes of the files contained in that directory will be given; the manual page for `ls`

d = 'directory'

indicates that option `-d` will list directories like other files, rather than listing their contents.
So you require

```
$ ls -id
```

'Dot' files

a = 'all'

Change to your home directory, and type `ls  -a` and you will see displayed the names of
the files in that directory including some other names that `ls` on its own does not produce.
These 'hidden' files all have names beginning with a dot (`.`). You will recognise the name
of the current directory *dot* and the parent directory *dotdot*, but some others will be there.
Typically you may expect `.profile`, `.mailrc` and `.xinitrc`; these files are all used

rc = 'run commands'

by a UNIX utility to enable you to customise that utility, and many of them end in `rc`.
When a utility requires such a file, the manual page will explain what data it should contain.
Never delete or edit a dot file unless you know what it should contain, even if it's empty –
that's why `ls` does not normally list them, to prevent you accidentally changing them.

If you wish to access a dot file, the procedure is exactly the same as for any other file –
it's just `ls` that hides them.

Groups

The System Administrator manages a database of **groups**. Each group is a list of users and
is given a name (such as `ugrads`, `general` or `proj`). The reason for having groups is
that when access to software or data needs to be restricted, a group can be used to specify
this. Each user will be a member of one or more groups, and each file will be allocated to
exactly one group. At any particular time, a user is allocated a group which is the default
group for new files they create.

id = 'identifier'

Each group has a unique name and also a unique number (its **group-id** or **GID**). The
command `id` is used to interrogate the database, and on its own will display the user's
name together with the groups they are a member of, both names and numbers, and the
user's user-id and current group-id. If you give `id` an argument which is another user's
username, then the information for that user will be displayed instead. For example,

```
$ id chris
uid=145(chris) gid=12(ugrads) groups=12(ugrads),417(proj)
```

shows that user `chris` is a member of groups `ugrads` and `proj`, with GID numbers
`12` and `417` respectively. Currently `chris` is allocated to group `ugrads`. Notice also
that `id` has displayed a number for `chris`, namely `145` – each user is also allocated a
unique number, their **user-id** or **UID**. In order to change your current group-id, command

newgrp = 'new group'

`newgrp` should be invoked. Followed by the *name* of a group *of which you must be a member* this will perform the required change. With no argument, it will return you to your default group-id as defined in the password file. For example, if you are user `chris`, and wish to change your allocated group to `proj`, so that you can control access to users in group `proj` when you create new files:

```
$ newgrp proj
$ id
uid=145(chris) gid=417(proj) groups=12(ugrads),417(proj)
```

File access control

Some data you store on the machine you will not want other users to read. If you are doing a programming assignment for your course, for example, you will not want other students to read it. If your institution has purchased software which has conditions attached to its use (as is often the case nowadays) it may be necessary to restrict its use to a specific group of users. UNIX has a flexible method of protecting files. First of all, each file on the machine divides the users of the machine into three categories:

- the file's **owner** (normally the user who created the file)

- a **group** of users

- **other** users.

For each of these categories of user, that user may be either given or denied the following **access privileges**:

- **read**

- **write**

- **execute**.

If a file has *read* permission, it can be examined at a terminal, printed (if it is a text file), viewed by an editor, and so on. If it has *write* permission, the contents of the file can be changed (for example, by an editor), the file can be overwritten or deleted. If it has *execute* permission, and is a binary program or a shell script, that program can be run (but copied only if it also has *read* permission). An example is given later on in this chapter.

The system first of all checks to see whether the user is the *owner* of a file, and if so the *owner* permissions are used. Otherwise, it checks to see if the user is a member of the group allocated to that file, and if so checks *group* file permissions. If the user is neither the file owner nor in the file's group, they come under the heading of *other* users. The group to which a file has been allocated must be a valid group which the System Administrator has already set up, as discussed above. The owner of a file can change the group to which it has been allocated.

Access privileges for directories have a different meaning than for ordinary files. If a directory has *write* permission, files in that directory may be created or deleted. If it has *read* permission, it is possible to see what files are contained in that directory (using `ls`, say); if it has *execute* permission it is possible to `cd` to it. A directory with *execute* but not *read* permission is useful if you wish to allow someone else to run one of your commands located in that directory, but do not wish them to see what other files you have.

To find out the access privileges for a file, use `ls`. As an example, consider user `chris` who has 6 files in the home directory (including two subdirectories). By typing `ls -l` the following output might be seen:

l = 'long'

```
total 561
-rw-r--r--  1   chris   ugrads      122 Dec 21 18:40 myfile
drwxr-xr-x  1   chris   general     512 Dec 22 14:55 dir1
drwx----    1   chris   general     512 Dec 22 14:55 dir2
-rw-r----   1   chris   proj       9912 Nov 22 17:55 prog.c
-r-x----    2   chris   general     147 Dec 22 17:56 foo
-r-x----    2   chris   general     147 Dec 22 17:56 bar
```

On BSD systems you need
ls -lg

In fact, `ls -l` will output most information you are likely to need about files for routine work. The general format for the output is:

```
-rw-r--r--  1   chris   ugrads      122 Dec 21 18:40 myfile
^^^^^^^^^^  ^   ^^^^^   ^^^^^^^^^   ^^^^ ^^^^^^^^^^^^ ^^^^

access     links owner   group    size  last change name
```

The access privileges are presented as a string of 10 characters. The first character is usually either a `d` or a `-`, indicating that the file is a directory or an ordinary file respectively. There are other values possible which we discuss later. Characters 2–4, 5–7 and 8–10 describe the access privileges for the owner, the group and for others respectively. Each of these 3-character substrings denotes whether read, write and execute privileges have been allowed or denied.

For *read* privilege, the first character will be `r`, otherwise `-`; for *write* privilege the second will be `w`, otherwise `-`. Lastly, for *execute* privilege, the third will be `x`, otherwise `-`.

For example, file `myfile` above can be read by anybody, but only Chris can write to it (that is, change the contents of the file in any way). File `prog.c` can only be written to by Chris, but only users who are members of the group `proj` can also read it. File `foo` can be read by Chris, and also executed, but no-one else can access it at all. Nor can Chris write to it – this is not necessarily a mistake, it is often useful to deny yourself write access to a file to prevent yourself accidentally deleting the file if it contains important data.

If a directory does not have write permission, then files in that directory cannot be deleted, nor can new ones be created. However, files within that directory which do have write permission can have their contents changed.

The other information that `ls -l` provides is as follows. The number of **links** to a file is printed, followed by the owner of the file and the group the file is currently assigned to. Then comes the size of the file in bytes and the date and time the file last had any of its contents changed. At the end of the line comes the name of the file.

A file has precisely one group associated with it; this can be changed to another group by `chgrp`. For instance, suppose our directory has the same contents as before, and recall that we have linked `foo` and `bar`, we might have the following dialogue:

chgrp = 'change group'

```
$ ls -l
```

```
total 561
-rw-r--r--    1    chris   ugrads      122 Dec 21 18:40 myfile
drwxr-xr-x    1    chris   general     512 Dec 22 14:55 dir1
drwx----      1    chris   general     512 Dec 22 14:55 dir2
-rw-r----     1    chris   proj       9912 Nov 22 17:55 prog.c
-r-x----      2    chris   general     147 Dec 22 17:56 foo
-r-x----      2    chris   general     147 Dec 22 17:56 bar
$ chgrp proj foo
$ ls -l
total 561
-rw-r--r--    1    chris   ugrads      122 Dec 21 18:40 myfile
drwxr-xr-x    1    chris   general     512 Dec 22 14:55 dir1
drwx----      1    chris   general     512 Dec 22 14:55 dir2
-rw-r----     1    chris   proj       9912 Nov 22 17:55 prog.c
-r-x----      2    chris   proj        147 Dec 22 17:56 foo
-r-x----      2    chris   proj        147 Dec 22 17:56 bar
```

Note that the other file linked to foo has also had its group changed, and that the access privileges for the file are not changed. chgrp allows one option, -R — with this option, if its file argument is a directory, all files and subdirectories will also have their groups changed. R = 'recursive'

The above information does not tell us that foo and bar are linked — it merely states that each of those two files has two links (but not necessarily to each other), and that they are the same size and created at the same time (to the nearest second). To check that two files are in fact linked, it is necessary to ask what their inodes actually are, and you should use ls -i as discussed earlier. The options -l and -i can be combined, giving

```
$ ls -il
```

but you may find the output becomes wider than your terminal is. Try it ...

Similar to chgrp is chown, which has similar syntax, but can be used to change the actual owner of a file. This is an operation you are unlikely to wish to perform, and most systems restrict the command so that only the SuperUser may use it. chown = 'change owner'

The most frequent change you are likely to make to a file, apart from its actual contents, is to the access privileges; chmod is used for this change. The syntax is chmod followed by a specification of changes to the access permission, followed by a file (or files) this change is to be applied to. chmod = 'change mode'

The specification can be done two ways — either the privileges for the user/group/other sets of users can be *set* or they can be *changed*. A character called a **who symbol** which is one of u (user), g (group), o (other) or a (all), or a sequence of who symbols, denotes for which users the specification will apply. For instance, go will refer to the group and others, but not to the file's owner. The symbol a is a synonym for ugo — this synonym is simply shorthand, as ugo is a very frequently used sequence of who symbols.

Following the sequence of who symbols comes one of +, - or =, followed by zero or more **perm symbols** (r, w, x or -), which represent permissions to be set or changed for the users specified by the previous who symbols. A + indicates *add* the permissions, - indicates *remove* those permissions, and = means *set* them. For example,

```
$ chmod go-w myfile
```

will deny write permission to group and to others,

```
$ chmod u+x myfile
```

will allow execute permission to the owner,

```
$ chmod g=r-x myfile
```

will set group access to r-x, so that users in the file's group will be able to read and to execute file myfile, but not write to it.

When a file is created, it has default access privileges which would be set by the System Administrator. These can be changed by the user by means of the command umask followed by a string with the same information as for chmod above. For example,

umask = 'user mask'

```
$ umask u=rwx,g=r,o=
```

will cause all new files created to have read, write and execute privileges for the owner, but to deny write and execute privileges for the group, and to deny all privileges for others. This state of affairs will continue during the current session until umask is again invoked.

Worked example 3.4

Create a file which no-one can read, and confirm that you yourself cannot read it.
Solution: First of all, choose a name for the file (myfile, say) and use cat or vi to create the file. In order to deny read access to everybody, the command is

```
$ chmod a-r myfile
```

the a for *all* users, r for *read*, and - to deny. To check that you can't read it, try examining the contents using cat and you should get an error message:

```
$ cat myfile
cat: myfile: Permission denied
```

File contents

Given a file, the question will come to mind: 'What does the file contain?' A simple answer to this question might be that it contains a sequence of bytes – but this would not be very helpful. We need to know what those bytes represent. We could start off by examining the filename; some UNIX files are required to have a particular suffix, and this information would indicate their contents. However, we should note that, for instance, if file `myfile.c` is to contain a C program, its suffix must be `.c`, but the converse does not hold. If we encounter a file called `myfile.c` then this does not mean that the file must contain a C program (although it would be perverse if in fact it did not).

It is not possible to infer from a file's suffix (if indeed it has one) what the contents of the file represent. Indeed, UNIX makes no stipulation of any sort as to what may or may not be stored in a file – a file is merely a sequence of bytes.

However, all is not lost. It is possible to make an intelligent guess as to what a file contains by examining the format of the data inside it. For instance, if the file contains words which occur in the C language, one might reasonably guess that the file contains C source code. Many sorts of data can have their type inferred from their format, and the command `file` is provided to do this. For example,

```
$ file prog.c
prog.c:         c program text
$ file libc.a
libc.a:         archive random library
$ file story
story:          English text
```

Don't worry about `file` telling you that a particular file is of a weird type you've never heard of! It probably means it contains something you aren't interested in anyway. Unfortunately, `file` is not infallible, and it is possible to confuse it, but nonetheless it's a pretty reliable aid.

What type of file is `/usr`?   **Worked example 3.5**
Solution: Use `file`:

```
$ file /usr
/usr:           directory
```

thus `/usr` is a directory.

We should also ask whether the question 'What does file X contain?' is a useful question. It is possible to define in a precise way what a C program must look like, but not, for instance, the data for transactions pertaining to a bank account. Rather than asking what type of data is in a particular file, we should instead be creating files whose contents are in a specified format.

Text files

We now concentrate on a particular class of files, **text files**, which are files divided into **lines** separated by a *NEWLINE* character. Such files, which would normally contain only printable characters, include text program source files, shell scripts, and in fact any files you would wish to use a text editor on. However, this is not a requirement and what we discuss in this section will also hold true for files containing other characters. Most of the files we will use as examples in the rest of this book will be text files.

Suppose we have created a file called story, which contains English text. Having established that it is a text file (by means of file or otherwise), we may wish briefly to examine its contents. We could, of course, invoke an editor such as vi and use the commands within the editor to move through the file and look at various bits of it, or we could use a pager. However, there are easier methods.

Often you will simply want to look at the first few lines of a file (for instance to verify that it was indeed the file you expected it to be). In this case, head will print out the first 5 lines of the file. In a similar vein, tail will print out the last 5. If you want to see the first (say) 10 lines, then the command would be head -n 10.

n = 'number'

Strictly speaking, tail copies its input to standard output *beginning at a designated place*, which is usually a number of lines from the end of the file. There are many options available to tail to allow you to specify what is meant by the designated place, and how many lines are output – refer to the manual page for further details.

As an example of simple use, suppose file myfile contains 100 lines, as follows:

```
line 1
line 2
 ...
line 100
```

Then we might have

```
$ head -n 3 myfile
line 1
line 2
line 3
$ tail -n 4 myfile
line 97
line 98
line 99
line 100
$
```

Worked example 3.6

Find the most recently modified file (excluding 'dot' files) in the current directory.
Solution: This has clearly somehow got to involve ls. With option -l we could examine by hand every file and see which one was last changed. That is not the UNIX way of doing

t = 'time'

things – by examining the manual page for ls we find an option -t which will sort the files it prints out so that the most recent is shown first. Option -l forces the output to be

one filename per line. Thus `ls  -t1` will produce a list of filenames with the desired one   1 is digit 'one'
at the top — use `head` to isolate it by piping the output of `ls` to `head` thus:

```
$ ls -t1 | head -n 1
```

There is only a limited amount of space on a machine, and it may be that each user has
been restricted (by the System Administrator) as to how much filespace they are allowed
to use. A quick way to find out how big files are is to use `wc`, which will indicate (i) the   wc = 'wordcount'
number of *lines*, (ii) the number of *words* and (iii) the number of bytes in a file. The latter
two are only meaningful if the file is a text file, though. For example,

```
$ wc myfile
27 124 664 myfile
```

indicates that file `myfile` has 27 lines, 124 words and 664 bytes (characters). With options
`-c`, `-w` or `-l` respectively only the byte, word or line count will be printed. Note that `wc`
does not work on directories.

A situation that often arises is that you are examining a file, and you discover a very
similar file, and require to know the differences between the two files. This can happen
when a file has been edited several times, and you lose track of precisely what changes have
been made. The command `diff` will come to your aid. Use it followed by the names of   diff = 'differences'
two files and it will tell you in the following manner. Suppose we have two files, `file1`
and `file2`, where `file1` contains the following text:

```
A
test
file
```

and `file2` contains

```
A
testing
file
```

then we would have

```
$ diff file1 file2
2c2
< test
--
> testing
```

indicating that line 2 containing `myfile` has been removed from `file1` and replaced by
a line containing `testing`.

Related to `diff` is `cmp`. Sometimes, especially within shell scripts, the verbosity of   cmp = 'compare'
`diff` is not required, and a terse indication of whether or not two files are identical is
required — `cmp` will give a short message if its two arguments are different, otherwise it

will stay silent. Also, diff can only compare text files — cmp will compare two files *of any type* and indicate whether or not their contents are the same.

Text files — especially ones containing 'raw data' — often contain repeated lines. It is sometimes useful to know either how often this occurs, or to filter out the repeated occurrences. The command uniq is provided for this purpose. For instance, supposing file A contains

uniq = 'unique'

```
aaa
bbb
bbb
bbb
bbb
bbb
ccc
ccc
aaa
ddd
```

then the following dialogue might take place:

```
$ uniq A
aaa
bbb
ccc
aaa
ddd
$ uniq -c A
1 aaa
5 bbb
2 ccc
1 aaa
1 ddd
```

c = 'count'
d = 'duplicate'
u = 'unique'

With no options, uniq simply filters out consecutive repeated lines; option -c prepends each line of output with a count of the number of times that line was repeated. Option -d causes uniq only to write out lines that are repeated, and -u only to write out lines that are not repeated consecutively. Thus

```
$ uniq -d A
bbb
ccc
$ uniq -u A
aaa
aaa
ddd
```

Another common situation arises when you have two or more files, containing what can be thought of as columns in a table. You require corresponding lines from the files to be concatenated so as to actually produce a table. Using the command `paste` will achieve this — corresponding lines of its arguments will be joined together separated by a single *TAB* character. For example, suppose file A contains

```
hello
Chris
```

and file B contains

```
there
how are you?
```

then the following dialogue can take place:

```
$ paste A B
hello there
Chris how are you?
```

Both `paste` and `uniq`, though only of use in limited situations, save a great deal of time editing files when they can in fact be used.

Sometimes, when dealing with files which are presented in a rigid format, you may wish to select character columns from such a file. The utility `cut` is a very simple method for extracting columns. Suppose we have a file `myfile` containing the following data (dates of birth and names):

```
17.04.61 Smith Fred
22.01.63 Jones Susan
03.11.62 Bloggs Zach
```

Then we can choose the years from each line by selecting character columns 7 to 8, thus:

```
$ cut -c7-8 myfile
61
63
62
```

c = 'column'

This command can also distinguish between **fields**, and to select family names from `myfile` (Smith, Jones and Bloggs), we could use `cut -f2 -d' '  myfile`, which specifies that we select field number 2 where the **delimiter** (option `-d`) is the space character:

A line is thought of as divided into fields separated by a known delimiter

```
$ cut -f2 -d' '  myfile
Smith
Jones
Bloggs
```

f = 'field'

Related to cut is fold; cut will assume you want the same number of lines in the output as the input, but you wish to select part of those input lines. On the other hand, fold assumes that you want all of your input, but that your output needs to fit within some lines of maximum width – for example, if you had a file with some very long lines in it that you needed printing on a printer which was fairly narrow. The action performed by fold is to copy its standard input, or names mentioned as arguments, to standard output, but whenever a line of length greater than a certain number (default 80 characters) is met, then a *NEWLINE* character is inserted at that point. With option -w followed by a number, that number is taken to be the maximum length of output lines rather than 80. Try the following:

w = 'width'

```
$ fold -w 15 <<END
Let's start
with three
short lines
and finish with an extremely long one with lots of words
END
```

For more sophisticated processing of files divided into records and fields we can use awk (see Chapter 9).

Another exceptionally useful command is sort, which sorts its input into alphabetical order line-by-line. It has many options, and can sort on a specified field of the input rather than the first, or numerically (using option -n) rather than alphabetically. So using file A above, we could have:

n = 'numerical'

```
$ sort A
aaa
aaa
bbb
bbb
bbb
bbb
bbb
ccc
ccc
ddd
```

A feature of uniq is that it will only filter out repeated lines if they are consecutive; if we wish to display each line that occurs in a file once and only once, we could first of all sort the file into an order and then use uniq:

```
$ sort A | uniq
aaa
bbb
ccc
ddd
```

There is an option -u which will automatically filter out such duplicated lines without the need to pipe the output into uniq. Try it ...

u = 'unique'

Find out how many separate inodes are represented by the files (excluding 'dot' files) in the current directory.

Worked example 3.7

Solution: Using ls -il we can list the files, one per line, preceded by their inode number. Piping the output into cut we can isolate the first six character columns, which contain the inode number, and sort with option -u will sort these into order and remove all duplicates. These can then be counted by counting the number of *lines* of output using wc -l:

```
$ ls -il | cut -c1-6 | sort -u | wc -l
```

We must address the question of what a file contains if it is not a text file. Clearly we cannot use the text utilities described above — not only will the file not be neatly split up into lines, the characters contained within it will in general not be printable. The file command gives us a rough indication as to what sort of data a file (binary or text) contains, but no more. If we need to know exactly what characters are contained in a file, od will give us precisely that information. Thinking of a file as a sequence of bytes, od will list each byte in a representation which can be printed. The name stands for **octal dump**, and by default it will list the bytes by their octal (base 8) codes word-by-word (a word being typically 4 bytes).

Since computers use binary code internally, when in the past it was necessary to examine data, it was often not possible to display that data in any way other than as a representation of binary numbers. One of the simplest ways of doing this was to group the bits (binary digits) together in sequences of 3, consider each 3-bit sequence as representing a digit in base 8, and print out the data as a string of octal digits. Hence we get the phrase *octal dump*.

A more useful output is with option -t c, whereby each byte is either printed as a 3-digit octal number which is the code for that character, or the character itself (if it is printable), or backslash followed by a character (if a standard escape sequence is known). For instance,

c = 'character', t = 'type'

The escape sequence for the newline character is \n

```
$ od -t c bintest
0000000 201 003  \n 013  \0 001 200  \0
0000010  \0  \0   @  \0  \0  \0 251 230
0000020  \0  \0  \0  \0  \0  \0
0000030  \0  \0  \0  \0  \0  \0  \0  \0
0000040 274 020      \0 320 003 240   @
0000050 222 003 240   D 225   *     002
0000060 224 002 240 004 224 002   @  \n
0000070 027  \0  \0   h 324   " 343 240
0000100 003  \0  \0  \b 302  \0   b  \b
```

. . .

We see that the first byte in the file has code 201_8 (which is 129 in decimal). The third byte is a *NEWLINE* character. Just for comparison, a file called `hellotest` containing one line which is simply the word `Hello` would be displayed thus:

```
$ od -t c hellotest
0000000 H e l l o \n
0000006
```

The command has several possible options, which we do not list here.

If you just want to examine a binary file quickly, and see what printable strings exist within it, use command `strings`. This can be useful if you have *compiled* a program, such as one written in C, and that program contains strings whose value is of interest to you (filenames, for instance). Going through the binary code with `od` would be tedious.

A useful command we introduce at this point is `touch`. This command has the effect of changing the date and time that its file arguments were last modified – they are altered to the current date and time. If the files which are its arguments do not currently exist they are created with size 0; `touch` is useful to create a file if you haven't yet decided what to put in it, but want it to be there. This might happen during the development phase of a program. It is also useful to indicate that the file is in some sense 'up-to-date'.

Printing files

`lp` = 'lineprinter'

On BSD systems `lpr` is used instead of `lp`

Although you will probably spend a lot of time sitting in front of a computer terminal, you will from time to time need to get 'hard copy' of documents, that is, you will need to print them onto paper. To do this, type `lp` followed by the name of the file or files you wish to be printed. If you omit filenames, the standard input will be printed, so that can have data piped into it. It is important that you only attempt to print text files. Most modern printers will be sensible if you send them unprintable files, and simply refuse to print them, but a few will go haywire.

`d` = 'destination'
`n` = 'numerical'

Each copy will normally start on a separate side of paper

Your machine will be set up with a 'default' printer, and your System Administrator will have told you which it is and where it is located. If you give to `lp` the option `-d` followed by the name of another printer, that printer will be used instead. The option `-n` followed by a number will cause that number of copies of the document to be printed (use with care!). For instance, to print 2 copies of file `myfile` on the printer named `def`:

```
$ lp -n 2 -d def myfile
```

It is a fact of life that documents stored on a machine are changed frequently. When a file is sent to a printer, it is often useful for an indication to be given as to when the file was printed (so the reader will be reminded how out-of-date it may be). It is also useful, when the document is long, for each page to be printed together with a header containing useful information such as the page number. When a file is printed with `lp`, that file is printed completely naked; nothing except the characters in the file will appear on paper. The command `pr` is designed to remedy this situation; it has numerous options, which allow you to tailor your files to particular printers. `pr` divides the input into *pages*, each commencing with a header naming the file and the date and time, and ending with a trailer of blank lines. The size (number of columns and width) of each page and the size of the header and trailer can be changed, output can be multi-column, and various other attributes of the output can be altered. The output of `pr` is to standard output, so must be piped to `lp`. For example, the following command will print file `abc` on the printer named `def`, 2 columns per page, 50 lines per page (using option -l):

1 is letter 'ell'

```
$ pr -2 -l 50 abc | lp -d def
```

To use `pr` effectively, you must know the characteristics of the printer (or printers) to which you have access; your System Administrator will provide you with that information.

It is common nowadays for laser printers to be available. Rather than having a fixed set of characters like a line printer, or a coarse selection of symbols which can be created by an artistic user such as in a dot-matrix printer, a laser printer is suitable for intricate graphical printing. In order to use such facilities, files for a laser printer must be in a special code. We discuss such printers in Chapter 10, however it is worth mentioning that most laser printers will accept text input just like other printers.

Such as PostScript

File archives and file compression

It will often be necessary to take a copy of a complete directory, either for the purpose of storing it in a safe place in case the computer system 'crashes', or to send it to a different computer system. There are two particular problems which utilities such as `cp` are unable to address. First, different machines and operating systems will store data in different formats, and it may be necessary to convert the format in which the files in the directory are stored. Second, `cp` will not handle links.

A 'backup'

There have historically been two commands, `tar` and `cpio`, which have been used. Both work by copying all the files in the directory, together with data describing the structure of the directory, into a single file known as an **archive**. Unfortunately, both `tar` and `cpio` work differently and produce archives in different formats. Although `tar` was used much more extensively than `cpio`, it was felt necessary to create a completely new command which would perform the functions of both rather than try to update `tar` so that it would also do everything `cpio` would do.

tar = 'tape archive'

cpio = 'copy in out'

Neither `tar` nor `cpio` became part of POSIX, but a new command `pax` has been written. We give a couple of examples illustrating both `pax` and `tar`.

pax = 'portable archive exchange'

To create a new archive, give `pax` the argument -w or `tar` the argument -c. The archive file will be sent to standard output. So to archive the contents of the current directory to the tape drive /dev/rst8, either of the following will work:

w = 'write'

c = 'create'

```
$ tar -c .  >/dev/rst8
$ pax -w .  >/dev/rst8
```

Alternatively, you can redirect the output to a file. To extract the contents of an archive, the standard input to `pax` or `tar` should be redirected from the archive, `pax` requires argument -r and `tar` argument -x. Naturally, when unpacking an archive, you don't

r = 'read'

x = 'extract'

want to overwrite any files or directories which you have already created. It is a good idea to check the contents of an archive by means of the `-t` option to both `tar` and `pax`, which will simply cause the names of the files in the archive to be listed.

Having multiple copies of directories – whether 'real' or archived – is bound to take up space. If you have created an archive – `mydir.pax`, say – you can **compress** the file and reduce its size, by means of the command `compress`. This will create a file `mydir.pax.Z` (note the `.Z` suffix) and delete `mydir.pax`; the file `mydir.pax.Z` will have a smaller size than `mydir.pax`. The actual reduction in file size will depend on what the file to be compressed contains. For example:

`compress` is not POSIX

Typically a factor of between 0.5 and 0.2

```
$ ls
mydir.pax
$ wc -c mydir.pax
206336
$ compress mydir.pax
$ ls
mydir.pax.Z
$ wc -c mydir.pax.Z
89473
```

To reverse the compression, use the command `uncompress`. If you have stored any large files which you do not use on a regular basis, you may wish to compress them.

Worked example 3.8

Copy the contents of your current directory to `/tmp/backup` preserving all links.
Solution: Using `pax -w` we can create a new archive; store this in a temporary file, create `/tmp/backup`, change directory to `/tmp/backup`, and read the archive.

```
$ pax -w .  >/tmp/backup.pax
$ mkdir /tmp/backup
$ cd /tmp/backup
$ pax -r </tmp/backup.pax
```

Other relevant commands

Many files have names containing a **suffix**, that is, a sequence of characters at the end of the name and commencing with a dot. For example, if you have a program written in the language C the file in which that program is stored will have a suffix `.c` of necessity. Let us suppose you have written a C program which is stored in file `myfile.c` in your home directory `/cs/ugrad/chris`. From the point of view of the UNIX kernel, it is irrelevant what name this file has. Only when you attempt to compile and run the program will the suffix become important, as the UNIX command for compiling a C program demands that the `.c` suffix be present, and indeed will create files with the same **base** `myfile` and different suffix. In this example, a file `myfile.o` would be created (the 'o' stands for 'object code', i.e. binary code for the processor). A standard POSIX command will make no demands on a file's suffix, although other utilities may well do so; the manual page for that command will tell you.

The command `dirname` will take as argument the name of a file and strip off the actual filename, leaving only the directories. Command `basename` also takes a filename as argument, but strips off the directory information leaving only the filename relative to its parent directory. If `basename` is given two arguments, and the second argument is a suffix of the filename, that suffix is also removed. For instance:

```
$ dirname /cs/ugrad/chris/test.c
/cs/ugrad/chris
$ basename /cs/ugrad/chris/test.c
test.c
$ basename /cs/ugrad/chris/test.c .c
test
```

The benefit of these two commands will not be apparent at this stage, but later on, when writing shell scripts which manipulate files, they are exceptionally useful.

When the command `mv` is called, the directory in which its first argument is located is updated so that the file's absolute name is changed. *The inode of the file is not changed* if the new filename is on the same filesystem. This command name is somewhat misleading, since the file doesn't really move at all.

We also need to know the *total* amount of space taken up by our files. Here the command `du` comes to our rescue. With argument the name of a directory (or the current directory, if no argument is given), `du` will print the total number of *kilo*bytes used to store the data in the files in that directory. For example,

`du` = 'disk usage'

```
$ du
12        ./dir1
7         ./dir2
27        .
```

indicates that directory `dir1` takes up 12k (kilobytes) and `dir2` takes 7k, whereas the total amount of storage used for the current directory is 27k (including `dir1` and `dir2`).

You can omit the rest of this chapter at first reading

There are some other standard commands which are not required for simple use of UNIX. Nevertheless, they are included within the standard, and are included here for completeness.

Suppose you have distributed some text files to a colleague, and you then make minor alterations to them. You want your colleague to have updated copies of the files. One possibility is to send them all the files anew, but this has the disadvantage that a potentially large volume of data must be transmitted, which may well incur costs. An arguably preferable method would be to send your colleague a list of the changes to the files. These changes can be displayed using `diff`, however it would be unreasonable for your colleague to edit all the files by hand to make the changes. Fortunately, command `patch` is provided which will perform the task automatically. It takes a file containing the changes, as output by `diff`, and the name of a file which those changes are to be applied to, and makes them.

The commands we have introduced in this chapter will be seen to perform only simple manipulations of UNIX files, especially when examining the contents of files. Three programs – `grep`, `sed` and `awk` – which we discuss later in the book – provide comprehensive facilities for processing file contents, and obviate the need for more 'simple' UNIX commands over and above those mentioned in this chapter.

Summary of utilities

`basename`	display non-directory part of filename
`cd`	change working directory
`chgrp`	change file group ownership
`chmod`	change file access privileges
`chown`	change file ownership
`cmp`	compare two files
`compress`	compress files
`cp`	copy files
`cpio`	copy files to and from archives
`cut`	select columns or fields from each line of a file
`df`	display free disk space
`diff`	show differences between two files
`dirname`	display directory part of a pathname
`du`	display file space usage
`file`	describe file contents
`fold`	fold lines
`head`	show the first few lines of a file
`id`	display information about a user's identity
`ln`	link files
`lp`	send files to a printer
`mkdir`	create new directories
`mv`	move files
`newgrp`	change your current group-id
`od`	dump files in various formats
`paste`	merge corresponding lines of text files
`patch`	apply changes to files
`pax`	file archiver and format translator
`pr`	a very basic formatter for text files
`pwd`	display working directory
`rmdir`	remove empty directories
`sort`	sort or merge text files
`strings`	display printable strings in a file
`tail`	show the last few lines of a file
`tar`	create tape archives, and add or extract files
`touch`	change last modification time of a file
`umask`	change access privileges when files are created
`uncompress`	uncompress files
`uniq`	filter out repeated lines
`wc`	word, line and byte count

Problems

3.1 Write a script which will list the three most recently altered files (including 'dot' files) in the current directory.

3.2 What type of file is `/bin/id`?

3.3 List the files (excluding 'dot' files) in the current directory, together with their inodes, in numerical order of the inodes.

3.4 How many subdirectories are there in `/usr`?

3.5 Write a script which will display the owner of the current directory *only*.

3.6 Write a script which will display the names of files in `/bin` and `/usr/bin` that have the same name.

3.7 Write a script which will list the files in the current directory (excluding 'dot' files) in 'long' format (that is, including the information that `ls` provides with option `-l`), and in increasing order of size (*difficult*).

3.8 List (without duplication) the groups which own the files in the current directory.

Chapter 4

Processes and devices

OBJECTIVES

In this chapter you will learn about:

☐ processes, jobs and the execution environment;

☐ how UNIX handles input and output devices.

The basic program unit apparent to a programmer working in a UNIX environment is the 'process'. An understanding of how processes are handled is fundamental to the effective use of UNIX.

Processes

So far we have considered a dialogue with a UNIX system as being a sequence of *commands* entered by the user, and the system taking *action* at each command. We now explore the mechanisms with which UNIX implements commands.

When describing an operating system, we need to remember that the computer system on which it is running contains electronics which run *only* machine code. Any command a user types in is translated into machine code, either directly by a process known as **compilation**, or is **interpreted** by another program which is already in machine code. A machine code program is known as a **process**. Every command given to a UNIX system, and every program run on a UNIX machine, relates to a process – either it creates one or more processes, or is interpreted by one which is already running. A UNIX shell has a mechanism for controlling processes which appears to the user to be independent of the electronics inside the machine.

Within a UNIX system will be one or more processing elements (which we will refer to as **processors**) which can only run a single process at any one time. At any instant, that process can be described completely by a sequence of bytes – some representing the memory contained within the processor, some describing the precise current state of the computation. It is possible to copy those bytes to memory, and replace them by a sequence of bytes from elsewhere in memory. Thus a partially completed process can be temporarily **suspended** (or **stopped**), and completed at a later time, and in the meantime another process can be run on that processor.

The kernel manages a large 'pool' of processes, most of which at any specific instant are not running, and moves them to and from the processor (or processors) as required. Much of this movement is automatic, and hidden from users – for instance, when there are several users on the machine each with a program which is running, then the relevant processes are moved in and out of the processor so that each gets a fair percentage of the time. However, a user will have a certain control over their own processes.

Known as 'time-sharing'

A process can be in a number of states, normally either **running** (currently being worked on by a processor), or **stopped** (not being processed, but available to continue evaluation when instructed). When a process completes its execution it is removed from the system entirely and **killed**. Not all processes have been invoked by a user – some are so-called *system* processes, and are constantly running while the system is operational.

When you initially login, you will invoke a program which is a copy of the shell, and known as your **login shell**. This program forms a process which must be present during the whole time you are logged in. Any subsequent process which is created by you will be **controlled** from the terminal (or window) where you were typing the command which created it.

If you type in a command to a shell, it can be of two possible types. Either it is a 'built-in' shell command, which is interpreted by the shell process directly, or a new process is created for it. In the latter case the binary code for it will be copied from storage, and will form the process to execute that command. The process which is the current shell will be suspended and the process for the new command will be run. After that process has finished running, it will be destroyed, and the shell process will be resumed.

You can find out which processes you have, either running or stopped, by means of the command ps. This will display a list of your processes, by default in a format similar to the following:

POSIX does not specify the default format of the output

```
$ ps
PID   TT         TIME COMMAND
10312 p7      00:02:23 sh
14277 p7      00:00:00 ps
```

Each process is given a unique identification number, its **process-id** or **PID**, which is indicated in the first column of the output from ps. The second column displays the name of the terminal from which that process is being controlled (normally your own terminal or one of your windows). The column headed TIME is the amount of processor time the process has so far consumed while actually running, a measure of how much work the computer has so far done for that process. In the final column the name of the command which that process is running is given. In the above example, the user has two processes running, the login shell sh, and the ps command which is being used to display the list of processes. The login shell (PID 10312) has already consumed 2 minutes and 23 seconds of processor time, whereas ps (PID 14277) has used less than 1 second (rounded down to 0 in the output from ps). The PID number is used internally by the kernel, and is not normally needed by the user.

Excluding all time when it has been suspended or has otherwise been moved out of any processor

Foreground and background

When running a command interactively – that is, when you type in a command and wait for the system to respond – that command is being run **in the foreground**. You can instruct UNIX to run a program **in the background** instead. What this means is that the program will begin to run but you will be prompted by the shell for the next command without waiting for the program to complete – your login shell and the background program are effectively running simultaneously. In order to instruct UNIX to run a command in the background, follow the command with an ampersand (&) – try the following:

```
$ date &
```

The exact meanings of the messages will be clarified later on in this chapter

A line will be printed confirming that the command has been sent to the background, then you will be prompted for your next command with $. Meanwhile date is executing, and shortly its output is displayed you are informed that date has completed running:

```
[1] 7293
$ Fri Aug  8 18:29:04 BST 1997
[1]+  Exit 0                        date
```

Process control

To illustrate how we can control processes, we use as an example the command sleep. Followed by an integer, sleep will *suspend* execution of the current shell for that number of seconds, so:

```
$ date
Fri Aug 8 17:22:21 BST 1997
$ sleep 15
```
(there is a delay of 15 seconds at this point)
```
$ date
Fri Aug 8 17:22:36 BST 1997
```

So sleep is a command which essentially does nothing, but a process is created for it nonetheless. So we might have:

```
$ sleep 100 &
[1] 16403
$ ps
PID TT        TIME COMMAND
10312 p7    00:02:25 sh
16403 p7    00:00:00 sleep 100
16425 p7    00:00:00 ps
```

Jobs are discussed later on in this chapter

After 100 seconds process number 16403 will terminate. The system confirms that the command has been sent to run in the background by printing a line containing **jobnumber** (enclosed in square brackets), and the process ID number (16403) of the command.

Signals

The kernel is controlling many processes, created by possibly many users, and including many which are 'system' processes, necessary for the system to function. The kernel allows these processes to communicate by sending 'messages' to each other. Any process in the system can send a message to any other process, and because there could be many processes and many messages being sent, UNIX restricts the messages to being very simple.

These messages are known as **signals**, and each takes the form of a single byte. They are instructions to processes such as *kill* (cease running immediately) and *stop* (become a suspended process). Signals are concerned with the **scheduling** of processes, that is, *when* and *in what order* they are executed. The command `kill` is provided for a user to send a signal to a specific process. A detailed discussion of signals is beyond the scope of this chapter, but one particular signal is important at this stage.

Named `kill` because the most commonly used signals that a user invokes will destroy a process

The signal `SIGKILL` when received by a process will cause it to be destroyed immediately. For example, to kill the `sleep` process above, you could type

```
$ kill -s KILL 16403
```

where `kill` with option `-s` causes the signal named after `-s` to be sent to the process whose PID is given as the final argument to `kill`. Note that, although this signal is referred to as `SIGKILL`, only the word `KILL` is passed to the command `kill`. This is because all signals are called `SIG`*something*, so the `SIG` is redundant in any context where the name of a signal is expected. There are many other signals, such as `SIGHUP` and `SIGTTIN`, some of which will be discussed later on.

`s` = 'signal'

This raises the question of why you might ever wish to destroy a process. It sometimes happens that a process which is running in the background is left there by mistake, for instance if the software which created it was poorly written. It also happens sometimes that you send a program to run in the background when you think it will run for a long time, and later on discover that because of an error in that program it is failing to finish.

It is important to remember that UNIX uses processes as its most basic concept of a 'program'. Remembering PIDs can be tedious, however. A more 'user-friendly' method of handling processes, called **job control** is available, which we now introduce.

Job control

A process can create other processes. Consider a shell script containing one line, which is `date`. When the script is executed, *two* processes will be created, one for the invocation of the shell, and one for the command `date`. The shell is referred to as the **parent** process, and `date` as a **child** process. Some UNIX commands which appear simple may create child processes, and it is seldom of interest to the users how many are created, and how they relate to the original command – the user is only interested in the original command.

Here the concept of a **job** comes to the rescue. A job is a collection of processes grouped together and identified by a small integer. In the example above, the job number for process `16403` was 1. When a UNIX command is sent to the background using `&`, a single job is created consisting of one or more processes. That job will initially be sent to the background, but can be moved into the foreground or destroyed in much the same way as an individual process can. Consider the following pipe:

```
$ cat testfile | wc &
[2] 2374
```

A single job (number 2) has been created in the background, but two processes are required, one for `cat` and one for `wc`. The process number `2374` is that of the last command in the pipe, namely `wc`. You can destroy that job, and consequently both those processes, with

```
$ kill -s KILL %2
```

(instead of giving the command `kill` the number of the process to send a signal to, we give it the number of the job preceded with a percent character).

Worked example 4.1

Arrange to be given an 'alarm call' after 2 minutes.
Solution: Create a script which uses `sleep` to cause it to suspend for 120 seconds, and then use `echo` to write a message to your screen. The script should be run in the background.

You could have used `vi` to create `myalarm`

```
$ cat >myalarm
sleep 120
echo Your alarm call ...
ctrl-D
$ sh myalarm &
```

If you now typed `ps`, you would find (amongst others) two processes:

```
23624 p2 S 0:00 sh myalarm
23625 p2 S 0:00 sleep 120
```

indicating that both the script `myalarm` and the command `sleep` had been invoked.

You may have several jobs running at any one time, and command `jobs` will list them. For example,

```
$ jobs
[1] Stopped testA
[2]- Running sh myalarm &
[3]+ Running testB &
```

The word `Suspended` is used on some systems instead of `Stopped`

indicates that you have 3 jobs. Numbers 2 and 3 are running in the background, whereas number 1 has been **stopped**. This means that the system is not running that job at all; it is suspended pending reactivation. You can try creating a few jobs yourself — the script `myalarm` from the last worked example is suitable to experiment with. Take a copy of `myalarm`, call it (say) `newalarm`, and execute both in the background; you should get a dialogue similar to:

```
$ cp myalarm newalarm
$ sh myalarm &
[1] 25816
$ sh newalarm &
[2] 25820
$ jobs
[1]- Running sh myalarm &
[2]+ Running sh newalarm &
```

If you have jobs running or stopped, one of them will be the **default** job, and is indicated in the output from jobs by the symbol + after its number – in the above example this would be job 3. The default job is the job which was most recently created (or sent a signal by you). If you have two or more running, one will be indicated by a - symbol, which indicates that were the default job to terminate, that one would then become the default. In the example above this would be job 2. The default job is also known as %%.

The rest of this section may be omitted on first reading

Any job which is in the background or is stopped can become the foreground job simply by giving the job number (preceded by %) as argument to the command fg. Similarly, any Stopped job can be reactivated to run in the background by the command bg:

fg = 'foreground'

```
$ bg %1
[1]+ testA &
$ jobs
[1] Running testA
[2]- Running sleep 120 &
[3]+ Running testB &
$ fg %%
```

bg = 'background'

The reason for having default jobs is that quite often, when you have sent a job into the background, you will either want it to be brought back to the foreground or perhaps killed. In practice, you tend to find that you have not created any new jobs in the meantime, and it is useful to have a shorthand for referring to the default job.

Any job sent to the background will still have its standard input, standard output and standard error streams set up as if the job were still in the foreground. What this means for the user is that if a background job wants to write to your terminal, it will do so (so you should not be surprised if, when running jobs in the background, messages do appear on your screen). Yet any input which you type on your terminal will be sent to the current foreground process or to the shell – if you had many background processes running, the system couldn't be expected to decide which job your input was intended for, so can only send it to a foreground process.

A background job must therefore do something sensible if it requires input from the terminal. What happens in this case is that the background job automatically stops – a signal called SIGTTIN is sent to it when it attempts to read from the terminal, and this signal has the effect of stopping the job. Consider:

TTIN = 'tty input'

```
$ cat &
[1] 13249
$
[1]+ Stopped (SIGTTIN) cat
```

The command `cat`, in the absence of any arguments, reads from standard input; `cat` is run in the background, so immediately demands input, but since it is in the background it cannot receive it. It therefore becomes suspended and you are sent a message to tell you of this fact.

   If you send a job to the background which requires input from your terminal, it will become stopped as soon as it requires that input, and you must bring it to the foreground if you wish it to complete executing. Try this with `mailx`:

```
$ mailx -s "Test" chris &
[1] 24545
[1]+ Stopped (SIGTTIN) mailx
$ fg %1
```
(you can type in your message now)

Command history list

UNIX keeps a record of the commands you have typed in to your shell. Each command is given a number, commencing with 1, and using the command `fc` you can re-execute previous commands. To list the commands you have already run, use option `-l`:

fc = 'fix command'
l = 'list'

```
$ fc -l
1      date
2      mailx sam
3      sh myalarm &
4      vi testfile
```

The mechanism for comm-
and history lists is based
on that used in the Korn
shell

If you run `fc` with no arguments, the shell will first of all create a temporary file (you don't need to know its name) containing one line, namely the last command you ran. In the above example, this would be

```
vi testfile
```

The shell would then run `vi` on that file without you having to type `vi` yourself. You can then edit that file, thinking of it as a script of commands to be run — you can change the last command you ran, or add extra commands to the file. When you leave `vi`, whatever is in that temporary file will be treated as commands to the shell and run immediately. Note that if, when leaving the editor, there is more than one line in the temporary file, each line in the file will be executed separately and in turn. An `fc` command is not itself entered in the history list.

   You can select a number of commands by specifying the first and last numbers of the commands you have already run — so to rerun commands 2 through 4 and edit them,

```
$ fc 2 4
```

would create a file containing three lines and then apply `vi` to that file.

Often you will simply wish to re-run commands that you have previously typed in without editing them. Using option `-s` this can be accomplished. In the above example, to re-run the alarm, you could just have

s = 'string'

```
$ fc -s 3
```

Running a job at a specific time

During a session on your UNIX system, most of the programs you run will be executed immediately. Sometimes this will not be desirable. If a program is likely to take a long time to run, you may wish it to run overnight since if a machine tries to execute too many processes at once, it becomes slow, to the detriment of all logged-in users. The command `at` can be used to schedule a job for a specific time in the future.

In its simplest form, typing `at` followed by a time and/or date will cause the standard input to be read, and those commands executed at that time, thus:

```
$ at 1530
echo "It's half past three"
ctrl-D
job 81 at Fri Aug 8 15:30:00 1997
```

The number of the job, together with confirmation of the date and time it has been scheduled for, will be printed on the terminal. The output (both standard output and standard error) will be mailed to you. Alternatively you can create a file (`test`, say) containing commands which you wish to be executed, and then you can use

The results will still be sent to you via email

```
$ at -f test 1530
job 81 at Fri Aug 8 15:30:00 1997
```

f = 'file'

The format allowed for you to specify the time is easy to use, but rather complex to specify — look in the manual page for `at` to check the exact syntax allowed. The following examples will give the general idea:

```
1645
16:45
16:45 GMT tomorrow
noon
4am Jan 25 1997
11pm today
now + 30 minutes
now + 1 month
```

Take care that your time/date specification is unambiguous, and it will probably be acceptable to `at`.

When a job has been created using `at`, it is placed on a **queue**. At the specified time and date, or as soon thereafter as the load on the system permits, an invocation of the shell will execute the commands given to `at`. The jobs on the queue can be examined (option `-l`) and jobs on the queue can be removed (option `-r`) by `at`:

l = 'list'
r = 'remove'

```
$ at -l
81 a Fri Aug 8 15:30:00 1997
$ at -r 81
$ at -l
$
```

a = 'at queue'

The second column of the listing of jobs contains an `a` indicating that the queue is named a. You should not normally need to be concerned about which queue a job has been placed on.

`batch` is the same as the command
`at -q b -m now`

Similar to `at` is `batch`. This command is used when you do not wish to specify exactly when a job should run, merely that the system load should not be high when you do it. A job submitted with `batch` is dealt with by the system in exactly the same way as `at`, except that `batch` will instruct the time of running to be now and will place the job on a separate queue. Jobs submitted to this **batch queue** can be listed (notice the name of the queue is b) and removed using `at`:

b = 'batch queue'

```
$ batch test
job 121 at Fri Aug 8 11:27:22 1997
$ at -l
121 b Fri Aug 8 11:27:22 1997
```

The 'jobs' described in connection with `at` and `batch` should not be confused with the 'jobs' in the section on job control. Jobs in an `at`-queue can only be created and removed by `batch` or `at`.

Worked example 4.2

Write a script which will list all the files in your filespace, and run that script in one minute's time.

R = 'recursive'

Solution: Using `man ls` you will discover that option `-R` to `ls` will all list files in the current directory and recursively through all subdirectories. So we can pass `ls -R` as the command to be processed by `at`. First of all, however, we must change directory to the home directory.

```
$ at now + 1 minute
cd
ls -R
```
ctrl-D

Running programs periodically

The facility also exists whereby you can specify, for instance, 'run program X every morning at 2 am'. This is enabled by the command `crontab`. The mechanism used by `crontab` is different to that for `at` or `batch`.

The word `crontab` is obscure, but probably means 'commands run over night table'

For each user, a file is kept on the system which specifies which commands are to be run periodically, and when. You can edit this file using `vi` by invoking `crontab` with option `-e`. Each line of this file commences with five columns, representing respectively minutes (0–59), hours (0–23) day of month (1–31), month (1–12), and day of week (1–7); each of these columns contains either a number, a comma-separated list of numbers, or an asterisk. The rest of each line is a command to be executed repeatedly whenever the five columns match the current time and date. An asterisk means 'every'. For instance, if the `crontab` file contains

e = 'edit'

```
30 15 * * * ls -R
0 0 * * 1 X
0 0 * 6 * Y
0 0 1,8,15,22 * * Z
```

then the command `ls -R` will be executed every day at 3:30 pm, command X will be run first thing every Monday, and command Y first thing every day in June. Command Z is run on days 1, 8, 15 and 22 of each month. If you try to create an entry in the `crontab` file which is inconsistent, such as specifying a non-existent date, you will be warned and the `crontab` file will not be changed.

Monday is day 1 in the week, Sunday day 7

To list the entries in your `crontab` file without using the editor type `crontab -l`.

Create an entry in your `crontab` file which will send user `jo` a friendly message every Christmas morning.
Solution: Using `crontab -e` create a line in the file which is

Worked example 4.3

```
00 09 25 12 * echo Happy Xmas | mailx jo
```

indicating that the message `Happy Xmas` will be piped to the mail program `mailx` at 0900 hours on the 25th of the 12th month each year. The day field is left as a * since having specified the date we do not need to worry about the day of the week as well.

Some sites will restrict the use of this command – if you find difficulties, check with your System Administrator first.

Big programs

Some programs take a lot of processing time before they complete. If you are running such a program, and the results are not awaited urgently, you would probably like it to be executing on a processor when the system is not busy, and for it to be suspended when the usage of the machine becomes high, in order not to slow down more urgent processes. The facility called nice exists to **prioritise** a job. If mycommand is a big program, then

nice is so called because
you are being considerate
to other users

```
$ nice mycommand &
```

will run mycommand in the background with low priority.

If a process is already running and you wish to reduce its priority, the command renice can be used, but we omit discussion of this command here – examine the manual page using man for further information.

HUP = 'hangup'

When you finish your session on the system, a signal SIGHUP is sent to all the processes you created during the session. Most processes, when they receive this signal, will terminate. If you have a job which you wish to continue running in the background after you have logged off – and this will probably be true for any big jobs you run – you must make the job immune to the signal SIGHUP by means of command nohup. The syntax is nohup followed by a command, and you will probably wish the command to run in the background:

```
$ nohup test &
```

You would only wish to run a command via nohup in the *foreground* if you were connected to the system using a communication link which might disconnect you without warning in the middle of a session. Standard output and the standard error stream from a job running with nohup are redirected to a file called nohup.out instead of to your terminal, if they are not already redirected, and the priority of the job is low (as with nice). The difference between nice and nohup is principally that a job run with nice will terminate when the user who invoked the job logs off.

Timing a program

It's often useful to know how long it takes to run a command. Perhaps you need to compare the speeds of different machines (if you have access to more than one) in order to choose the fastest machine. Perhaps you need to know if a program takes a long time to run so that you can schedule it when you run it again at a quiet time of day. The command time will provide this information. With no options, time followed by a *simple* command (that is, not a pipeline or other complex shell construct), will print out on the standard error stream some statistics.

Precisely which statistics
and the format will vary on
different systems

A more concise output can be obtained by running time with option -p. In that case, only three numbers will be given. First, the total **real** (or **elapsed**) time (in seconds) that the command took to run is printed, then the **processing** time spent by the user's command executing on the processor. Finally, the time spent by the **system** (for example, moving processes in and out of the processor) is printed:

That is, by the kernel

```
$ time date
Fri Aug 8 09:46:48 GMT 1997
0.1user 0.5system 0:00.13elapsed 56%CPU 80pagefaults 0swaps
$ time -p date
Fri Aug 8 09:47:02 GMT 1997
real 0.6
user 0.1
sys 0.4
```

p = 'POSIX'

If the system is busy, the real time will be larger, since there will be many users running processes, all of which demand their fair share of processor time. However, for a particular command (such as date) the user and the system times ought to remain fairly constant, since that command will do the same work each time it is run. Try timing the sleep command:

```
$ time sleep 5
real 5.7
user 0.3
sys 0.3
```

You will see that the total time for the command to run was slightly over 5 seconds, but the amount of processing time – and thus the work the system had to do – was very small in comparison. This is to be expected, since sleep does nothing anyway.

The times for the *system* and *user* are the actual processing time, and exclude any idle time when the relevant processes are not running, so that the *real* time will always be *at least* the sum of the *user* and *system* time.

If you wish to time a complex command, which is not a single word with arguments, then a simple way to do it is to create a shell script containing the command and time the execution of that script.

Running programs in order

You may wish a program to run only when another has completed. Suppose a large program (myprogram, say) is to be run, and you require to be mailed a message when it has run, you could create a file containing

```
sh myprogram
echo "Program completed" | mailx chris
```

and then run the commands from that file in the background using sh and &. This is not always convenient – and once myprogram has begun to execute you cannot go back and edit the file. Another possibility is to use command wait. In order to do this, you require the PID of the command you wish to wait for. As an example, create a file called myprogram containing

```
sleep 200
date
```

Run this in the background:

```
$ sh myprogram &
```

```
[1]+ 14523
```

and you will be informed of the PID of the process running `myprogram`, in this case
`14523`. Now, create another file (say `notify`):

```
$ cat >notify
wait 14523
echo "Program completed"
```
ctrl-D

The command `wait` is similar to `sleep`, except that instead of waiting a specified number
of seconds, it waits until a process (which is its argument) terminates. If we now run
`notify` in the background,

```
$ sh notify &
```

then as soon as `myprogram` has finished, `notify` will write `Program completed`
on your terminal.

There are restrictions on the use of `wait` – you can only wait for a process to complete
if that process has been spawned from the current shell. Thus you cannot wait for someone
else's process to complete. If you call `wait` with no arguments, it will wait for all child
processes to terminate – therefore if you are running many jobs in the background `wait`
will not complete until each of them has finished. Normally you would use `wait` with a
process ID as argument.

Environment

Another communication mechanism employed by UNIX is that of the **environment**. If
you are already familiar with a programming language, the environment is a collection
of **variable** names together with an associated value for each one. Unlike most other
languages, variables in UNIX are usually regarded as character-strings, and only interpreted
as numbers (or other data types) in specific circumstances.

A *variable* in UNIX is a name with which is associated a **value**. For instance, there
is a name LOGNAME which has as its value your own username. Variable names are by
convention formed of upper-case letters, whereas names of files are normally lower-case.
The value of a variable can be referred to by prefixing the name by a $:

Some systems also have a variable USER with the same value

```
$ echo LOGNAME
LOGNAME
$ echo $LOGNAME
chris
```

Some variable names are set by the UNIX system for you; other names you can set for yourself. The syntax for assigning a value to a name is *name* = *value*, for instance

```
$ ADDRESS="1 High Street"
$ echo I live at $ADDRESS
I live at 1 High Street
```

If the value of a variable includes whitespace (*SPACE*s or *TAB*s) or symbols known to the shell (such as & and |), the value should be enclosed in quotes. For the moment, just think of the value as being a string; if it contains numbers, they are still just sequences of characters, and you will not (yet) be able to do any arithmetic on it. Check the values of the predefined variables listed in Figure 4.1 using echo as above.

EDITOR	Your preferred editor
HOME	The absolute pathname of your home directory
LOGNAME	Your login name
PATH	The 'search path' for commands (see below)
PRINTER	The 'default' printer that lp uses
PS1	The shell prompt
PS2	The shell 'continuation' prompt (see below)
SHELL	The pathname of the shell you use
TERM	The type of terminal or window you are using
VISUAL	Your preferred *full-screen* editor (possibly the same as EDITOR)

Figure 4.1   *Some predefined variables.*

Of these PATH and PS1 deserve further discussion. When a UNIX shell encounters a command which is not built in to the shell, it looks at the variable PATH – as you will have noticed, the value of this variable is a sequence of pathnames, known as **pathname components**, separated by colons. UNIX then examines each of these pathnames in order, assuming each to be a directory, to see whether there is an executable file whose name is the same as that of the command. If it finds one, that is executed, otherwise an error message is generated when all the directories in PATH have been examined. Typically PATH will have been set up on your system so as to contain the directories which the System Administrator knows you will need; a typical instance might be:

```
$ echo $PATH
/bin:/usr/bin:/usr/local/bin
```

For the moment, do not try to reset the value of PATH.

If you wish a variable's value to *contain* the dollar symbol, prefix the dollar with a backslash, or enclose the value in **single quotes**:

```
$ X='This is a $'
$ echo $X
This is a $
```

The variable PS1 controls the prompt that the shell gives you; this variable you can safely play with ...

```
$ PS1="Type in a command: "
Type in a command: echo $PS1
Type in a command:
```

The concept of a variable is one which is understood by any process; a variable can be assigned a value by other utilities, not just by the shell. However, the value of a variable is not automatically available to other processes.

You may ask 'What happens if I change the value of LOGNAME?' Try it ... the system will not stop you changing it. The only problem which will arise is if you run a command which needs to know about LOGNAME, such as one you may have written yourself. The system knows who you are, and does not need to examine LOGNAME to find out – using LOGNAME is an aid to you when writing shell scripts.

env = 'environment'

You can list all the variables set for you by use of the command env with no arguments, which we discuss in more detail later on. Try it ... you may need to pipe the output through a pager, since your system may have set many variables for you:

```
$ env | more
```

Worked example 4.4

Find out the name of the type of terminal you are using.
Solution: Examine the contents of the environment variable TERM:

```
$ echo $TERM
xterm
```

Global and local variables

Suppose a process assigns a value to a variable. That value cannot be passed to the parent process, but may be passed to child processes. To illustrate this, consider a variable called X which we set to be the number 42. Then invoke a second copy of the shell using sh; you will get the usual prompt, but this prompt is from the new shell, not from your login shell. The new shell is a child of your login shell. Now check the value of X, and you will see it is not assigned a value:

```
$ X=42
$ echo $X
42
$ sh
$ echo $X
(blank line)
$
```

The new value of X is not passed down to the child process. We say that the value of X is **local** to the process which assigned it a value, and no changes will be recognised by any child process. If you now cause the child shell to finish by typing *ctrl-D*, you will get the $ prompt again, this time from your login shell, and if you examine the value of X again, you will see it is 42, as that was the value assigned to it in that login shell.

We can cause a variable instead to be **global** by means of the command `export`, which means that its value will be passed down to all the child processes, and their children, and so on. Do the same example as above, but immediately after setting X to 42, type a line exporting X:

```
$ export X
```

Change your prompt from $ to `enter command`:
Solution: The variable PS1 contains the prompt; reset it and `export` its value:

```
$ PS1="enter command: "
enter command: export PS1
```

Another method for assigning a variable a value is by means of the command `read`. Followed by one or more variable names `read` will read words from the standard input and assign them to the successive variables. The following script will request the name of a user and send them a greeting by mail:

```
echo "Whom do you wish to greet?"
read RECIPIENT
echo Hello | mailx -s Greeting $RECIPIENT
```

Generally you will `read` one variable at a time, but it is possible to read several at once from a single line of input. In that case you must be careful if the number of variables, and the number of words on the input line, are different. If there are fewer variables than words on the line, the initial variables will be assigned one word each, and the final one the rest of the line; if there are more variables than words on the line, the final variables will be assigned the null string. Suppose script `testread` has the following contents:

```
read X Y Z
echo "X=$X Y=$Y Z=$Z"
```

then we might have the following:

```
$ sh testread
hello there chris
X=hello Y=there Z=chris
```

```
$ sh testread
hello
X=hello Y= Z=
$ sh testread
hello there chris jo and sam
X=hello Y=there Z=chris jo and sam
```

Worked example 4.6   Write a script which will prompt the user for the name of a file and then print the file on their terminal.

Solution: Use echo to prompt the user, read to input a filename into a variable, and cat to print out that file:

```
echo Type in a filename
read FILENAME
cat $FILENAME
```

A use of read which is not apparent from the above discussion is that it can be used to allow the user control over the speed with which a shell script is executed. Try creating a file (say cat2files) containing the following:

```
echo Type in 2 file names
read FILE1 FILE2
cat $FILE1
echo Press RETURN to continue
read X
cat $FILE2
```

Now execute that script ... it will print out the first file on the screen, then pause for you to press *RETURN* before displaying the second file. The second read assigns a value to the variable X (which is not actually used for anything else), but waits for you to type in something before moving on to the next line.

Suppose file myprogram contains

```
echo The emperor is $MY_NAME
```

and you wish to run the commands in the file with MY_NAME set to a value. You could set MY_NAME, then export it, then run the file, so:

```
$ MY_NAME="Julius Caesar"
$ export MY_NAME
$ sh myprogram
The emperor is Julius Caesar
```

There is a problem with this, namely that you have reset MY_NAME in the current shell as well. You may not wish to do this. You may wish to test myprogram with the variable MY_NAME assigned a different value. This would be especially important if you were writing a script which used system-defined variables, such as TERM or LOGNAME, where it would be confusing if you were to reset them. You can use the following:

```
$ MY_NAME="Julius Caesar" sh myprogram
The emperor is Julius Caesar
```

This does not affect the current value of MY_NAME, but has the same effect as inserting the single line

```
MY_NAME="Julius Caesar"
```

at the start of the file myprogram. An equivalent effect can be achieved using the command env:

```
$ env MY_NAME="Julius Caesar" sh myprogram
The emperor is Julius Caesar
```

In both cases, the environment is amended either by the given variables having their names changed or by being added to the environment.

Executable scripts

Suppose you have written a script, called (say) myprogram. In order to execute the commands in that file we have indicated that they must be passed to the shell; using

```
$ sh myfile
```

a copy of the shell command interpreter is created for the sole purpose of executing the commands in myfile, and when it has finished with them that new shell terminates. Typing sh each time can be tedious, especially if you have written many scripts; if you change the permissions on myfile so that you have *execute* permission for it, then it can be run as any other command:

```
$ chmod +x myfile
```

This is the same as

```
$ chmod a+x myfile
```

which gives execute permission to all users. You can now type just the name of the file and it will run:

```
$ /cs/ugrad/chris/myfile
```

For example, suppose you create a file called mydate and containing

```
echo The date and time is:
date
```

then you could run the script by

```
$ $HOME/mydate
```

Alternatively, give it the name relative to the current directory:

```
$ ./mydate
```

Examine the value of your PATH:

```
$ echo $PATH
```

. is the current directory

If there is a dot as one of the components of PATH the current directory will also be searched, and you can then simply type mydate

```
$ mydate
```

Worked example 4.7

Update your PATH so that it includes the subdirectory bin of your home directory.
Solution: We assume that you have created the subdirectory by moving to your home directory using cd and then typing mkdir bin. The value of $HOME is the name of your home directory, so the subdirectory bin can be referred to by $HOME/bin. The variable PATH contains the directories, separated by colons, which are searched for. We want to replace the value of PATH by a new value, which is the old value with a colon then $HOME/bin added on at the end. You will then need to export the value of PATH so that child processes will use the new one.

```
$ PATH=$PATH:$HOME/bin
$ export PATH
```

Note that we have added $HOME/bin to the *end* of $PATH; it would be unwise to place it at the start, in case you accidentally include a command in $HOME/bin which has a name identical to another command on the system. If this happened, your command would be executed in preference to the other one, which might have unexpected consequences. Of course, you might wish to write your own version of a system command, in which case having $HOME/bin at the *start* of $PATH would be necessary, but you are strongly advised against rewriting system commands.

Not to be confused with directory .

There is a command . which, when followed by a file which is a shell script, will cause the commands in the script to be executed by the calling shell. A new shell is not created. For most purposes it does not matter whether or not you use sh or ., but if you use sh you should bear in mind that any environment variables defined in the calling shell must be exported to be recognised within the script. If you use . changes you make to the environment will alter the environment of the current shell.

Worked example 4.8

Write a command `changeprompt` which will request you to enter a new shell prompt and will then reset it to its new value.

Solution: The variable PS1 has as its value your prompt. Create a file which resets its value, and then execute the file using . (not sh) to run the commands in that script.

```
echo Type in the new prompt:
read PS1
export PS1
```

Quotes and escapes

A number of characters are understood by the shell to have a special meaning, such as $, > and <, for example, which we have already used. The purpose of quotes and backslash is to enable characters which are part of the shell's reserved characters to be used in a context where they are not recognised as such. In this section we discuss the three characters ′ (**single quote**), " (**double quote**), and \ (**backslash**). The following other characters are reserved for the shell:

```
< >  |  & * @ # ?  !  - $ ( ) [ ] { } ; = %      ‘
```

If you wish to use any of these characters in any context other than that which the shell defines for them, they must be either quoted or escaped. In general, if it's a single character, preceding it with a backslash will indicate that its literal value is to be used. Alternatively, if there are several such characters, enclose the whole string in single quotes:

A single quote refers to an 'close' single quote '

```
$ X='hello <$Chris>'
$ echo $X
hello <$Chris>
```

There are two important points here that you need to remember. First of all, the shell strips off pairs of quotes, and matches an opening quote with its nearest possible closing match, so:

```
$ X='abc >''>&def'
$ echo $X
abc >>&def
```

This implies that a single quote cannot occur within a quoted string which is quoted using single quotes. The second point is that quotes must come in pairs. Notice what happens if they don't:

```
$ X='abc
>
```

At the end of the first line the shell is looking for a single quote; not having found one, it assumes that the *NEWLINE* character you entered when you typed *RETURN* is part of the string, that you intended a space instead, and that you wish to continue entering the rest of the string on the following line. The > is the **continuation prompt** (different to $) indicating an unfinished command. If we then complete the dialogue:

You can change the prompt by setting PS2

The newline is not part of the string, and is replaced by a space

```
$ X='abc
> def'
$ echo $X
abc def
```

Double quotes can be used in the same way as single quotes, except that not all characters enclosed between them become literal. In particular, variable names preceded by $ are replaced by their values. Double quotes may be used to include a single quote in a string:

```
$ PS1="$LOGNAME's prompt "
chris's prompt
```

Without quotes, the shell would assign $LOGNAME to PS1 and then try to execute prompt as the next command.

Having set up variables, you may wish to protect some of them to avoid accidentally changing them. The command readonly will prohibit you changing the value of a variable:

```
$ X=42
$ readonly X
$ X=99
X: read-only variable
$ echo $X
42
```

If a read-only variable has been exported, it will not be read-only for any child processes — 'read-only-ness' is not exportable.

Devices

A **device** is any piece of equipment connected to a computer system which performs communication between 'the outside world' and the system, such as a printer or a terminal. Although normally hardware, a device might be software which behaves, from the perspective of UNIX, in the same way as hardware. When you have run commands that use input and output streams, their behaviour as 'streams of characters' does not depend upon where they originate or are directed to. They are simply streams of characters. It does not matter whether input comes from a terminal or from a file, nor whether output is piped to a printer, sent to the terminal, or redirected to a file. In fact, UNIX treats devices *exactly* the same as files.

From the perspective of a UNIX programmer, every device *is* a file.

Type `tty` to discover what the name of your current terminal (or window) is (say, `ttyp9`). Now change directory to `/dev` and use `ls` to examine which files are in it. You will find a very large number of files. Look now closely at file `ttyp9`:

`dev` = 'device'
Substitute the name of the terminal you are using for `ttyp9`

```
$ ls -l ttyp9
crw--w--- 1 chris tty 20, 2 Mar 26 12:02 ttyp9
```

This looks very much like an ordinary file, except that the first character in the output of `ls -l` is the character `c`, indicating that the file is a **character special file**, the technical jargon used to describe a device such as a terminal. You own the file, and can write to it. Try:

Defined in POSIX.1

```
$ date >ttyp9
```

and the date will appear on your screen just as if you had typed `date` on its own.

Every device has a filename in the directory `/dev`.

If you attempt to write to a device which is owned by another user, you will not be allowed to. If you have several windows on your terminal you will normally be allowed to write to other windows – use `tty` to discover their names, and then try the above example with one of them. There is also a file in `/dev` called `tty` which is always a synonym for the current terminal's filename – so

```
$ date >tty
```

would produce the same output as above.

Standard input is received from, and standard output and standard error are sent to, the file which is your terminal, unless you redirect them elsewhere. They are not files, they are simply concepts to enable redirection of streams to take place – at the ends of pipelines, unless these streams are redirected they are automatically directed at `/dev/tty`, thus

You can overload a device and direct input and/or more than one output at it

```
$ sh myprogram
```

is equivalent to

```
$ sh myprogram 0</dev/tty 1>/dev/tty 2>/dev/tty
```

Other devices you may encounter include `/dev/audio`, if your terminal has a loudspeaker and microphone, `/dev/console` if you are using a workstation, and devices with names similar to `/dev/rst8` if you ever need to use a magnetic tape drive. There is, however, one device which you will need, and will have to use by name.

Suppose you have written a program which outputs diagnostic messages as well as its output, and you wish to view only the output. You could send the standard error stream to a file:

```
$ sh myprogram 2>test.errors
```

but this would be wasteful of filespace. You can discard this stream by redirecting it to a file (device) known as `/dev/null`:

```
$ sh myprogram 2>/dev/null
```

This file behaves in the same way as any other file or device, but it simply junks any output sent to it, and if you try to read from it it is always at end-of-file. Use `/dev/null` with care, and only when you know that you want output discarded.

Worked example 4.9   Write a script which will read in the name of a file and display a message only if it cannot be read.
Solution: Use `cat` to read the contents of the file. If `cat` fails, the file is unreadable, and the error message, sent to standard error, should be displayed. However, we do not actually wish to see the file's contents, so junk them by directing the standard output to `/dev/null`:

```
echo Type the name of a file:
read FILENAME
cat $FILENAME >/dev/null
```

Backquotes

Sometimes redirecting output from a command is not quite what you want to do. If you need to set the value of a variable to be the output of a command, the mechanisms we have already met will not work. As an example, suppose you wished to set a variable YEAR to the current year. We can easily find the current year using `date`. Either use the

Use the manual page to find out about formatted output from `date`

formatting argument `+"%Y"` to `date`, or pipe the output through `cut`, as was discussed in the previous chapter.

```
$ date +"%Y"
1997
$ date | cut -f6 -d' '
1997
```

However, printing the output of `date` on your terminal or sending it to a file will not allow it to be on the right-hand side of the equals symbol in an assignment. This is where ` (**backquote**) is used — if you enclose a command in backquotes, that command is executed and its standard output becomes a string which is then passed to the shell in place of the original command. This is known as **command substitution**. So

```
$ YEAR=`date +"%Y"`
```

will achieve the desired result. Alternatively, enclose the expression in $ (and) thus:

```
$ YEAR=$( date +"%Y" )
```

As for double quotes, variable names preceded by a $ symbol will be replaced by their values between backquotes.

Reset your shell prompt to the name of the shell followed by a > symbol.   **Worked example 4.10**
Solution: the variable SHELL holds the name of the shell as an absolute pathname:

```
$ echo $SHELL
/usr/local/bin/sh
```

The command basename can be used to remove the directory portion of that name, so basename $SHELL will extract the name of the shell you are using. Use backquotes to turn the output from basename to a string, and remember that >, since it is a special symbol, must be quoted:

```
$ PS1=$( basename $SHELL )"> "
sh>
```

Summary of utilities

at	execute commands at a specified time
batch	execute commands when system load permits
bg	run a job to the background
crontab	schedule periodic background work
env	set environment for a command
export	set export attribute for a variable
fc	process command history list
fg	run a job to the foreground
jobs	list the jobs in the current session
kill	send a signal to a process
nice	run a command with changed priority
nohup	run a command immune to hangups
ps	display information about processes
read	read a line from standard input
readonly	set read-only attribute for variables
renice	change the priority of a running process
sleep	suspend execution for a time interval
time	display execution time for a command
wait	suspend process until completion of another process

Problems

4.1 Arrange for a 'Good Morning' message to be mailed to you at 8 am every Monday morning.

4.2 Arrange for a list of *all* your files (including 'dot' files) and directories to be mailed to you every weekday at 6 pm.

4.3 Arrange for an 'alarm call' message to be written on your terminal in one hour.

4.4 What is the Process-ID (PID) of your login shell?

4.5 Write a script which will write your username, your home directory, the type of your terminal, and the printer that lp uses, so the output looks like:

```
Your username is chris
Home directory is /cs/ugrad/chris
You are using a terminal which is a vt100
The default lineprinter is cs/p1
```

4.6 Write a script which will prompt you for the name of a directory and then list the files in it.

4.7 Set an environment variable called MY_NAME to be your name in the form *first name* followed by a space followed by *family name*.

Chapter 5

Introduction to shells

OBJECTIVES

In this chapter you will learn:

- [ ] why a shell is needed;

- [ ] simple syntax for the shell, including conditional statements and loops.

We have in previous chapters considered UNIX *commands* together with related concepts such as *process* and *environment*. In this chapter we consider the shell — the command interpreter — in more detail, and introduce the constructs which are a part of the shell and which make it a programming language in its own right.

Why do we need a shell?

This question may be on your mind. Most of the commands discussed so far are to be found in directories mentioned in your PATH. You can edit files, print files, and run programs. You can schedule commands. You have access to languages such as Pascal or C on your system, and they can be used for complex programming tasks. So what else does the shell have to offer?

The shell allows you to check on *success* and *failure* of commands, on the *state* of the filesystem, on the *values* of environment variables, and to process this knowledge. It is a programming language in the full sense — it has the power of other programming languages — but tailored for use in conjunction with an operating system. It contains built-in features that allow the user to get the maximum amount of information from the kernel in an easy manner. By writing shell scripts you can create your own commands.

Although the shell is a powerful programming language, it is designed as a user interface to a UNIX machine, and is not an ideal language for doing complex numerical calculations. If you have a particular application which does not clearly have a need to be written in the shell, then it is good practice to write it in another language more suited to it, and then call that program from the shell.

It is not possible to give exact instructions as to where the boundary lies — when you should decide that the shell is unsuitable and use another language. The examples in the following chapters will give you a feel as to what sorts of task are typically programmed in the shell. Some people use a UNIX system happily and hardly ever use any of the shell facilities, some are quite at home with the most complex scripts.

Shell syntax

Any computer language has a **syntax** – that is, a set of rules defining what you can write in the language, and what you are forbidden to write. The shell uses symbols and words in a very precise way. We will not attempt to give a formal definition of the shell's syntax here, but we will describe most of its features.

Recall that a *script* is a file containing commands which the shell is able to interpret. If a script is two or three lines long, it is likely to be clear to anyone reading the file what the commands do, and therefore what the purpose of the script is. If a script is a hundred lines long, it will not be so easy to see what is happening. Not only will it be difficult for someone else reading your scripts, but if you make an error while writing it, you may yourself find trouble discovering exactly where the error has occurred.

It is good practice to include **comments** in your scripts. These are messages which the shell *ignores* – they are there merely for the benefit of anyone reading the scripts.

= 'hash'

If you write a script, and include a # symbol, then the rest of that line (including the #) is ignored by the shell (unless that # appears within quotes or is within a word). For instance, the following script

```
MESSAGE="Hello $LOGNAME"
echo $MESSAGE
```

Comments only work in scripts, and will not work interactively, when you are giving the shell instructions from a terminal

will cause a message to be printed on the terminal screen. The next script does exactly the same thing, but has had comments included.

```
# This script prints a friendly message on standard output
# Written by Chris, 8 August 1997
#
# This script requires variable LOGNAME to be set

MESSAGE="Hello $LOGNAME"      # Set MESSAGE to the message
echo $MESSAGE                 # ... and echo it to stdout
```

The sort of information that should appear in comments includes

- who wrote the script,

- what the script does,

- when it was written,

- what the individual parts of the script do.

For very short scripts, this may appear rather trivial, but for long scripts comments are essential, and you should get into the habit of commenting all your scripts. Try creating a file (`messagefile`, say) containing the above script, and run it using:

```
$ sh messagefile
```

When the shell reads input, it reads the input line-by-line looking for commands, and each line is first of all stripped of comments. A command is normally terminated by the end of the line it is on, with the exception that if the end of a line is premature, and the shell knows you haven't completed typing in the command, it will recognise this and expect you to continue the command on the next line. If the shell is interactive, it will prompt you with a > to continue with a command which was started on the previous line. For instance, suppose you tried to echo a string and typed only one quote; the shell would think that you had not finished typing in the string, and that you would continue on the next line. Try it:

Or whatever the value of PS2 is instead of >

```
$ echo "Hello
> Chris"
Hello
Chris
```

You can also try creating a file containing

```
echo "Hello
Chris"
```

and executing the file as a shell script. Remember that the only difference between a shell script (which is a file containing shell commands) and the commands you type in on your terminal, is where the input to the shell comes from. In the case of an interactive shell, such as your login shell, the shell commands are typed in by you at your terminal; when a script is run, the shell reads commands from the script file.

You can also terminate a command with the symbols & or ; — so you can have several commands on a single line. If you separate them with semicolons they will run one after the other, as if you had written them on separate lines. If you separate them by ampersands, they will one after the other be sent to run in the background, and will therefore be executed concurrently. A semicolon terminates a command and causes it to be run in the *foreground*. Try the following:

```
$ date; sleep 5; date
$ date & uname & who &
```

A sequence of commands separated by semicolons or *NEWLINE*s is called a **sequential list**, and a sequence separated by ampersands is an **asynchronous list**.

Types of shell command

We must now distinguish between two concepts — **utility** and **command**. A utility is the name of a program, such as wc, date or uname. A command is an instruction to the shell to perform a task. A very simple command may well just be the name of a utility, but in general will be more complex. Consider

```
$ uname -a >outputfile
```

which will display the 'vital statistics' of the system you are running the command on, redirecting the output to file outputfile. We have as *command* uname -a >outputfile, which comprises of *utility* uname with argument -a and standard output redirected to outputfile.

In order to combine the utilities we have met, and the sorts of command we already know about, into more complex structures, we need to be very precise about what sorts of command are available. The shell allows five different types of command:

- **simple command**

- **pipeline**

- **list command**

- **function definition**

- **compound command**.

When we use the word *command* we mean any of the above five types of command. We discuss all of the above in this chapter, with the exception of functions which are found in Chapter 7. Of the five types of command, we will explicitly define the first four, and all other commands we introduce come under the heading of compound commands. Don't worry if these names look complex — we need them so that later on we can be completely unambiguous when we discuss shells, and you may then need to refer back to here. For now, you should remember simply that command types are neatly categorised.

Simple commands

A **simple command** is a name (understood to be a valid UNIX utility name) together with options and arguments, any input or output redirection, and possibly preceded by variable assignments. Examples which we have met in previous chapters would be:

```
date
```
Just the name of a utility which displays the current time and date.

```
cat 0< inputfile 1> outputfile
```
A utility with input and output redirected — this command copies `inputfile` to `output-file`.

```
VAR=42 NAME=Chris mycommand argument1 argument2
```
A utility (`mycommand`) run with two arguments and variables `VAR` and `NAME` set — see Chapter 4.

Pipelines

A **pipeline** is a sequence of commands separated by the pipe symbol (|); a single command is also technically a pipeline. We can string any number of commands together to form a long pipeline. The following are valid pipelines:

Subject to limits which are system dependent

```
date
```
A simple command, displays the time and date.

```
who | cut -c1-8 | sort
```

A pipeline of three simple commands; this will list the users currently logged-in in alphabetical order, without any of the extra information that who displays. The first command in the pipeline lists users together with more information, including the terminal they are using the system from, and the second — cut — will extract the first eight characters from each line of the output of who. These eight characters are precisely the character columns that contain the usernames. The output of cut is then piped to sort to place the usernames in alphabetical order.

Assumes usernames are at most 8 characters long

```
ls -l /usr/local/bin 2> errorfile | wc -l > outputfile
```
A pipeline of two simple commands, each redirecting some of its output, which counts the number of files in /usr/local/bin. If directory /usr/local/bin exists, the number of lines produced by ls -l — and hence the number of files in /usr/local/bin — will be counted by wc, and the result sent to outputfile. If /usr/local/bin does not exist, an error message will be sent to errorfile.

```
who | VAR=42 mycommand | VAR=99 mycommand
```
A pipeline of three simple commands, the latter two run with variable VAR set to a specific value; since mycommand is not a system utility — it is the name of a script which you will have written — the effect of this pipeline will depend on what you have written in that script.

Exit status

Every time a UNIX command terminates, that command returns a number, called its **exit status**, to the shell which caused it to run. The shell can then take action dependent on that number. By convention, the exit status of a command is 0 if the command is successful. If a command fails, for whatever reason, a value different to 0 is returned (although typically 1). We can find out the exit status of the previous command executed by means of the special parameter $?. Immediately after running a command, type echo $? and the exit status of that command will be displayed. The exit status of a pipeline is the exit status of the last command in that pipeline.

We discuss special parameters in detail later on in this chapter

As an example, create a file (testfile, say), protect it so that you cannot write to it using chmod and then try to write to it:

```
$ chmod -w testfile
$ cat >testfile
testfile: Permission denied.
$ echo $?
1
```

The 1 which is the value of $? indicates that the cat command failed.

Worked example 5.1

What is the exit status of

```
mv  ~/X  /
```

Solution: We would expect this command to fail. If ~/X does not exist, it will return exit status 1 for that reason. If it does exist, you will not have write permission for the root directory, and the command will fail. Anyhow, check the exit status by typing the command and then echo $?:

```
$ mv  ~/X  /
```
an error message
```
$ echo $?
1
```

List commands

A simple use of exit status is when using a **list command**. A list command is a sequence of pipelines separated by either || or &&. In the case of an **or-list**

|| is pronounced 'or'

```
$ pipeline1 || pipeline2
```

pipeline1 is run, and if a non-zero exit status is returned *pipeline2* is run. The exit status for this list command is 0, if *pipeline1* returns 0, otherwise the status of *pipeline2*. Thus the or-list succeeds if either the first command or the second succeeds. In the case of an **and-list**

&& is pronounced 'and'

```
$ pipeline1 && pipeline2
```

pipeline1 is run, and if a zero exit status is returned *pipeline2* is run. The exit status for this list command is that of *pipeline1*, if non-zero, otherwise that of *pipeline2*. An and-list succeeds if both its first and its second component succeed. Both or-lists and and-lists can be strung together, in which case the pipelines separated by || and && will be evaluated from left to right.

Simple examples for || and && would be to check whether a command has in fact completed successfully:

```
$ mycommand || echo Cannot run mycommand
$ mycommand && echo mycommand ran OK
```

In the first, if mycommand fails — that is, returns exit status not zero — the following echo command is run which informs you that mycommand failed. In the second, if mycommand succeeds the following echo command is run.

Compare files named `file1` and `file2`, and if they are different mail yourself a message indicating the differences.

Solution: Using `diff` to compare the two files, we see from the manual page for `diff` that an exit status of 0 is returned only when the two arguments to `diff` are identical. You can therefore send the output of `diff` to a file and then mail yourself the contents of that file. `||` can be used so that the mail will only be performed if the `diff` returned non-zero exit status.

```
$ diff file1 file2 >diffout ||
> mailx -s "Output of diff" chris <diffout
```

Using `&&` we can sequence commands so that subsequent commands will only run if earlier ones have been completed successfully.

Compare files named `file1` and `file2`, and if they are identical delete `file2`.

Solution: Since we do not require a *list* of any differences it will be quicker to use `cmp`, which, like `diff`, returns 0 exit status if its arguments have the same contents. Use `&&` to perform `rm` upon successful completion of `cmp`.

```
$ cmp file1 file2 && rm file2
```

Parentheses can also be used to **group** list commands – so that, for instance,

command1 `||` (*command2* `&&` *command3*)

would cause *command1* to be run, and if it failed the and-list *command2* `&&` *command3* would then be run.

Two other commands which it is appropriate to introduce here are `true` and `false`. Both these commands do nothing at all, but return exit status 0 and 1 respectively. We shall use them later on in this chapter.

There is also a command : (colon) which has the same effect as `true`

Arithmetic

The shell itself does contain some rudimentary facilities to do arithmetic, which we shall discuss later. However it is not itself designed for doing such calculations, unlike most high-level languages. It is recognised, however, that non-trivial arithmetic will be required by some shell programmers. The solution adopted is to introduce a utility known as `bc`, which is a sophisticated calculator. Use of this utility deserves a chapter in its own right, and we shall merely touch on the possibilities that `bc` offers. The characteristics of `bc` include

bc = 'basic calculator'

- arbitrary precision arithmetic,

- a complete programming language including *for* and *while* loops and variables, and

- ability to perform arithmetic in bases other than 10.

We omit here the complex structures in bc and concentrate on using bc to perform simple calculations in decimal.

By default, bc takes input from standard input; commands are one per line or separated by semicolons. Each command to bc is either an *expression* which it evaluates, or a statement which affects the subsequent output. As a short example, consider the following dialogue:

```
$ bc
1+2
3
100/7
14
scale=5
100/7
14.28571
sqrt(2)
1.41421
```

Most of this dialogue is self-explanatory; scale=5 indicates that subsequent calculations should be output correct to 5 decimal places, and sqrt is a predefined **function** which works out the square root of its argument.

To use a function in bc, type the name of the function followed by its *argument* enclosed in parentheses. Thus to evaluate 'log base e of 10' the expression would be l(10). The available operators and functions are summarised in Figures 5.1 and 5.2. If the 'scale' is set to 0, no calculations are done on digits after the decimal point, and integer arithmetic is performed. In this case the operator % will yield 'integer remainder' so that 11 % 3 would yield 2. Some of the operators require bc to be called with option -l, and these are indicated in Figure 5.2. Trigonometric functions assume you are working with radians (and not degrees), and the exponential function e raises e (the base of natural logarithms,

l = lower-case 'ell'

l = 'library'

+	addition
-	subtraction
*	multiplication
/	division
%	integer remainder
^	'to the power of'

Figure 5.1   *Operators used by* bc.

```
sqrt      square root
length    number of decimal digits
scale     scale
s         sine, requires option -l
c         cosine, requires option -l
a         inverse tangent , requires option -l
e         exponential, requires option -l
l         natural logarithm, requires option -l
```

Figure 5.2   *Functions used by* bc.

2.718...) to the power of its argument. In bc you can use parentheses to group parts of an
expression together, so the expression

```
10 * (3 + 4)
```

would evaluate to 70. You can use as many parenthesised expressions as you like, provided
you ensure that each opening parenthesis is matched by a closing one — i.e. the usual
conventions in a programming language apply. Note that *multiplication* and *division* take
precedence over *addition* and *subtraction*, so that

```
1 + 3 * 4
```

is equivalent to

```
1 + (3 * 4)
```

and not to

```
(1 + 3) * 4
```

If in doubt about prece-
dence, use parentheses

Use bc to find the number of seconds in a day.
Solution: The calculation we require is $24 \times 60 \times 60$, and the dialogue that would follow is

```
$ bc
24 * 60 * 60
86400
ctrl-D
```

Worked example 5.4

Since bc takes input from standard input, to leave bc you type *ctrl-D* on a line of its own.
We can also pipe expressions into bc, and

```
$ echo "1 + 2" | bc
```

would be a valid way of using bc, since the pipe ensures that the standard output of echo
becomes the standard input to bc.

Worked example 5.5

Write a script which will read in two numbers and display their product.

Solution: Use `read` to input the numbers, and then construct the expression which represents their product using the `*` operator in `bc`. This expression can then be passed to the standard input of `bc` using `echo`.

```
echo Input two numbers:     # Prompt the user ...
read N1 N2                  # read in two numbers ...
echo "$N1 * $N2" | bc       # pass their product to bc
```

Making decisions

Consider the following problem: 'If file `A` is smaller than 100 lines then display it on the terminal, otherwise tell me that it's bigger than 100 lines.' How would you set about programming that using the shell? We can find out how many lines are in `A` using `wc`, we can print a file, and we can output a message. However the only method we have so far met for deciding to execute commands conditionally is to use `||` or `&&` and the exit status of a command. We would ideally like a command `A_is_small` which succeeds (exit status 0) if `A` is smaller than 100 lines. Our script might then look like:

```
(A_is_small && more A) || echo A is too big
```

The fundamental method by which the shell allows you to make choices as to what to do next in a script is by use of the exit status of a command. We can't in general expect commands such as `A_is_small` to exist already – there must be a more general method of translating such statements into something the shell can understand, which will return an appropriate exit status. We need to be able to compare numbers (such as file sizes) and strings (values of environment variables), and to interrogate easily the existence and access permissions of files.

The command which accomplishes this is `test`. Followed by arguments, `test` will give an exit status of 0 if the arguments *evaluate* to True. There are two ways of invoking `test`:

`test` *arguments*

`[` *arguments* `]`

and we shall use the latter for the rest of this book. To give you the flavour, the following will check whether file `testfile` exists and print out a suitable message if it does:

```
$ [ -e testfile ] && echo Testfile exists
```

Using the alternative syntax this would look like:

```
$ test -e testfile && echo Testfile exists
```

-d *filename*	True if *filename* exists and is a directory
-e *filename*	True if *filename* exists
-f *filename*	True if *filename* exists and is **regular**
-r *filename*	True if *filename* exists and is readable
-s *filename*	True if *filename* exists and has size non-zero
-w *filename*	True if *filename* exists and is writable
-x *filename*	True if *filename* exists and is executable

A regular file is essentially one which is not a directory; there are other sorts of non-regular files, such as FIFO files, but they do not concern us here

Figure 5.3   *File operators used by* test.

-n *string*	True if *string* has length non-zero
-z *string*	True if *string* has length zero
string	True if *string* is not null
s1 = *s2*	True if strings *s1* and *s2* are equal
s1 != *s2*	True if strings *s1* and *s2* are not equal

Figure 5.4   *String operators used by* test.

The *operator* -e, when presented as an argument to test, examines the following argument, and if that file *exists* the command succeeds (exit status 0), otherwise it fails with exit status 1. Various options are available to test; those listed in Figure 5.3 relate to files, and with the exception of -f are self-explanatory.

Write a script which will read in the name of a file and print out a message indicating whether or not it is a directory.
Solution: Use test with option -d to check the file, and || and && to control which message is output.

Worked example 5.6

```
echo Input a file name:    # Prompt the user ...
read FILENAME              # input a file name ...
([ -d $FILENAME ] &&       # check it's a directory ...
                           # then confirm this if so
     echo $FILENAME is a directory) ||
   echo $FILENAME is not a directory
```

The options given in Figure 5.4 relate to strings. For instance, to check whether variable NAME has been set a value which is not the null string, we might have:

```
$ [ "$NAME" ] || echo NAME is unset
```

n1 `-eq` *n2*	True if numbers *n1* and *n2* are equal
n1 `-ne` *n2*	True if numbers *n1* and *n2* are not equal
n1 `-gt` *n2*	True if *n1* is greater than *n2*
n1 `-ge` *n2*	True if *n1* is greater than or equal to *n2*
n1 `-lt` *n2*	True if *n1* is less than *n2*
n1 `-le` *n2*	True if *n1* is less than or equal to *n2*

Figure 5.5   *Arithmetic operators used by* `test`.

Note that we have enclosed `$NAME` in double quotes; `test` expects to get an argument, and if we did not enclose it in quotes, and `NAME` was unset (or contained only whitespace), the line would become

```
[ ] || echo NAME is unset
```

prior to execution, which would give an error, whereas

```
[ "" ] || echo NAME is unset
```

would be OK.

Worked example 5.7   Write a script which will greet the person running it if they are logged on as user `chris`. **Solution**: Use `logname` to check the user's name (not the variable `LOGNAME`, which might accidentally have been changed), and `test` to compare it with `chris`.

```
[ "$( logname )" = chris ] && echo Hello Chris
```

We will not cover such aspects of `bc` here

The numerical checks listed in Figure 5.5 that `test` can perform are the principal way of doing numerical comparisons using the shell. They only work with whole numbers, however, and if you wish to perform complex tasks using floating-point numbers you are advised to use `bc`. As an example, we code the solution to the question posed at the start of this section, which was: 'If file A is smaller than 100 lines then display it on the terminal, otherwise tell me that it's bigger than 100 lines.'

```
FILESIZE=$( wc -l A )     # Use wc -l to count the lines
([ "$FILESIZE" -gt 100 ] && echo File too big) || cat A
```

There is a difference between the operators `=` and `-eq` for instance,

```
[ 0 -eq 00 ]
```

succeeds, as 0 and 00 are numerically equal, but

```
[ 0 = 00 ]
```

fails, as they are different strings of characters.

Write a script which will request you to type in a number, and then to guess its square; it should then either congratulate you or tell you the correct answer.

Worked example 5.8

Solution: After reading in a number into variable NUMBER, construct an expression $NUMBER * $NUMBER to be piped to bc, assigning the output of the calculation to SQUARE. Then, after reading in the user's guess into variable GUESS, use test to check whether GUESS and SQUARE are the same.

```
# Prompt the user and read in the number
echo Type in a number:
read NUMBER

# Evaluate the square of the number using bc
SQUARE=$( echo "$NUMBER * $NUMBER" | bc )

# Prompt the user and read in the guessed answer
echo Guess its square:
read GUESS

# If the guess is equal to the square, confirm ...
([ "$GUESS" -eq "$SQUARE" ] && echo Correct) ||
# otherwise display the correct answer
     echo The correct answer is $SQUARE
```

Notice the different 'style' of comments used here — each on a line of its own; this style is preferred with long command lines

Since test requires arguments, you must separate those arguments from the word test by whitespace. Similarly, if you are using the square bracket notation for test, you should separate the square brackets from what is inside the brackets. Otherwise, the brackets themselves would become part of the strings which they should enclose. For instance,

WARNING!

```
[ hello = hello]
```

would attempt to compare string hello with string hello] and think that you had forgotten to provide the closing square bracket.

Grouping commands

Occasionally it will be necessary to group commands together so that they appear to the shell as a single command. For instance, suppose you wish to print a text file (myfile, say) on the printer, and you wish to append lines both at the start and at the end of the file. If this is to be performed in a script you cannot use vi, since vi does not use standard input and standard output in a simple manner. What you also cannot do is to send the standard output of the echo and cat commands to lp separately — you would then get the header and footer messages printed on separate pages. There are several solutions that you will already be able to use. The first involves creating a temporary file to store the output, and then catting that file:

```
$ echo "This is the start" > temp
$ cat myfile >> temp
$ echo "This is the end" >> temp
$ cat temp | lp
```

This is inelegant and to be discouraged – proliferation of temporary files causes confusion and wastes storage space. The second involves creating a script to perform the task – so:

```
$ cat <<END >temp
echo "This is the start"
cat myfile
echo "This is the end"
END
$ sh temp | lp
```

This method also uses a temporary file, but we can substitute the occurrence of `temp` for standard output, and pipe it to `sh`:

```
$ cat <<END | sh - | lp
echo "This is the start"
cat myfile
echo "This is the end"
END
```

By using the latter method we have overcome the need for a temporary file by taking the commands for `sh` from standard input explicitly by using the hyphen. What we have done is to anonymise the temporary file. However, we can improve on the here-document method by means of a technique called **command grouping**.

By enclosing a list of commands in parentheses, a new invocation of the shell is formed to execute that list of commands, just as if you had placed those commands in a file and run that file as a separate shell script. The solution to the above problem then becomes:

```
$ ( echo "This is the start"
> cat myfile
> echo "This is the end" ) | lp
```

If a sequence of commands (which can be separated either by newlines or by semicolons) is enclosed in *parentheses*, then they will be executed in sequence, and their output streams will be concatenated together to form a single stream, which can itself then be redirected.

Without creating any temporary files, and using a single shell command, instruct your shell to display the names of files in the current directory, preceded by an explanatory message, and *paged* (in case you have a large number of them).

Solution: Use `ls` to list the files, `echo` to produce a message, and `more` as the pager. Then use command grouping to join the outputs of `ls` and `echo` together:

```
$ (echo "Your files are:"; ls) | more
```

Worked example 5.9

The 'if' statement

For making simple decisions based on a command's exit status, | | and && are fine, but if many commands are involved it may become quite difficult to read. For this reason another syntax for checking the exit status of a command is provided, taking the form of an `if` statement. To illustrate this, recall the example used to introduce | | and &&:

```
$ mycommand || echo Cannot run mycommand
$ mycommand && echo mycommand ran OK
```

This could be rewritten using `if` as follows:

```
$ if mycommand
> then echo mycommand ran OK
> else echo Cannot run mycommand
> fi
```

The line which starts with `else` is optional

The keyword `fi` denotes the end of the statement

This mechanism is very similar to that used in Pascal or C. You may find it easier, or clearer, to use than | | or && . It should be stressed that an `if` statement fulfills the same function as | | and && — it is simply another syntax.

Write a script which will inform you whether or not you have used more than 100k of disk space.

Solution: Using `du` with option `-s` will give you a number which represents the number of kilobytes of storage you have used, and will also display the name of the directory for which it performed that calculation. You can use `cut` to extract the first field of that output, namely the number. Then `test` can check whether this number is greater than 100, returning an exit status of 0 if that is the case, then `if` will check this exit status and run `echo` to display a message if that is indeed the case.

Worked example 5.10

Refer to Chapter 3 for a discussion of `cut`

```
# Evaluate the number of kilobytes of storage used
KBYTES=$( du -s ~ | cut -f2 -d' ')

# Check the value of KBYTES ..
if   [ $KBYTES -gt 100 ]
# and display message if >100
```

```
then echo "You have used more than 100k"
# and display message if <=100
else echo "You have used less than 100k"
fi
```

Using | | and &&, this could have been coded so:

```
KBYTES=$( du -s ~ | cut -f2 -d' ')
( [ $KBYTES -gt 100 ] &&
     echo "You have used more than 100k" ) ||
  [ $KBYTES -gt 100 ] ||
     echo "You have used less than 100k"
```

'For' loops

The `for` loop is a method of executing a section of a script a specified (and fixed) number of times. For instance, to page, in sequence, each readable file in the current directory:

r = 'readable'

```
$ for i in $( ls )
> do
>    [ -r $i ] && more $i
> done
```

The syntax for the `for` loop is

```
for name in values
do
commands
done
```

and this causes the variable *name* to be set in turn to each word in *values*, and *commands* executed with *name* set to that value. So in the above example, $(ls) becomes a list of the files in the current directory, and variable i is set to each one in turn. The filename, which is the value of i, is tested to see if it is readable, and if so it is paged using more.

Worked example 5.11

Send a personalised greeting (such as Hello jo) to each of users jo, sam and george:
Solution: You cannot simply use mailx jo sam george, as they would then each receive the same (unpersonalised) message. So you should instead use a for loop to create each message in turn and then mail it to the appropriate user.

```
$ for user in jo sam george
> do
> echo "Hello $user" | mailx $user
> done
```

'While' and 'until' loops

You may wish to execute a sequence of commands a variable number of times while a certain specified condition holds. The `if` statement allows a single test to be carried out; multiple tests can be carried out using `while`. The syntax is

```
while  command1
do       command2
done
```

indicating that *command1* is executed repeatedly. Each time its exit status is checked, and if the exit status is zero, *command2* is executed. As soon as *command1* yields a non-zero exit status the `while` loop ceases immediately. As a simple example of a while loop, the following will print `tick` on your terminal repeatedly once a second:

```
$ while true
> do
>     echo tick
>     sleep 1
> done
```

The exit status of `true` is always 0

Don't forget to press *ctrl-C* to stop it.

Use a `while` loop to print out the 'twelve times table':

Worked example 5.12

```
1 x 12 = 12
2 x 12 = 24
 . . .
12 x 12 = 144
```

Solution: Use a `while` loop and `bc` to do the calculations. Set a variable `i` to start at 1 and then become in turn 2, 3, up to 12. While the value of `i` is less than or equal to 12 evaluate `$i * 12` using `bc`, storing the answer in variable `result`, print out the line of the table, and add one to `i` using `bc` again.

```
$ i=1
$ while [ $i -le 12 ]
> do
>     result=$( echo "$i * 12" | bc )
>     echo "$i x 12 = $result"
>     i=$( echo "$i + 1" | bc )
> done
```

Similar to `while` is `until`; the syntax is the same as `while`, but instead of the condition *command1* being evaluated before the shell commands *command2* are executed in the loop, it is evaluated after, and the loop finishes when the condition gives exit status 0. So

```
until   command1
do      command2
done
```

indicates that *command1* is executed repeatedly. Each time its exit status is checked, and if the exit status is *not* zero *command2* is executed. As soon as *command1* yields a zero exit status the `until` loop ceases.

Worked example 5.13

Write a script which will repeatedly request names of files to be printed, until you type in QUIT to stop.

Solution: Use an `until` loop repeatedly to read in the name of a file, then (after having checked that it can be read) print it out. Note that we commence by setting the value of the filename, stored in the variable FILENAME, to " " (i.e. the null string). This is advisable, just in case the user running the script has already set FILENAME to QUIT — in which case the script would stop immediately it had begun to run. This may appear highly unlikely, but you should always err on the side of caution.

```
FILENAME=""                         # Initialise FILENAME
until [ "$FILENAME" = "QUIT" ]      # Finish when value is QUIT
do
    echo "Name of file to print (or QUIT to finish):"
    read FILENAME                   # Read in FILENAME
    if   [ -r "$FILENAME" ]         # If it's readable ...
    then lp "$FILENAME"             # print it
    fi
done
```

Two other commands are provided for use in `while`, `until` and `for` loops. The first one is `break` which is a method of breaking out of a loop. If a `break` command is encountered the immediately enclosing loop will terminate immediately. The other command is `continue`; unlike `break`, instead of completely leaving the loop, control passes back to the beginning of the loop.

Worked example 5.14

A file called `core` is sometimes created when a program 'crashes' — they are very big, and you will often need to delete them

Write a script which will once a minute check to see whether you have created a file called `core` in your home directory, and will terminate with a message on your terminal warning you of this fact.

Solution: There are several ways of approaching this, and we present two possible solutions. Both use loops, check the existence of the file `core` using the `test` command, and `sleep` for 60 seconds between tests. The first uses `until`:

```
until [ -f $HOME/core ]     # Stop when $HOME/core exists
do
    sleep 60                # Wait one minute
done
echo core file created      # Notify the user
```

The second solution involves looping forever, and within each loop does the test, and if
this detects the file uses break to leave the loop:

```
while true                  # Forever ...
do
    sleep 60                # Wait one minute ...
    if   [ -f $HOME/core ]  # If $HOME/core exists ...
    then break              # leave the loop
    fi
done
echo core file created      # Notify the user
```

Instead of writing a shell script, you might have considered crontab for this task

Try running one of these scripts in the background. You can create a file core yourself,
using touch, say, to check that it does indeed work:

```
$ touch core
```

Searching for files

In spite of files being arranged in a directory structure, the complexity of the file structure is
still high. Using ls may not be an easy way of finding some files — suppose, for instance,
that you had a large number of files and many subdirectories, and that somewhere you had
created a file myfile. How would you find it? In any event, searching for files other
than by name is hit-and-miss using ls — how could you print out the names of all your
executable files of size greater than 1k, for instance? You would, at this stage, have to list
all your files, send the output to a file, and edit that file.

There is a command find which can be used to examine all files within a directory
(and all subdirectories of it) and select them according to criteria such as the *group* the file
belongs to, the *time* of last modification, its *name*, its *access permissions*, its *size*, and so
on. The syntax is find, followed by a pathname (which should normally be a directory,
but it will work if it is just a file) then the criteria find is to use. For instance, to print the
pathnames of all files in your home directory called myfile, you could have:

```
$ find ~ -name myfile -print
```

This will search your home directory (~), looking for files whose name (-name) is myfile,
and display (-print) the full pathname of each such file to standard output. Note that the
criteria for find selecting files are real words, not single letters. Note also that in order
for find actually to print out the names of the files found, you must explicitly state this by
using -print. You can instead of printing the names of the files found, tell UNIX to run

The criteria are simply arguments to find, not options

any other command on those files. It is likely that you will normally only use find to print out the names of files, but instead of simply displaying names, find can be instructed to perform other actions on files it has selected. The following instructs find to perform wc on all files in the current directory (and any subdirectories) owned by user chris:

```
$ find .  -user chris -exec wc {} \;
```

The directory find is searching is . (the current directory), the criterion it uses to select files is -user chris, meaning files owned by chris. The action it takes when it has selected a file is to execute (-exec) the command wc on the file. The notation {} is shorthand for the name of that file. The semicolon terminates the action to be taken (otherwise the shell command used as the action for find would get confused with the find command itself), and must be escaped with a \.

The arguments to find are of three varieties: *options* which affect the command's behaviour, *tests* which specify which files are to be selected, and *actions* which specify what will be done with the selected files. Figures 5.6 and 5.7 list useful tests and actions.

Worked example 5.15

Remove all files named core from your filespace.

Solution: Use find to locate the files then -exec to call rm to delete them:

```
$ find ~ -name core -exec rm {} \;
```

-empty	file is empty, either a regular file or a directory
-gid *n*	file's group ID is *n*
-group *name*	file's group name is *name*
-inum *n*	file's inode is *n*
-links *n*	file has *n* hard links
-name *pattern*	filename matches *pattern*
-perm *mode*	file's permissions are (exactly) *mode*
-size *n*	file has size *n* blocks of 512 bytes
-type *c*	file's type is *c*
-user *name*	file's owner is *user*

Figure 5.6   *Tests used by* find.

-exec *command*	execute *command*
-printf *format*	print the filename

Figure 5.7   *Actions used by* find.

Formatted output

To display messages on standard output we have so far used echo. This command can only write a single string on a single line. A command printf is provided which will format a message any way you desire. Use of printf involves giving it as first argument a string known as the format, followed perhaps by subsequent arguments. The format string is copied to the standard output with certain changes made. A simple example is

The shell printf is very similar to printf() in the language C

Some shells do not yet support printf

```
$ printf "Hello"
Hello$
```

Note that Hello is precisely what has been printed – no extra spaces and no *NEWLINE* character after it, so that the next dollar prompt follows it immediately.

If a \ is encountered, it is treated as an **escape character**, the following character examined, and the pair replaced according to the table in Figure 5.8. Not all of these characters will be interpreted sensibly by all terminals, especially formfeed and vertical tab.

\ = 'backslash'

\\	\
\a	'alert' (bell)
\b	'backspace' (moves cursor left one space)
\f	'formfeed' (skips one 'page' if possible)
\n	'newline' sequence
\r	'carriage return' (moves cursor to start of current line)
\t	'tab'
\v	'vertical tab'

Figure 5.8   *Escape sequences.*

Perhaps the most common escape sequence you will meet is \n, to terminate a line:

```
$ printf "Hello\nthere\n"
Hello
there
```

When a % is included, the following several characters represent a **conversion specification**, which will instruct how one of the arguments is to be displayed. There should be the same number of conversion specifications as arguments following the format string, and they are paired up with the arguments in order. The next example illustrates the use of %d to insert a number into the output:

% = 'percent'

```
$ printf "%d is a square number\n" 64
```

The string %% is not a specification, and is replaced by a single % in the output:

```
$ printf "%s is %d%%\n" "one half" 50
```

> d   integer (printed in decimal, base 10)
> o   integer (printed in octal, base 8)
> x   integer (printed in hexadecimal, base 16)
> s   string
> c   character

Figure 5.9   *Conversion characters.*

Common specifications are given in Figure 5.9. Between the % and the conversion character may come a number indicating the **field width** in which the argument should be printed, and preceding this number may come a - (hyphen) indicating that the argument should be displayed left-justified within the field (it would by default be right-justified). If the data is numeric, then following the % immediately with a + would cause the number always to be displayed with a leading + or - sign. Note that if you wish printf to terminate a line, you must do so yourself by including a \n within the format string. The following examples illustrate printf:

```
$ printf "Hello %s\n" $LOGNAME
Hello chris
```
The string value of LOGNAME is substituted for %s.

```
$ printf "The temperature is %+7d degrees\n" 21
The temperature is      +21 degrees
```
The number 21 is substituted for %d, preceded by a + sign, and padded out with blanks to fill 7 character positions.

```
$ printf "You are %s\nyour home directory is: %s\n" \
$( logname ) $HOME
You are chris
your home directory is: /cs/ugrad/chris
```
The string which is the result of executing the command logname, and the value of the variable HOME, are substituted for the two %s specifications. Note the *NEWLINE*s within the format string, and the use of a backslash to continue the statement onto another line when it becomes long.

Worked example 5.16

Write a script which will read the standard input, and print each word from the input, right-justified in one column of width 30. A blank line (or end of file) will terminate the script.

Solution: This is formatting, so we need printf. Use a while loop to continually read in words until a 'null' one is read in (which happens with a blank line or end of file).

```
read X                  # Read first word
while [ "$X" ]          # while a "real" word ...
do
  printf "%30s\n" $X    # print it ...
  read X                # and read next one
done
```

Scripts which take arguments

Just as a UNIX command can take arguments, so can a script. After all, a script is a command written by a user. The first argument of a script is referred to within the script as $1, the second by $2, and so on. These are known as **positional parameters**. They can be manipulated like any other variables, except that they cannot be reset using =. Create a file (argfile, say) containing one line:

```
echo $1 $2
```

Now run that script, but give it two arguments:

```
$ sh argfile hello 99
hello 99
```

There are some other 'variable names' which have special meanings when used within a script. The name of the script (i.e. the name of the file containing the script) is denoted by $0, and the number of positional parameters by $#. Suppose the following script, called showargs, is invoked:

In this context # does not introduce a comment

```
This script is $0, and it has $# arguments
First argument is $1
```

the output we would get would be:

```
$ sh ./showargs foo bar
This script is ./showargs, and it has 2 arguments
First argument is foo
$ sh showargs "foo bar"
This script is showargs, and it has 1 arguments
First argument is foo bar
```

Note that the name of the script that $0 uses is that name by which the script has been called

In the second invocation the first argument of showargs is the string "foo bar", not foo – the quotes around it cause it to be considered as a single word.

When a script is given many arguments, accessing them one-by-one using positional parameters is often awkward. We can use $* to refer to them all at once. In other words, the value of $* is the *single* string "$1 $2 $3 ...". In order to experiment with these parameters, create a script containing

```
for i in $*
do
echo $i
done
```

and call it testfile. When it is run, the $* will be replaced by the arguments of the script; thus calling testfile with arguments jo, sam and george so:

```
$ testfile jo sam george
```

would be equivalent to running a script containing:

```
for i in jo sam george
do
echo $i
done
```

You can omit the rest of this section at first reading We must be careful, though; the shell will strip out quotes before passing arguments to a command, and we need to be able to handle

```
$ sh testfile jo "Sue Smith" sam
```

in a sensible manner. To this end we can use $@, which is similar to $*. Edit testfile to replace $* by $@. In both cases the result is the same, namely

```
$ sh testfile jo "Sue Smith" sam
jo
Sue
Smith
sam
```

indicating that the quotes have been stripped before the arguments have been passed to testfile. If, instead, the first line of the script is

```
for i in "$*"
```

the quotes are stripped from the arguments, which are then enclosed by a new pair of quotes. Thus the string jo Sue Smith sam is the expansion of $*, which is then quoted within the script indicating a single string, and the output is:

```
$ sh testfile jo "Sue Smith" sam
jo Sue Smith sam
```

If, however, "$@" is used, the arguments to the script are passed without modification, including quotes, to replace "$@", and the quotes are then interpreted within the script:

```
$ sh testfile jo "Sue Smith" sam
jo
Sue Smith
sam
```

If a script requires an indeterminate number of arguments, you may wish to discard the earlier ones — for instance, if they are options and you have finished processing all the options. The command `shift` will remove `$1` from the positional parameters, `$2` will become `$1` (etc.), and `$*`, `$@` and `$#` will all be changed accordingly.

Write a script called `mypager` which will take arguments that are files and page each of them in turn using `more`. Additionally, `mypager` may take a single argument, `-i`, which will cause a message to be displayed on the screen before each file is paged, giving the name of the file, and requiring the user to press *RETURN* to continue.

Worked example 5.17

Solution:

```
IFLAG=no
if [ "$#" -gt 0 ]            # Make sure there are some files
then    if [ "$1" = "-i"]    # Check if the option is called
        then IFLAG=yes       # If so, reset the flag ...
             shift           # and delete the argument
        fi
fi

for i in "$@"                # Go through each file in turn
do
   if    [ "$IFLAG" = "yes" ]   # If "-i" ...
   then echo "Paging $i"        # output message ...
        echo "Press RETURN to continue"
        read j                  # wait for RETURN
   fi
   more "$i"                 # Page the file
done
```

Parameter expansion

We have already considered assigning values to variables in the previous chapter. In this section, we look at the shell's features which allow it to examine in detail whether variables have been set values and what form those values take.

Often you will write scripts where you will use variables which you assume will have certain values. They may be variables you have created yourself for your own benefit, they may be 'system' variables, such as PATH, which have been set for you. However, there is always a possibility that such a variable has not been assigned a value. A case in point is the variable NAME which is not mentioned in the POSIX standard, and commonly contains the user's real name. Many shells and utilities (especially mailers) use it, and it's quite reasonable to assume that it has been set a value. Unfortunately, this is not guaranteed.

It is thus good practice whenever writing a script which relies on a variable that is not defined as necessarily existing in POSIX, to check that it has in fact been assigned a value, and that that value is of the correct format. **Parameter expansion** is the mechanism usually employed.

Let's for a moment consider NAME. Suppose a particular script requires that variable; we could include the following code to check whether it indeed does have a value, and if not we could give it a *default* value:

```
if [ -z "$NAME" ]
then NAME="A.N. Other"
fi
```

This will work. It is also verbose — a script which used many variables would be tedious to write if you included checks for all the variables in that script. It should be emphasised that it is a very good idea to check that variables have in fact been assigned values before you attempt to use those variables. Parameter expansion will not do anything that cannot already be done using test, but it provides a concise and easy to read notation which avoids saturating scripts with tests.

At this point we need to discuss an apparently minor — but nonetheless important — feature of variables. If a variable has not got a value, this can be for two reasons. Either it has not been mentioned at all before, in which case it is **unset**, or it has been set, yet has the null string as its value, so:

A null string "" has length zero

```
$ NAME=""
```

or alternatively, since it would not be ambiguous,

```
$ NAME=
```

For most purposes the two situations have the same result. If you wish to unset a variable rather than just set its value to null, use unset:

```
$ unset NAME
```

To ensure that a variable is set, the form is

${*variable*: -*default*}

which expands to the value of *variable*, if that variable has been set or is null, otherwise to *default*. For instance, instead of the test example above, the first time you use NAME, replace $NAME by

```
${NAME:-"A.N. Other"}
```

The following script will check to see if variable NAME has been set; if not it will be replaced by the value of LOGNAME, and output a welcome message:

```
$ echo Hello ${NAME:-$LOGNAME}
```

Try this, first of all without NAME set, and then after you have given it a value.

The form of *default* can be anything that returns a value – the above could be accomplished equally well using:

```
$ echo Hello ${NAME:-$(logname)}
```

Create a welcome message which initially checks variable NAME to find out your name; if that is unset, checks LOGNAME, and if LOGNAME is unset uses command logname as a last resort.

Worked example 5.18

Solution: As in the example above, if NAME is unset we fall back on the value of LOGNAME, but then we also have to check that LOGNAME has been assigned a value. So we can replace $LOGNAME by the result of running the command logname.

```
$ echo Hello ${NAME:-${LOGNAME:-$(logname)}}
```

If a variable is unset, the : - mechanism will not assign the default value to it – that default is merely substituted for the expression at that single instance. If you also wish the variable to be set to the default, use : = instead of : -, so:

```
$ unset NAME
$ echo Hello ${NAME:=$LOGNAME}
Hello chris
$ echo $NAME
chris
```

Another behaviour which might be desirable is for the shell to give you an error message if a variable is unset – especially useful if there is no sensible default value you can substitute for the variable – replace : - by : ? so:

```
$ unset NAME
$ echo Hello ${NAME:?}
NAME: parameter null or not set
```

If you follow the ? by a string, that message will be printed instead of parameter null or not set:

```
$ echo Hello ${NAME:?"who are you?"}
NAME: who are you?
```

Don't forget to enclose the string in quotes if it contains blanks

Worked example 5.19

Ensure that PATH is set; if it is not reset it to /bin:/usr/bin, and inform the user of its value.

Solution: Use positional parameters

```
$ echo The PATH is ${PATH:="/bin:/usr/bin"}
```

When using : - the default value is substituted if the variable is null or unset. If you use : + the reverse happens – the default value is substituted only if the variable is set and not null:

```
$ unset NAME
$ echo ${NAME:+Chris}
(blank line)
$ echo ${LOGNAME:+Chris}
Chris
```

We can discover the **length** (i.e. the numbers of characters) of a string:

```
$ echo $LOGNAME
chris
$ echo ${#LOGNAME}
5
```

does not begin a comment when used in this way

Worked example 5.20

Use a loop to print out a line of 50 plusses so:
++
Solution: Use an until loop, and store the plusses in a variable LINE (say). Start off by setting LINE to null, and repeatedly add a single + to it until its length has become 50.

```
LINE=""                         # Set LINE to null
until [ ${#LINE} -eq 50 ]       # Until its length is 50 ...
do
   LINE=$LINE+                  # add another "+" to it ...
done
echo $LINE                      # and finally display the line
```

Summary of utilities

`bc`	calculator
`break`	exit from `for`, `while` or `until` loop
`continue`	continue `for`, `while` or `until` loop
`false`	returns 'false' value, exit status 1
`find`	find files
`printf`	write formatted output
`shift`	shift positional parameters
`test`	evaluate expression
`true`	returns 'true' value, exit status 0

Problems

5.1 List all regular files in your home directory whose size is less than 512 bytes.

5.2 What is the maximum length of a line in `/usr/dict/words`?

5.3 Write a script called `mcat` which will be identical to `cat` with the following difference: if any argument given to `mcat` which is a file either does not exist or is unreadable, `mcat` will not send *any* output to the standard output. The behaviour of `cat` is that all its arguments which are readable are copied to standard output.

5.4 List the name of each file in the current directory (or any subdirectory of it) which is a *regular* file, together with the first line of the file.

5.5 List all users currently logged in to the system, in 4 columns of width 10 characters, so:

```
    chris        jo       sam    george
     pete       sue      dave      jane
     emma      bill
```

5.6 Write a script which will prompt the user for two numbers, representing the width and height of a rectangle in cm, and output the area of the rectangle both in square metres and in square inches (1 inch = 2.54 cm).

5.7 Write a script which will take text input from standard input, and copy it to standard output with each line preceded by a line number in the same manner as `cat -n`. Do not use the command `cat`.

Chapter 6

More on shells

OBJECTIVES

In this chapter you will learn about the following shell features:

- □ arithmetic expansion, pattern matching and 'case' statements;

- □ scripts which require options;

- □ file system conventions.

In this chapter we examine shells in more depth. Much of this chapter is dependent on you being comfortable with Chapter 5, and if you have not yet familiarised yourself with the material in that chapter you are strongly encouraged to return to it.

Simple arithmetic

The utility bc was discussed in the previous chapter, and will perform any calculations required, to any accuracy, just as if you had a pocket calculator available. Since bc does have all the facilities required, it is in many circumstances 'overkill' – the overheads of calling and executing a utility such as bc are high. It is therefore desirable to have another method of doing simple arithmetic tasks which are a part of the shell, thus obviating the need to call a utility like bc. The mechanism is known as **arithmetic expansion** and takes the form of

On some non-POSIX systems, use $[...] instead of $((...))

```
$(( expression ))
```

where *expression* is a valid arithmetic expression, using only integers (no floating point arithmetic), and the operators described below. Boolean expressions are represented by 1 for True and 0 for False. The operators, which are listed in Figure 6.1, are a subset of those available in the C programming language, and parentheses may be used to group subexpressions. Thus the following dialogue could take place:

Do not confuse with the shell commands true and false

```
$ echo $(( 1 + 2 + (3 * 4) ))
15
$ echo $(( 1 > 2 ))
0
```

+	plus
*	times
/	integer division
%	integer remainder
==	equal to
!=	not equal to
>	greater than
>=	greater than or equal to
<	less than
<=	less than or equal to

Figure 6.1   *Operators for arithmetic expansion.*

```
$ echo $(( 1 < 2 ))
1
```

As an example, the following script will read in a number, assumed to represent pounds
weight and write to the standard output a message translating that to stones and pounds: One stone = 14 pounds

```
echo Type in a whole number representing pounds weight:
read POUNDS
STONES=$(( $POUNDS / 14 ))
SMALLPOUNDS=$(( $POUNDS % 14 ))
echo $POUNDS pounds is $STONES and $SMALLPOUNDS pounds
```

Write a script `convertsec` which will read in a number, thought of as representing   **Worked example 6.1**
seconds, and print out the number of hours/minutes/seconds it represents, so:

```
$ convertsec
Enter a number of seconds:
12345
12345 seconds is 3:25:45
```

Solution: First of all, check that the number is not less than zero, then do the calculation,
which is self-explanatory.

```
# Prompt the user and read in number of seconds
echo Enter a number of seconds:
read SECONDS

if   [ $SECONDS -lt 0 ]              # Check it's positive
then echo Number must be positive
else MINUTES=$(( $SECONDS / 60 ))   # Total minutes
     RSECONDS=$(( $SECONDS % 60 ))  # Residual seconds
```

```
   HOURS=$(( $MINUTES / 60 ))     # Total hours
   MINUTES=$(( $MINUTES % 60 ))   # Residual minutes
   printf "%d seconds is %d:%02d:%02d\n" $SECONDS \
                         $HOURS $MINUTES $RSECONDS
fi
```

You may wish to compare arithmetic expansion with using bc. The example in the previous chapter which will display the '12 times table' would be coded as a script using arithmetic expansion as follows:

```
i=1
while [ $i -le 12 ]
do
    result=$(( $i * 12 ))
    echo "$i x 12 = $result"
    i=$(( $i + 1 ))
done
```

Try out both — you will find that when you use arithmetic expansion it is much faster. Where possible, you should use arithmetic expansion in preference to bc, but if you are in any doubt as to whether arithmetic expansion can give you sufficient precision, you should play safe and use bc.

expr = 'expression'

The command expr performs a similar function to arithmetic expansion. In fact, it can be considered just a different syntax — just as [*expression*] can be replaced by test *expression*, so can $((*expression*)) be replaced by expr *expression*. Non-POSIX shells will probably only support expr.

We do not explore here non-arithmetic capabilities of expr

There is, unfortunately, a catch. You can also use expr to perform more functions than just arithmetic — it is also capable of rudimentary operations on strings. If you give expr an argument which is not a 'sum', it will assume it is a string and print it:

```
$ expr hello
hello
```

Between $((and)), the shell knows it is expecting an arithmetic expression. Following expr the shell does not know that what follows will be such an expression — it might be simply a string. For instance,

```
$ expr 1+2
1+2
```

In this example, 1+2 was not recognised by expr as ' 1 + 2'. In order for expr to work correctly with arithmetic, each 'token' — that is, number/operator — must be separated by whitespace:

```
$ expr 1 + 2
3
```

Since `expr` is simply a command like any other, any characters within the expression which are special to the shell (such as `*`) must be escaped, for instance:

```
$ expr 6 \* 7
42
```

If you had not escaped `*` in this example it would have been replaced by the names of all the files in the current directory. Another difference between arithmetic expansion and `expr` is that the equality operator for `expr` is =, not ==.

For historical reasons

Write a script which will read in a number and decide whether that number is prime or not. **Solution**: This calculation is one which you would typically code in another programming language — it is not too complex to use the shell for, although efficiency considerations would discourage it. Using a variable `I` to iterate from 2 to half the possibly prime number `N`, keep checking whether or not `I` divides `N` exactly. If a divisor is found, set `RESULT` to 1.

Worked example 6.2

If we used `bc` for this, it would be extremely slow

```
echo "Type in a number"
read N
RESULT=0
I=2
HALFN=$(( $N / 2 ))              # HALFN is N/2
while [ $I -le $HALFN ]         # Stop when I equals N/2
do
   if [ $(( $N % $I )) -eq 0 ]  # If I divides N exactly
   then RESULT=1                # ... RESULT is 1
        break                   # ... and leave the loop
   fi
   I=$(( $I + 1 ))              # Increment I
done
if [ $RESULT -eq 0 ]           # If no divisor found
then echo "$N is prime"
else echo "$N is composite"
fi
```

A better algorithm would have been to iterate to $\sqrt{N}$ rather than N/2, but arithmetic expansion doesn't allow for the square root function. Try this example using `expr` instead of arithmetic expansion.

Pattern matching

Using a notation known as **pattern matching**, we can consider concepts such as 'all files with suffix `.c`' or 'all arguments to the command which are three characters long and commence with a digit'. Pattern matching is used in several situations by the shell, and we shall introduce those particular instances as we meet them. If the shell encounters a word containing any of the following symbols (unless they are 'escaped' by being preceded by a backslash or contained within (single) quotes)

```
?    *    [
```

then it will attempt to match that word with filenames, either in the current directory, or absolute pathnames (if they commence with/). A ? will match any *single* character, * will match *anything at all*, and [introduces a list of characters which it will match. If the word commences with a * or a ?, it will only match filenames in the current directory not commencing with a dot. When the shell has worked out which filenames the word matches, it will replace the word by all those names. Try:

```
$ echo *
```

echo * won't format file-
names into neat columns,
and the output might be
longer than your terminal is
wide

Since * matches anything it will match any files in the current directory, and the resulting output will be similar to that from ls. Suppose you have a file mycommand — try

```
$ echo m*
```

since m* matches all filenames in the current directory commencing with m, all those filenames will be displayed, including mycommand.

Worked example 6.3

Use ls -ld to list all 'dot' files in your home directory.
Solution: Use ls -ld, but instead of giving it argument ~ or $HOME to list files in your home directory, you must isolate only those whose names commence with a dot. The 'dot' files in your home directory will each be matched with either ~/.* or $HOME/.* and one solution is therefore:

```
$ ls -ld $HOME/.*
```

A * will match any number of characters, a ? will match one single character, but is otherwise used in exactly the same way as *, so

```
$ echo ????
```

will display all filenames in the current directory which have 4 characters in their names (but do not commence with a dot). Pattern matching does not extend to subdirectories of the current directory, and ??? would not match a/b.

Worked example 6.4

How many directories/files located in the root directory have names which are of three characters?
Solution: Use pattern matching and ls to select the files and wc -w to count them.

```
$ ls /??? | wc -w
```

Many files on a UNIX system come equipped with a specified **suffix**, that is, a sequence of characters at the end of the filename.   Some also give meaning to other parts of their filenames – look at the files in /lib, for instance, which contains files of the form lib*something*.a and are library files used by the C compiler. Pattern matching is useful for isolating files whose names you know to be of a specified 'shape'.

Such as .c for C programs and .o for files containing object code

---

Print detailed information on all files in the current directory with the .c suffix.
Solution: Using ls -l, we need to give it as arguments those files with suffix .c, and the pattern *.c will match precisely those files:

Worked example 6.5

```
$ ls -l *.c
```

Between symbols [and] comes either a list of characters, one or more *ranges* of expressions, possibly preceded by the ! character. A range, which is denoted by two characters separated by a hyphen, means all those characters which are lexically between (and including) those two characters. Thus [m-q] matches any lower-case letter between m and q inclusive. The ! indicates that the word will match any single character not specified between the brackets.

! = exclamation mark

The character to the left of the hyphen in a range must lexically precede the character to the right or the range matches nothing

[abc]	matches a or b or c
[l-z]	matches all lower-case letters l to z inclusive
[A-Cb-k]	matches upper-case letters A to C and lower-case b to k
[XYa-z]	matches upper-case letters X and Y and any lower-case letter
[-a-z]	matches any lower-case letter or a hyphen
[!0-9]	matches any character which is not a digit

List all commands stored in /bin whose names consist of two characters, the second one being a vowel.
Solution: Use ls with an argument which will match this pattern. ? matches a single character, and [aeiouAEIOU] matches any vowel, thus:

Worked example 6.6

```
$ ls /bin/?[aeiouAEIOU]
```

We shall use pattern matching later on in this chapter in the context of case statements, and you should remember that it is a much more powerful tool than simply one for checking filenames. In the meantime, using ls followed by a pattern is an excellent method of getting used to pattern matching. Remember that *, ?, [and] all involve patterns, and that if you use them in a script and don't want them to relate to patterns, they must be escaped using \ or single quotes. In later chapters we shall introduce a similar concept to pattern matching, known as **regular expressions**.

Worked example 6.7

Create a script which will remove all files with suffix . o in the current directory, prompting you for each one as to whether you do in fact wish to delete it, and confirming whether or not it has been removed.

Solution: These files are matched by *.o, and we can pass the files one-by-one to rm -i using a for loop. rm yields exit status 1 if it fails to remove its argument/s.

```
for i in *.o                        # Loop through files
do
  if    rm -i $i                    # If deleted ...
  then echo File $i deleted         # confirm this ...
  else echo File $i not deleted     # otherwise not
  fi
done
```

WARNING: rm * deletes all files in your current directory – be careful using patterns with rm

We could not simply have used

```
rm -i *.o
```

since we would then have been unable to generate the 'confirmation' message.

The 'case' statement

A statement which involves pattern matching is case. The way it works is you start off with

```
case expression in
```

where *expression* has a value (and would typically be a variable preceded with a $). Following that is a sequence of

pattern) *command-list* ; ;

and the case statement is terminated with esac. The value of *expression* is evaluated, and the first of the patterns which matches it has the following *command-list* executed. For example, a very simple version of the command file which only examines the suffix of its first argument might look like:

Double semicolons are required, because a single semicolon is used to separate multiple commands occurring on a single line

```
case $1 in
  *.c)        printf "%s:    %s\n" "$1" "c program text" ;;
  *.a)        printf "%s:    %s\n" "$1" "archive library" ;;
  *.o)        printf "%s:    %s\n" "$1" "object file" ;;
  *)          printf "%s:    %s\n" "$1" "unknown type" ;;
esac
```

Where patterns appear in a case statement they are matched with the expression at the start of the case statement, and not with any filenames. If a pattern appears within a command-list in a case statement, however, the pattern is matched to filenames as before. The following script will list the files in the current directory, but will ask you whether you wish to list the 'dot' files:

```
echo "List dot files as well? "   # Prompt user
read YESORNO                      # Read reply

case "$YESORNO" in               # Check reply
    [Yy]*)   ls * .* ;;          # Commence with a Y?
    [Nn]*)   ls * ;;             # Commence with an N?
    *)       echo "Sorry, don't understand";;
esac
```

Note the technique used here for asking the user a yes/no question – the answer is assumed to commence with a Y or an N, in upper or lower case, and that is sufficient. This script would happily accept input Yqwerty as a positive response. If you required the user to type in exactly the word YES, the pattern, instead of [Yy]*, would be [Yy][Ee][Ss].

Write a script compile which will take a single argument representing the name of a program written in a high-level language, and then compile that program using one of cc (for C), pc (for Pascal) or f77 (for FORTRAN). File suffices .c, .p and .f respectively are assumed to indicate the language type.

Solution: We need to check the file suffix using a case statement.

```
# First, check we do have a single argument
case $# in
    1)  ;;
    *) echo "$0: Incorrect number of arguments";;
esac

# Now examine the suffix of argument 1
case $1 in
    *.c) cc $1 ;;
    *.p) pc $1 ;;
    *.f) f77 $1 ;;
    *)   echo "Unknown language";;
esac
```

Worked example 6.8

The names for the compilers may be different on your system, and are not specified in POSIX

Where the same command is required for two separate patterns, rather than duplicating the line (or lines) of commands, you can combine the two (or more) patterns. So the pattern

sam|chris

would match *either* sam *or* chris.

Worked example 6.9

This is not an exhaustive
list of the types of number
available in the UK

Write a script which will read in a string representing a telephone number as dialled from
the UK, and indicate whether it is an overseas number (commencing 00 or 010), a *value
added* number (commencing 0898 or 0891), a freephone number (commencing 0800), a
service number (3 digits commencing with a 1) or a *national* code (10 digits commencing
0 or 11 digits commencing 01).

Solution: We could use many if statements, but the script would be very messy. This is
the sort of problem for which a case statement is ideal.

```
# Prompt user and read in the number
printf "Input phone number: "
read N

# Examine the various patterns that might match N
case $N in
  00*|010*)    echo "International" ;;
  0898*|0891*) echo "Value added" ;;
  0800*)       echo "Freephone" ;;
  1??)         echo "Service number" ;;
  0?????????)  echo "National code (pre 1995)" ;;
  01????????)  echo "National code (after 1995)" ;;
  *)           echo "Unknown code" ;;
esac
```

Entering and leaving the shell

In this section we look at the command sh – the shell. As we have discussed, the shell is
a program. It is treated just as any other utility, and as such can take arguments. If it takes
one argument, which is a filename, the action taken is to take its input, the commands for
that shell, from that file, which is called a **shell script**. With no arguments the shell reads its
commands from the standard input. When a shell terminates, just like any other command
it returns an exit status, which is normally the status of the last command executed by that
shell.

Create a file (mycommand, say), containing a single line which is the shell command
false. Run the command and check its exit status using $?:

```
$ sh mycommand
$ echo $?
1
```

Add an extra line to the end of mycommand (using vi or >>) which is the shell command
true; run the command again and check the exit status. This time it will be 0.

A shell can be forced to terminate with a specific exit status by means of command
exit. Add the following line to the end of mycommand, run it again and see what exit
status you then get:

It is good practice explicitly to use exit to leave a
script, rather than allowing
a default exit status

```
exit 42
```

Any commands which might be executed after an exit command are discarded; exit kills the shell immediately. The same is true of an interactive shell.

Type sh to start a new interactive shell, and reset the prompt (so you know which is the new shell, and which the previous one) then type exit followed by a number. You will see that the new shell terminates (since you are back to the original prompt), and $? confirms that the new shell did indeed return an exit status to the original shell.

```
$ sh
$ PS1="--> "
--> exit 99
$ echo $?
99
```

Write a script called morning which will exit with exit status 0 (if it is run before noon) and status 1 (if run after noon).

Worked example 6.10

Solution: Use date to check the time, then test to check whether the time is am or pm.

```
HOUR=$( date +"%H" )      # HOUR is a number between 0 and 23
if   [ $HOUR -le 11 ]     # Check HOUR is AM
then exit 0               # ... then exit with status 0
else exit 1               # ... otherwise status 1
fi
```

This command can then be used, for instance, in the following manner:

```
$ if sh morning
> then echo "Good morning"
> else echo "Good afternoon"
> fi
```

You could have piped the output from date to cut instead of using the formatting option to date, as in previous worked examples. By now, however, you should be getting into the habit of using man to find out more information on commands.

The shell supports various **options**, just like other commands. A very useful option is -x, which instructs the shell that, each time it is about to execute a command, it displays on the standard error stream the name of that command. This is performed after all variable names have been replaced by their values, and other substitutions done; it is thus a very good method of **debugging** shell scripts in the event of them not working as planned. For instance, supposing file badcommand contains

x = 'eXpand'

```
date              # This is OK ...
cat $LOGNAME      # but file chris doesn't exist
```

We could then run this with option -x set:

```
$ sh -x badcommand
+ date
Mon Aug 11 17:39:52 BST 1997
+ cat chris
cat: chris: No such file or directory
```

Shell options can be set during a shell session by means of the command `set`:

```
$ set -x
```

Not unset and can be **unset** as follows:

```
$ set +x
```

Within a script − or indeed when using an interactive shell − you can set the positional parameters $1, $2, etc., without passing them as arguments to the script. This uses `set`, and in the same way as before. Suppose we have a file `testfile`, which contains a script. Having `set -x` at the start of the file and executing the file using `sh` would be equivalent to not having `set -x` in the script, and running the script with `sh -x testfile`. If we wanted to pass other arguments to `testfile`, we could either have:

```
$ sh testfile arg1 arg2 arg3
```

or we could `set` the extra arguments at the start of the script with

```
set arg1 arg2 arg3
```

in which case $1 would become `arg1`, $2 would become `arg2`, $3 would become `arg3` and $# would become 3. This is handy when debugging scripts which use positional parameters. After setting positional parameters, you can list what they are, together with the values of all other environment variables, by just typing `set`. You can unset all of them with:

```
$ set --
```

Try the following:

```
$ set --
$ set Chris
$ echo Hello $1
Hello Chris
$ set Sam
$ echo Hello $1
Hello Sam
```

The line `set Sam` has reset the value of the first positional parameter $1 to Sam.

More about writing scripts which require options

Writing a script with arguments is straightforward – you just need to examine $1, $2, etc. – but what about options? Suppose you wanted to write a command `mycommand` which if given option -h would print a 'help' message rather than executing:

An option is an argument which commences with a hyphen

```
$ mycommand -h
Usage: mycommand [-h]
```

You could check whether $1 is equal to ' -h', but if you had several possible options, not just one, the number of permutations would make this a very messy programming exercise. If `mycommand` took option -a in addition to -h, you would have to check for:

```
mycommand -h
mycommand -a
mycommand -ah
mycommand -ha
mycommand -a -h
mycommand -h -a
```

in addition to any invalid options it might be presented with. The utility `getopts` is provided to assist in writing shells which have options. Consider the instance above – we could have as the contents of `mycommand`:

```
while getopts h OPTIONNAME
do
    case $OPTIONNAME in
        h)   echo 'Usage: mycommand [-h]' ;;
        ?)   echo '"mycommand" allows only option -h'
             exit 1 ;;
    esac
done
echo "Arguments were $@"
```

The action `getopts` performs is to look at `getopt`'s first argument, which should be a list of letters – representing the valid options allowed by the script – and possibly colons. It then looks at the next argument to the script in which it occurs. If the argument to a script is an option (i.e. preceded by a minus sign), `getopts` checks to see whether the option is in the list of valid options. If not, an error message is displayed. The second argument to `getopts` is a variable name, which is set to the option that `getopts` has discovered. Only one option at a time will be checked, so you need to enclose `getopts` in a `while` loop. Let's see what happens when `mycommand` is called:

Options must precede all other arguments which are not options

```
$ mycommand -h hello
Usage: mycommand [-h]
Arguments were -h hello
$ mycommand -x hello
mycommand: illegal option -- x
```

```
Bad option to mycommand
$ mycommand hello there
Arguments were hello there
$ mycommand hello -h
Arguments were hello -h
```

In this case -h is not an option

Some commands take options which require arguments — such as lp, whose option -d must be followed by the name of the destination printer. This is handled by getopts by using colons.

If you intend to write scripts which require options, then using getopts is the preferred method

If an option requires an argument, then a colon should follow the option name in the list of allowed options to getopts. When that option is encountered, the value of its argument will be stored in the system variable OPTARG. For instance, suppose a script called mymessage takes one option -m, followed by a string, and prints out that string. With no arguments mymessage prints Hello. The string would be an argument to the -m option. This script might be coded thus:

```
MESSAGE=Hello                      # Variable to store message
if getopts m: OPTIONNAME           # If an option found
then
   case $OPTIONNAME in             # Check which option found
      m)   MESSAGE=$OPTARG;;
      ?)   exit 1;;                # Exit if not -m
   esac
fi

echo $MESSAGE                      # Output the message
```

The number of the next argument to be processed by getopts is stored in OPTIND, so that by using shift you can strip off the options from the command and leave the rest of the arguments for processing later.

Worked example 6.11

Write a script mymail which will call mailx to send messages. The script should take an optional argument -s (to specify the subject) and one or more other arguments to specify the recipients (just like mailx). No other options apart from -s should be allowed. If mymail is called without option -s it should prompt the user for a subject.

```
$ mymail -s "Test message" sam
```
(message)
```
$ mymail sam
Subject: Test message
```
(message)

Solution: Use `getopts` to process the command line the script is invoked from:

```
SUBJECT=""
if getopts s: OPTNAME                    # Valid option is 's'
then                                     # which takes an argument
    case $OPTNAME in
        s)  SUBJECT="$OPTARG";;          # The argument to 's' is
                                         # SUBJECT
        ?)  echo "Usage: $0 [-s subject] users"
            exit 1;;                     # Exit if invalid option
    esac
fi

shift $(($OPTIND - 1))                   # Remove the options
USERS="$*"                               # The rest of the line
                                         # is the recipients
if      [ -z "$USERS" ]                  # ... which is compulsory
then    echo "Must specify recipients"
        exit 1                           # Exit if no recipients
fi
while   [ -z "$SUBJECT" ]                # Loop until subject
do                                       # is not null
        printf "Subject (no quotes): "
        read SUBJECT
done

mailx -s "$SUBJECT" $USERS"
```

Symbolic links

In Chapter 3 we introduced *links*. Recall that a file is represented by a name and by an inode, and that a single inode can have several names. We use a *link* to create an extra name for an inode using the command `ln`, so

```
$ ln fileA fileB
```

will cause `fileA` and `fileB` to be two names for the same file. If you delete one of them, the other continues to exist, and the file only disappears when both are removed. They share the same inode.

Hard links could only be used within a single filesystem. Hard links can also only be used on *ordinary* files, and not on directories. If you try, for instance,

```
$ ln / rootdirectory
```

you will get an error message.

Not POSIX

There is another type of link referred to as a **symbolic link** or **soft link** which can get around these problems.

A hard link is an entry in a directory associating a filename with an inode. A soft link is an entry in a directory associating a filename with another filename. This is an important distinction — hard links are names for inodes, soft links are names for other filenames. To create a soft link, use `ln` with option `-s`. Consider:

s = 'symbolic'

```
$ ln -s fileA fileB
```

which will create a symbolic link, called `fileB`, to a file `fileA`, which should exist. Examining your files with `ls -l` would give something like

```
lrw-r--r--  1 chris ugrads 122 May 21 18:40 fileB -> fileA
```

indicating that `fileB` is a symbolic link (1 in column 1), and that it points to (`->`) `fileA`. Whenever you use `fileB`, UNIX will assume you want to access `fileA` and treat `fileB` accordingly. If `fileA` does not exist, and you try to access `fileB`, you will get an error message telling you `fileB` does not exist.

You can make a symbolic link to any file, provided that file does exist. The advantage of symbolic links is that you do not have to worry about the filesystems the system's storage is divided into. There is a danger, though: if the file a symbolic link points to is deleted, the link remains in place. Try:

```
$ ln -s fileA fileB
$ rm fileA
$ cat fileB
cat: fileB: No such file or directory
```

Thus you must be careful when deleting files which are pointed to by symbolic links.

Worked example 6.12

Create a symbolic link called `systmp` in your home directory, which is linked to `/tmp`.
Solution: Use `ln -s`, as just described. You cannot use a hard link, since `/tmp` will (almost certainly) be on a different filesystem.

```
$ ln -s /tmp $HOME/systmp
```

Now try the following to confirm it works:

```
$ ls $HOME/systmp
$ ls /tmp
```

Setting up terminals

With a bit of luck, you'll never have to worry about the 'characteristics' of your own terminal, but it is possible that you may have to hook up a terminal to the system and then find it's not quite in order. The command `tput` is provided to help you check basic characteristics of your terminal, using knowledge provided by the environment variable TERM. It can do operations such as 'reset' or 'initialise' your terminal (if either is possible) and cause your screen to 'clear'. The usability of this command depends entirely on the type of terminal you are using, and only three actions are specified by POSIX. To clear the terminal screen, invoke tput with argument clear:

```
$ tput clear
```

The reset and initialise procedures require arguments reset and init respectively, and their actions depend on the system you are using. Typically you may need tput reset if your terminal starts to respond unexpectedly, which is sometimes due to having received spurious data which it has interpreted. This can sometimes happen if you cat a binary file by mistake. Check the manual page for tput to find out precisely what effect they will have on your system.

The *TAB* key will input a *TAB* character to the system. For most purposes a *TAB* can be treated as a *SPACE*, and both are sometimes collectively described as **whitespace**. The effect of touching a *TAB* key is to move the cursor to the next **tab position**. You can reset the tab positions on your terminal (just for the duration of your current session) using the command tabs. Followed by a comma-separated list of numbers, tabs will reset the tab positions to those column numbers. So, to set the tab positions to columns 5, 10 and 15 you would type:

This command only works on some terminals

```
$ tabs 5,10,15
```

Tabs are useful in text files if you want to line up columns, and don't wish to involve yourself in any complex text formatting programs. It is a good idea when writing shell scripts to 'line up' the first character of each command so that commands inside a loop are clearly so. For instance, in the following script the 'body' of the for loop is made up of two commands which have been indented by several spaces.

```
for i in *
do
    printf "File %s has size " $i
    wc -c $i
    printf "\n"
done
```

Rather than count the number of spaces each time you may find it easier to insert a *TAB* character instead:

```
for i in *
do
TABprintf "File %s has size " $i
TABwc -c $i
TABprintf "\n"
done
```

Conventions used in UNIX file systems

In Chapter 3 we introduced the hierarchy of UNIX directories and files. In this section we look in detail at *which files* are stored *where*. Your home directory will be located at least one level down the hierarchy, and whatever subdirectories you create are your own business. There are some conventions which it would be unwise to ignore, although they are not always followed, even in parts of the file hierarchy which contain system files, and there is no requirement for them in the standards.

Executable files, whether they are binary files or executable shell scripts, are usually held in directories called `bin`, or which have `bin` as part of their name. For instance,

```
/cs/ugrad/chris/bin
/cs/ugrad/chris/import/bin
/cs/ugrad/chris/bin/star4
/cs/ugrad/chris/bin/scripts
```

If `bin` is the *last* component of the pathname, the previous components would typically indicate some property of the commands held in the directory. The directory `/cs/ugrad/chris/import/bin` might well hold commands which `chris` has been mailed by colleagues. If `bin` is not the last component, subsequent names in the pathname might indicate the type of machine the commands can run on. Commands in `/cs/ugrad/chris/bin/star4` might be binary commands which will only run on a Star4 system, and `/cs/ugrad/chris/bin/scripts` might contain shell scripts.

Devices are contained in directories called `dev`; most systems will simply have `/dev` as the only such directory, as they cannot be created by users at will. Manual pages are always contained in a hierarchy with `man` as the last component. Source code (such as C or Pascal programs) is often held in directories called `src`. Files which have to be stored temporarily while being sent to a printer or waiting to be sent off by the electronic mail program, are held in directories called `spool`. Files and directories whose size is known to vary considerably are often held in a directory called `var`. It would not be uncommon for `chris`'s **mailbox** – the file in which incoming mail is stored before being read – to be the file `/var/spool/mail/chris`. Libraries – that is, sets of data required by specific utilities such as the C compiler – are held in directories called `lib`, and 'include' files – also required by the C compiler – are held in directories called `include`. Have a look at the root directory, and you will see several of these directories.

There is a wide variety of practice across manufacturers and institutions, but these conventions are broadly adhered to, even if minor variations are added; if you find a directory called `4lib` you would be fairly safe guessing it to be a 'library' directory.

The last directory name which interests us here is `tmp`. This directory is used for **temporary files**. Many commands – including several of the scripts in this book – use temporary files which are only required while the command is running, and the existence of these files is of no interest to the user running the command. Instead of using the current directory to store the temporary files in, it is good practice to use a completely different directory. There are two principal reasons for this. First, it avoids the problem of the current directory filling up with unwanted files (should they accidentally not be deleted) and secondly, it prevents existing files being overwritten (should their names happen to coincide with that of the temporary file). There is also an advantage from the viewpoint

Hence 'imported'

Recall that binary code is machine-specific

var = 'variable size'

of the System Administrator – provided the locations of the tmp directories are known, they can periodically have their contents removed, so that unwanted temporary files do not waste storage space.

You can expect to find a directory called /tmp, and you can choose names for temporary files to place in that directory by using $$ as part of the filename.

$$ is the current process number

Write a script which will repeatedly request you to type in the names of files, and will concatenate them and print on the terminal the resulting file after all the concatenation has taken place. The script should terminate when you enter a blank line in response to the request for a filename.

Worked example 6.13

Solution: We need to concatenate the files to a temporary file, cat that file, then delete it.

```
# Start off by choosing a unique name for the temporary file
TMPFILE=/tmp/$LOGNAME.$$

# Double check that it doesn't exist - just in case
if    [ -f $TMPFILE ]
then echo "Temporary file exists"
      exit 1       # The command fails ...
fi

while true       # Forever ...
do    printf "New file (RETURN to finish): "
      read NEXTFILE
      if    [ -z "$NEXTFILE" ]
      then break # Leave the while loop
      fi
      cat $NEXTFILE >>$TMPFILE
done

cat $TMPFILE     # Print the temporary file
rm $TMPFILE      # Remove the temporary file
exit 0           # Exit cleanly
```

First of all, a filename is chosen to store the concatenated text as it is produced; a check is made to ensure that it does not in fact exist. This is necessary – in the unlikely event that another user had chosen the same temporary filename, and you did not make this check, the results of running the script would be at best unpredictable. A more sophisticated solution would try generating other filenames until it found one which did not exist. The script then loops continuously, requesting the user to enter a filename, reading that name from standard input, and storing it in the variable NEXTFILE. If NEXTFILE has zero length (i.e. the user has typed in a blank line) the loop is left using break, otherwise the named file is appended to the end of the temporary file. Finally, after the loop has been left, the temporary file is sent to standard output then removed.

Summary of utilities

`exit`	cause the shell to exit
`expr`	evaluate an arithmetic expression
`getopts`	parse options for a utility
`set`	set options and positional parameters
`tabs`	reset the tab positions
`tput`	change terminal characteristics
`unset`	unset options and positional parameters

Problems

6.1 Write a script `cm2ftin` which uses arithmetic expansion to convert from centimetres to feet and inches, rounded down to the nearest whole number of inches. Input should be a whole number of centimetres, and you may assume 1 foot is 30 cm.

```
$ cm2ftin
Enter cm: 42
42 cm is 1 foot 5 inches
```

6.2 Repeat 6.1 using `expr` instead of arithmetic expansion.

6.3 Write a script which will read a single argument, representing the name of a text file, and output the average number of characters per line (excluding *NEWLINE* characters) to two decimal places. Make sure that the script can handle the cases when it is called with the wrong number of arguments and when it cannot access the required file. *Hint:* use `read` and `wc`.

6.4 Write a script called `pythagoras` which will take two numerical arguments, representing the base length and height of a right-angled triangle, plus one or two options `-a` and `-h` (meaning *area* and *help*). With option `-a`, the area of the triangle will be printed on standard output preceded by the message `Area is`, and with option `-h` a short help message will be printed. With no options, there will be no output; any other option will be ignored, except that a warning message will be output on standard error.

6.5 Write a script called `hello` which will print out one of `Good morning`, `Good afternoon` or `Good evening` depending on the time of day. You should use the output of `date` and pattern matching.

6.6 Write a script called `saytime` which will print out the current time in words.

6.7 Write a script called `drawsquare` which takes as argument a single number, between 3 and 15 inclusive, and will draw on the standard output a square, using the symbols + (plus), - (hyphen) and | (vertical bar), so:

```
$ drawsquare 4
+--+
|  |
|  |
+--+
```

If drawsquare is presented without arguments, with more than 1 argument, or with a single argument which is not a number between 3 and 15, it should output an error message and exit with status 1.

6.8 Write a script called drawcube which takes as argument a single number, between 3 and 15 inclusive, and will draw on the standard output a cube, using the symbols + (plus), - (hyphen), / (slash) and | (vertical bar), so:

```
$ drawcube 4
   +--+
  /  /|
 /  / |
+--+  +
|  | /
|  |/
+--+
```

If drawcube is presented without arguments, with more than 1 argument, or with a single argument which is not a number between 3 and 15, it should output an error message and exit with status 1.

6.9 Write a script called eurhello which will output a greeting in one of several languages. With option -e, or with no options, eurhello should use the greeting Hello, with option -f it should use the French Bonjour, and with option -g it should use the German Guten Tag. It should also allow an option -G, which takes an argument, allowing an arbitrary greeting. Following any options, an argument is required which is a string representing the name of the person to whom the greeting is addressed:

```
$ eurhello Chris
Hello Chris
$ eurhello -f "Monsieur le President"
Bonjour Monsieur le President
$ eurhello -G "Hi there" Sam
Hi there Sam
```

If several of the three possible options are given as arguments to the script, the last (rightmost) one takes precedence.

Chapter 7

Advanced shell programming

OBJECTIVES

In this chapter you will learn about:

- □ trapping signals;

- □ shell functions;

- □ the 'exec' and 'eval' mechanisms;

- □ mailing files which are not text files;

- □ other POSIX utilities not covered elsewhere in this book.

In this chapter we examine briefly those aspects of shells which are not required later in the book, and which may be considered as 'advanced' in comparison with those topics already covered. The other chapters in the book will enable you to use the shell quite adequately, and the contents of this chapter are by no means necessary for you to be a competent shell programmer. However, even if you do not at this stage make use of the facilities discussed in this chapter, knowledge of their existence is important should you in the future decide to study shell programming in greater detail. Also, should you read shell scripts which have been written by other people, and you encounter unfamiliar utilities, you will at least recognise them.

Sending and trapping signals

In some circumstances you will wish that accidentally typing *ctrl-C* will not kill the current process. For example, the execution of a complex script which makes non-trivial changes to files, where your filespace would be left in a mess if the script died when only half-completed. There is a mechanism, known as **trapping signals**, whereby a shell will take action which you specify when it receives a signal, rather than taking the default action. The command used to intercept a signal is `trap`, and is used in the following manner:

`trap` *'action' signal*

The *action* is either null or a string containing a command, and the *signal* is one of the signal names. Create a script `interrupts` containing:

```
trap 'echo Ouch' INT
echo Beginning
sleep 10
echo ten seconds
sleep 10
echo twenty seconds
sleep 10
echo thirty seconds and ended
```

The signal SIGINT is sent when ctrl-C is pressed

The SIG in the name of a signal is omitted when naming the signal to trap

and execute it using sh. Try to interrupt it by typing *ctrl-C* at your terminal a couple of times and see what happens. You should see

```
$ sh interrupts
Beginning
```
ctrl-C
```
Ouch
ten seconds
```
ctrl-C
```
Ouch
twenty seconds
```
ctrl-C
```
Ouch
thirty seconds and ended
```

Similar to SIGINT is SIGQUIT. This signal can usually be generated from your terminal by typing **ctrl-**. The difference between the two is that SIGQUIT will on many systems generate a **coredump**, that is a file named core which contains information about the interrupted command when it received the signal. The file core can be used to examine the state of the program when the signal was received. A core file can be interrogated by an experienced UNIX programmer using utilities such as dbx, but at this stage you will not be interested in its contents. A coredump is usually a big file and should be removed unless you intend to use it. Try the following:

```
$ sleep 1000 &
[1] 17465
$ kill -s QUIT %1
[1]+ Quit (core dumped) sleep 1000
```

Check which files you have using ls and you should find that one named core has now been created.

When a shell script exits, a signal is sent to it called EXIT, which can be trapped. To see which signals you have trapped, use trap with no arguments. Be careful which signals you trap — in particular, don't try KILL (or you would have difficulty using kill to destroy the process) or HUP (or unpredictable things would happen if you tried to suspend the process). If you have set a trap on a signal, you can remove it by giving it the action - so:

You will not be allowed to trap KILL

- = minus symbol

SIGEXIT	trapped by all shells immediately before exit
SIGHUP	hangup – sent to child process when parent dies
SIGINT	Sent by *ctrl-C*
SIGQUIT	Sent by *ctrl-* and may coredump
SIGKILL	'Sure kill' signal – cannot be `trapped`
SIGALRM	'Alarm' – used by e.g. `sleep`
SIGTERM	The 'default' signal used by `kill`

Figure 7.1   *Signal names.*

```
trap - INT
```

will restore *ctrl-C* to its normal function.

Worked example 7.1

By setting a trap on your login shell, arrange to be given the message `Goodbye` when you logout.
Solution: The signal `EXIT` is sent to your login shell when you logout, so use `trap` to perform an `echo` when this signal is intercepted:

```
$ trap 'echo Goodbye' EXIT
```

There are various other signals – the main standard ones are listed in Figure 7.1, although most UNIX systems will support many more.

Functions

The shell supports **functions**, which are a way of grouping commands together in a non-trivial manner without needing to write a new shell script. In complexity, functions lie between a straightforward pipe (or similar shell command) and a script.

To create a function, you first of all choose a name for a function, then enter that name, followed by (), followed by a shell command enclosed in braces. For example, a simple function myls which performs `ls -l $HOME`, might be **defined** thus:

Separate the braces from the function definition by blanks

```
$ myls() { ls -l $HOME }
```

To execute a function, simply type its name:

```
$ myls
```

A function can only be used by the shell in which it has been defined, and subshells or child processes cannot use it. A function will use the environment of the current shell (so that you will not need to `export` variables which the function may use).

Worked example 7.2

Write a function `myusage` which will print the total disk used by your home directory, preceded by a message reminding you of that directory's pathname.

Solution: Standard syntax for defining a function is followed. To find the disk usage, `du` is used; the output from `du` with option `-s` consists of two fields: the size of the directory which is its argument, and the name of the directory; use `cut` to isolate the size. The output from `du` thus piped to `cut` will print the size of your home directory on standard output.

```
$ myusage() {
> printf "Directory %s uses " $HOME
> du -s $HOME | cut -f 1
> }
```

`cut` is discussed in Chapter 3

You may be wondering why functions are needed — at first sight, they may appear an added complication to the shell which duplicate the purpose of executable shell scripts. There are some operations which *cannot* be performed by a script. Consider writing a command which will alter the value of a variable in the current shell; to run that command, if it is implemented as a shell script, involves creating a child process whose parent is the current shell. Any change in that variable's value will be done by the child process. However, there is no way that the child process can communicate the new value back to its parent, and the variable's value in the current shell thus remains unchanged. A function, however, would be executed by the current shell without sparking a child process, and could therefore be used successfully.

Having defined one or more functions, you may wish to run a command without looking up the function definitions. You may, for instance, have a shell script which runs a command called `myls`. You would not wish the command run by the shell script and called `myls` to be confused with the *function* called `myls`. Since a function is not the name of a file, you cannot use the value of `PATH` to perform the disambiguation.

As a simple example, supposing you had called the function above `ls` instead of `myls`. Then to run the original utility called `ls`, simply prefix the command with `command`:

```
$ command ls
```

The effect of `command` is identical to typing a command not preceded by `command`, except that user-defined functions are not looked up.

Functions can be defined interactively, or within a script — in which case they can be used from within that script only, unless the script is run using **dot** (`.`) (see Chapter 4).

Another reason for using functions is efficiency. Executing a function involves the shell in less work because it does not have to create a new process. It can also be argued that functions are easier to understand than shell scripts. One common function that many users define, in order to speed up their sessions, is `ll`:

```
$ ll() { ls -l }
```

If you wish to exit from a function before the end you should use `return` − this is equivalent to the use of `exit` to leave a shell script early.

Aliases

Functions are general-purpose, and can be arbitrarily long. A mechanism similar to functions, but which is suitable for naming short commands only, is that of **aliasing**. The format is

`alias` *alias-name=string*

and whenever the alias-name is encountered it is replaced by the string, whose value is then executed as a command. For instance, instead of naming `ll` above using functions, we could have

```
$ alias ll='ls -l'
```

The command `alias`, with no arguments, lists all the aliases you have set up, and `alias` followed by a name (assumed to be the name of an alias) will display the string which that alias represents. To remove an alias definition, the command `unalias` can be used.

When the shell encounters a name, it first of all checks to see whether it is an alias; if not, the shell sees if there is a function definition for it. If both of these fail, it examines the `PATH` to find an executable command of that name.

The 'exec' mechanism

When you execute a script, a copy of the shell is created. Thus when that script itself executes a command, a process is created for that command as well as the process for the calling shell. This is potentially inefficient, especially if the script is relatively simple, but essentially unavoidable.

In a few instances, however, the calling shell is redundant − in particular, if a utility is executed as the last command in the shell. The shell will terminate precisely when the utility has terminated. During the time that the utility is running, the shell's process continues to run, but is simply waiting for the utility to finish − nothing more. This is inefficient because the kernel still needs to manage the shell process, and the shell is a 'big' program. The command `exec` is provided which will reduce this redundancy.

Using `exec` the final command can be executed by the same process as the calling shell. UNIX accomplishes this by replacing the machine code which the shell process contains by the machine code for the command, and the shell cannot therefore execute any later commands. Suppose file `sleepfile` contains one line `sleep 100`:

```
$ sh sleepfile &
[1] 28409
$ ps
PID TT STAT   TIME COMMAND
15826 p4 S     0:21 sh
```

```
28409 p4 S      0:00 sh sleepfile
28410 p4 S      0:00 sleep 100
28417 p4 R      0:00 ps
```

There are 4 processes, your login shell 15826, the ps process, process 28409 for the shell which interprets the script, and the process 28410 for the command in the script. Now, replace the first line of the file by exec sleep 100, and we get:

```
$ sh sleepfile &
[1] 28547
$ ps
PID TT STAT   TIME COMMAND
15826 p4 S     0:22 sh
28547 p4 S     0:00 sleep 100
28551 p4 R     0:00 ps
```

The shell script was created with PID 28547. When we look at the processes, we have the login shell and the ps process as before, but process 28547 is the sleep command, not a shell.

Write a script which will take one argument, assumed to be a filename, and run vi on that file using exec. If no arguments are given, the script should exit with return status 1.
Solution:

Worked example 7.3

```
# Check number of arguments
if [ $# -ne 1 ]

# If too few arguments, warn user
then   echo $0 requires exactly 1 argument
       # and exit with status 1
       exit 1
# otherwise run vi
else   exec vi $1
fi
```

The 'eval' mechanism

Suppose you are using variables which contain values representing the names of other variables. For instance, you wish to check the values of variables X1 through X100, and you need a loop to perform this task. You cannot choose another variable N, loop the value of N from 1 to 100 using expr, and examine the value of X$N. It simply won't work. Nor does the shell allow *indexed* variables, such as arrays as in Pascal or C. You must use eval instead; eval will examine its arguments, and concatenate them to form a command which it then executes. The arguments to eval are examined and any environment variables are

This section may be omitted at first reading

replaced by their values. This forms the command which is then executed. So to print out the values of PS1, PS2 and HOME, we might have:

```
for i in HOME PS1 PS2
do
    eval echo The value of $i is '$'$i
done
```

For the first iteration of the loop, the value of i is HOME; the command

```
eval echo The value of $i is '$'$i
```

is then executed; the first thing that eval does is to replace $i by HOME and remove the quotes, and then the remainder of the line after eval is executed as a command itself:

```
echo The value of HOME is $HOME
```

This process is then repeated with i set to PS1 then to PS2.

Worked example 7.4 Create a script which will read in a single-line command and execute it.
Solution: Use read to read in the command into a variable (say CMD) and eval to execute that command.

```
echo "Type a command:"      # Prompt the user ...
read CMD                     # read in the command ...
eval $CMD                    # and run it
```

Note that the last line of the script must not be simply $CMD – see what happens if you change that line to $CMD and then enter ls $HOME as the command. You will get a message

```
ls: $HOME: No such file or directory
```

indicating that it was trying to find a file whose actual name is $HOME.

If you find yourself needing to specify an array of variables while shell programming, then using eval is the only method available to you. Your problem is likely to be solved more effectively using another utility, and awk – which is introduced in Chapter 9 – is recommended.

Sending data across networks

If you send electronic mail to someone the message you send must consist only of printable characters. If you wish to send other data you must code it into a form containing only ordinary text. The reason for this is that some networks interpret some non-printing characters as instructions, which could cause messages to go astray or their contents to be changed. The command uuencode will take a file and write to standard output a representation of that file containing only ASCII characters; the command uudecode takes a file and

performs the reverse operation. Either one or two arguments are needed by uuencode
– the second one is the name of the file as it will be known when decoded (which is not
necessarily the same as the name of the file which you are encoding). The first argument,
if there are two, is the file to be encoded (standard input is encoded if there is only one
argument). The format of the file after encoding is a sequence of lines commencing with a
header line and terminating with end on a line of its own. The header line consists of three
fields – the word begin, the access permissions the file should have after it is decoded, and
the name of the file after decoding. For example, suppose we have a file A containing an
'alert' character (*ctrl-G*), which we wish to mail to sam, and we wish it to be received with
name chris_file. We can check what the file contains using od which will confirm
that \a is indeed included in chris_file

od is discussed in Chapter 3

```
$ od -t c A
0000000    h   e   l   l   o   \a  \n
0000007
```

This file can now be coded using uuencode. Note that the output is sent to standard
output:

```
$ uuencode A chris_file
begin u=rw,go= chris_file
':&5L;&\'"@CP
```
(line containing a single blank space)
```
end
```

So, to send the encoded file to sam, we merely pipe the output to mailx:

```
$ uuencode A chris_file | mailx -s "Binary file" sam
```

The resulting file can then be recreated by sam storing their mail message in (say)
mailfile and typing:

```
$ uudecode mailfile
```

Any lines before begin and after end will be ignored by uudecode, so you don't need
to worry about an extra header lines the mailer inserts into your message. Try this yourself
– choose a file, uuencode it, mail it to a friend, and get them to uudecode it. Have a
look at the encoded version, and the final decoded file, and convince yourself that it does
in fact work.

Try now encoding a large file, say /usr/dict/words:

```
$ uuencode /usr/dict/words tmpfile
```

Look at the output – it consists of lines of fixed width (61 characters) commencing with
the letter M:

```
    . . .
M=&4*87)B;E86P*87)B;W)E='5M"F%R8G5T=7,*87)C"F%R8V%D90I!<F-A
M9&EA"F%R8N80IA<F-A;F4*87)C8V]S"F%R8V-O<VEN90IA<F-H"F%R8VAA
M90IA<F-H8C"F%R8VAA:7-M"F%R8VAA;F=E; IA<F-H8FES:&]P"F%R8VAAD
    . . .
```

It is therefore possible to write scripts which will read in a file containing several encoded files and automatically separate them.

Often to 64k bytes Some mailers and networks restrict the size of messages they can send so that if you wish to mail a large file you cannot send it in a single message. You could, of course, edit the message into several smaller files and send each one in turn, but that would be tedious. The command `split` will split a file automatically for you into similar sized pieces. For instance, try

```
$ split /usr/dict/words
```

and you will find a large collection of files have been created in the current directory with names xaa, xab, xac, etc., all of which (with the exception of the last one) are 1000 lines long (test this with wc). With option -1 followed by a number `split` will chop a file into a collection of files each of that number of lines. The reason for having 1000 lines as the default size of the file is not only that 1000 is a 'nice round number', but also that 1000 lines of text with 61 characters per line (uuencode outputs lines which are 61 characters wide) comprise just less than the 64k limit which some mailers impose on files.

l = 'lines'

Worked example 7.5

You have a long file called bigdata, which contains control characters, and you wish sam to have a copy of it. Arrange to send sam a copy via electronic mail.

Solution: First of all, bigdata must be encoded and then split into small enough chunks to pass through the mailer. Each of those chunks must be individually mailed to sam.

```
$ uuencode bigdata bigdata | split
$ for i in x??
> do
> mailx -s "File $i" sam <$i
> done
```

You must ensure that you have no files whose names are of three letters commencing with an x before attempting this exercise. The xaa files will be overwritten by split if files of the same name already exist in your current directory. The files sam receives can be joined together and then uudecoded to recreate the original file bigdata. Although uudecode will strip away headers and footers from a *single* file, it will not cope with extra lines inserted in the middle of a file. The recreated file will have to be edited to remove all headers and footers introduced by the mailer.

It is to be hoped that sending data across a network will result in the message received being identical to that sent. Regrettably, this is not always the case. If the communications medium is prone to interference (such as a crackly telephone line) it sometimes happens that data becomes corrupted. The command `cksum` can be used to identify quickly whether this has happened. Followed by a filename, `cksum` will print a large number, known as a **checksum**, based on the contents of the file, together with the number of characters in that file. If anything is altered in the file, the number created will be very different:

On some non-POSIX systems the command `sum` is provided instead of `cksum`

```
$ echo "To be or not to be" | cksum
3740407258      19
$ echo "to be or not to be" | cksum
1143317160      19
```

If the sender and the recipient of data both run `cksum` on the message, and this yields the same number, then they can both be confident that the message has not been corrupted during transmission. To try out `cksum`, create two files (say `data1` and `data2`) using `vi`, and containing the same piece of text (a short poem would be suitable). Then see what happens if you first of all use `cksum` to check whether they are the same, and then try `diff`.

Makefiles

When developing software you will frequently create files which depend on the existence and/or state of other files. Consider the situation where you have a C program, which you wish to call `myprogram`, which is stored in two files, `prog1.c` and `prog2.c`; in order to compile the program you would compile each of the two source code files, creating files `prog1.o` and `prog2.o` respectively which contain object code (binary code). Those two files would then be **linked** to create the final file `myprogram`. That is, the binary code in `prog1.o` and `prog2.o` will be joined together to produce a single binary file – this is in fact not a trivial operation. We therefore have the dependencies:

Note the suffix `.c`

Not related to file links

- `prog1.o` depends on `prog1.c`

- `prog2.o` depends on `prog2.c`

- `myprogram` depends on both `prog1.o` and `prog2.o`.

In order to compile this C program using the command `cc`, you would have three commands to perform:

`cc` = 'C compile', which is the normal name for the command; in the POSIX standard it is named `c89`

```
$ cc -c prog1.c
$ cc -c prog2.c
$ cc -o myprogram prog1.o prog2.o
```

The first two, which translate the two source files to object code, can be performed in either order. The final command, which links two object code files together, must wait until the first two have been completed.

If you were to type in these commands each time, there would be a danger of making an error and accidentally forgetting to recompile one of the source files after editing it. Alternatively, you could place all three commands into a file and then execute that file as a shell script. This would have the disadvantage that if you edited (say) `prog1.c` you would also have to recompile `prog2.c` even though this was not necessary.

In this small example, this might seem a minor problem, but when performing serious system development it is not unusual to have large volumes of code that take a long time to compile. In such a case, it is sensible to minimise the amount of work that has to be done when small changes to the code are made.

A tool which makes use of file dependencies is known as `make`. This works in the following way: a file, called a **makefile**, is created (usually in the same directory containing the software which is being developed), and a program called `make` reads that file. The makefile contains information indicating

- which file depends on which other file/s, and

- what commands must be performed to bring a file 'up-to-date'.

The above example could have as the contents of its makefile:

```
myprogram: prog1.o prog2.o
        cc -o myprogram prog1.o prog2.o

prog1.o: prog1.c
        cc -c prog1.c

prog2.o: prog2.c
        cc -c prog2.c
```

You will notice two types of line in this file. There are lines which are not indented — they take the form of a word (known as the **target**) followed by a colon followed by some other words, where the words would usually be names of files. These lines indicate that the word (file) on the left of the colon is dependent on the filenames on the right of the semicolon. Thus `myprogram` depends on both `prog1.o` and `prog2.o`, etc.

The indented lines (which must be indented with a single *TAB*, not with *SPACE*s) indicate the action to be taken if the dependency (which would be shown on the previous line) is not up-to-date. So if `myprogram` was older than either `prog1.o` or `prog2.o`, the command `cc -o myprogram prog1.o prog2.o` would be executed.

In order to use makefiles, data in the format discussed above should be stored in a file with name either `Makefile` or `makefile`. Then, to bring the software up-to-date, simply type `make` followed by the target which you need updated:

```
$ make myprogram
```

If you invoke `make` without any arguments, it will assume that the target is the first target mentioned in the makefile. If you run `make` with option `-n` it will display the commands that it would execute, but will not actually run them. If you are unsure of the correctness of your makefile, it is wise to run `make` with the `-n` option initially simply to ensure that the actions it performs are in fact the actions you expect. For instance, taking the above example would give:

```
$ make -n
cc -c prog1.c
cc -c prog2.c
cc -o myprogram prog1.o prog2.o
```

If, while running `make`, one of the commands fails (for example, you had not created `prog1.c` at all, or there was an error in that C program), then `make` would terminate at that point.

This utility has many other features, and can handle much more complex dependencies than the simple ones indicated here. If you are creating programs as part of a course in Pascal or C (say), then a simple makefile such as this one will be adequate. Only when you move on to more complex programming tasks will you need to examine `make` in greater detail.

Two other standard commands – which are principally used within makefiles – are worth mentioning briefly. Command `ar` is used to maintain 'archives' of files, and is used principally for maintaining libraries of object code. When an executable file consisting of binary code is produced, it contains information used by debugging utilities which is not required simply to execute it. This redundancy can be eliminated from such a file by means of the command `strip`.

Produced by a compiled language such as C

Safe programming

To write a script which always works as you want it to, it is good practice to perform as many checks as you can. Whenever you try to use a file, make sure that a suitable action is taken if you cannot access that file. Whenever you write a script which is called with options or arguments, make sure that the first few lines check that it has been called with sensible options and arguments.

So far we have met ways of checking access to individual files, and have remarked that names of files may be subject to certain limits. A utility called `pathchk` is available which will give more information than `test`. Followed by the name of a path, `pathchk` will check that it does not breach any of those limits, by (for example) being simply too long. It will also check that no component of the pathname cannot be searched because it does not have *execute* permission. With option `-p` it will also indicate any potential problems where the name may be acceptable for the current system, but breaches certain minimum limits defined by POSIX, and might thus present problems if the name were to be used on a different system.

p = 'portable'

Worked example 7.6

Is it sensible to write a script which creates and uses a file called `instrumentation` and expect this script to work on all systems?

Solution: This is a problem which concerns the portability of a filename; use `pathchk` with option `-p`:

```
$ pathchk -p instrumentation
pathchk: name 'instrumentation' has length 15; exceeds
limit of 14
```

This message indicates that any filename of length above 14 may not be allowed on every system, therefore the answer is 'no'.

If, during the course of a session logged on to a UNIX system, you have reset a number of variables, it may be that you accidentally change the value of a system variable which was defined when you logged in. You can find what the values of the system-defined variables are with command `getconf`. This can also be useful in a shell script if you wish to check that such variables have the required values. Perhaps the clearest example of where this would be useful would be in the case of `PATH`. It is common to reset the value of `PATH`, as we have already discussed, so that it includes directories within your own file space. If you were to make an error while doing this and left out one of the system directories, you might be unable to proceed as some commands you needed to use would be denied you. By using

```
$ getconf PATH
```

the default value would be printed out and you could reset `PATH` to a sensible value which would allow you to continue.

There are a number of variables which are not 'environment' variables (and which you cannot change) which indicate the system limits (such as the maximum length of a filename allowed, and the maximum number of processes you can have running at any one time). These values can only be accessed using `getconf`.

getconf = 'get configuration'

PATH is discussed in Chapter 4

Setting up a terminal

We have assumed that your System Administrator has set up your terminal and the system so that the terminal will work. This is a very reasonable expectation, but sometimes you may need to communicate with a UNIX machine from an unusual terminal which has not been set up for you. If you have a problem with your terminal, then in the normal course of events it can be corrected using `tput`; this will not help though if the system does not already have all the information it needs about the terminal.

The command `stty` is used to specify to the UNIX system the characteristics both of the terminal and of the communication device linking the terminal and the system. Clearly, if you cannot communicate at all with the UNIX system, `stty` is of no use to you. If you can get the system as far as reading a line containing `stty`, you are then in a position to

tput is discussed in Chapter 6

WARNING! Be careful using *stty* — mistakes may be difficult to correct

correct such things as the size of terminal screen that UNIX thinks you have, which control
characters are matched to which keys, and so on. Try this command with option `-a` to
display the current settings for your terminal. You will get several lines of output, which
will look something like:

```
$ stty -a
speed 9600 baud; rows 25; columns 80; line = 2; intr = ^C;
...
-parenb -parodd cs8 -hupcl -cstopb cread -clocal -crtscts
...
```

In this instance, the terminal has 25 rows and 80 columns and communicates with the
processors at 9600 **baud**. The keystroke necessary to send an interrupt signal SIGINT is   baud is 'bits per second'
ctrl-C. Look at the manual page for `stty` to discover the meaning of the other information
it displays. In order to change any of the settings, follow `stty` by the setting you wish to
change and its new value. For example, to cause your terminal to have a width of only 30
character columns, you would type:

```
$ stty columns 30
```

If you try this example, remember to reset the terminal to its original settings afterwards.

More on files

UNIX supports **named pipes**, also known as **FIFO** files. A named pipe is like an ordinary   FIFO = 'first in first out'
pipe, except it has a name by which it can be referred to from within a program (normally
pipes are anonymous). In order to implement a named pipe, UNIX creates a file which *is*
the named pipe, and whose name is the name of the named pipe. The command `mkfifo`
is available to create such a file. The use of such a file is that many processes can write
to it at once, the file will temporarily store the data it receives, and when the contents are
requested by another process the contents of the file will be 'flushed'. Try the following:

```
$ mkfifo pfile
$ ls -l
$ echo Hello >pfile &
$ echo There >pfile &
$ cat pfile
```

You will notice that the `ls -l` indicates that `pfile` exists as a file in the current directory,
but the character in the first column is a `p` indicating that it is a named pipe. Once a named
pipe is 'opened', when you start to write something to it or read something from it, you can
write to it from several processes (such as the two `echo` processes in the above example)
— the pipe therefore can have several input streams. The input streams are then merged and
the result can be read by reading the named pipe just like any other file.

   As soon as all the processes which are writing to the named pipe have terminated the
named pipe closes and any processes attempting to read it receive the end-of-file character.

The named pipe acts as a 'buffer' temporarily storing characters sent to it from its input streams, and after sending these characters to the standard output they are deleted.

There is one 'feature' of named pipes – all processes which read from or write to a given named pipe must be running on the same processor as that which created the pipe in the first place. If your UNIX system contains many processors you must take care. We do not discuss named pipes further here, save to indicate that if you are familiar with programming in C you may wish to investigate them in greater detail.

If you create a binary file using (say) C, that file will contain **symbols**, that is to say, the names used within that file for data which may need to be communicated to and from the file. Although discussion of the format of object files is outside the scope of this book, the command nm is provided to list names in such a file, and will be of interest to a C programmer. To see how nm works, look in directory /usr/lib and see what files are in that directory with suffix .a and choose one of them (say libc.a). A large volume of output will be produced, so you will probably wish to pipe it through more:

Type ls /usr/lib/*.a

```
$ nm /usr/lib/libc.a | more
```

And some other language constructs

A similar task can be accomplished on the *source code* files written in C or FORTRAN using ctags, which will create a file called tags listing the named functions defined in those files given to ctags as arguments.

When creating text files which include *TAB*s it will sometimes be inconvenient to have those *TAB*s there – or vice versa, you may wish a file to include *TAB*s where otherwise it might not. Situations where this may be important include preparing input for utilities such as awk or make. *TAB*s sometimes are included in text files automatically, especially by some editors, in order to utilise space more efficiently. The command expand will take input containing *TAB*s and produce standard output which is the same as the input but with the *TAB*s replaced by the appropriate number of spaces. The command unexpand does the reverse – a file containing spaces will have some (or all) of the spaces replaced by *TAB*s, where tab stops are assumed to occur at every eighth column. See also the command tabs discussed previously.

Using the standard collating sequence

If you have two text files, whose lines have been sorted into order, the utilities comm and join may be of use. To select those lines common to both files, or which occur in only one of them, use comm. This command is complementary to diff and to uniq. The output of comm, when given two arguments representing filenames, is a sequence of lines containing three tab-separated columns. The first column contains the lines unique to the first file, the second column the lines unique to the second, and the third column those lines common to both. For instance, if file A contains

diff, uniq and paste are discussed in Chapter 3

```
apple
orange
pear
pomegranate
strawberry
```

and file B contains

```
apple
peach
pomegranate
raspberry
```

then the effect of comm would be

```
$ comm A B
```
TAB TAB apple
```
orange
```
TAB peach
```
pear
```
TAB TAB pomegranate
TAB raspberry
```
strawberry
```

To join lines from the two files which contain a common **field**, use join – this command is complementary to paste. The two files are considered to contain a number of blank-separated columns. Lines which have an identical first column cause a line to be output which is that first field followed by the other fields from the line in the first file, then the other fields from the second. To illustrate this command, suppose A and B contain lists of fruits together with other data; then join will output a sequence of lines which commence with the fruit names and then include the extra data from A and B. Suppose A is

```
apple 2 kilos Monday
orange 4 kilos from Jones' shop
pear none
pomegranate 3 kilos Tuesday
strawberry 2 boxes
```

and file B contains

```
apple 1 kilo Wednesday
peach none
pomegranate 1 kilo Thursday
raspberry none
```

then the effect of join would be

```
$ join A B
apple 2 kilos Monday 1 kilo Wednesday
pomegranate 3 kilos Tuesday 1 kilo Thursday
```

Miscellaneous utilities

Although the structure of files on a UNIX machine is uncomplicated, other operating systems may impose a more complex structure on how their files are represented. If you need to convert a file, either to export it to or to import it from a non-UNIX system, use

This section may be omitted on first reading

dd. For example, some systems require that files be structured as having a sequence of fixed-size **blocks**, or might use a different character set to ASCII. This command can also perform simple translation of characters – for instance, if you received a file funny which contains only upper-case letters then dd can create a file which has lower-case letters in place of the upper-case ones:

dd = 'disk-to-disk'

```
$ dd conv=lcase < funny
```

conv = 'convert'
lcase = 'lower case'

You can try this. More seriously, if you do need to read from or write to a file which is to be used on a non-UNIX system, you should examine the manual page for dd carefully.

Suppose you wished to run a utility with the arguments to that utility piped to it. This might be the case if the arguments were to be split over several lines. A simple example might be if you had a file list containing filenames, and you wished to ls -l each of them. Using the mechanisms so far discussed, the resultant script would be inelegant:

```
$ X=$( cat list ); eval ls -l $X
```

By use of the $(...) mechanism we have concatenated all the lines of list into a single string, and have passed that string to ls -l. The utility xargs can help: it takes as its arguments a command, and then reading from its standard input appends options to that command, and then runs it. The above example would then become:

```
$ xargs ls -l <list
```

A more serious, and frequently quoted example of the use of xargs is in conjunction with find, where with the -exec argument find might create a large number of processes. Suppose your home directory contains a large number of subdirectories, and you wished to perform ls -ld on each of them. One possibility would be:

find was introduced in Chapter 5

```
$ find ~ -type d -exec ls -ld {} \;
```

but this would create as many processes as directories – this is inefficient. More effective – and quicker – would be:

```
$ find ~ -type d -print | xargs ls -ld
```

The final three commands that are mentioned in this chapter are introduced for completeness; they are included in the POSIX standard, and you should know of their existence.

There is a command logger which can be used to save a message for reading later on by the System Administrator. It might be used (say) to inform the Administrator if a batch job failed to read a system file correctly; the user would not be in a position easily to forward the message, and the action to be taken would definitely be for the Administrator to perform.

logger = 'log error message'

Although you are likely to be using UNIX where English is a normal medium of communication, the concept of **locale** is supported whereby both messages from commands and the character set used can be customised to other languages. The command locale allows you to examine the current locale, and localedef to define a new locale.

Unless your Administrator has given you specific instructions on how it should be used, you are probably advised not to use logger

Summary of utilities

`alias`	define or display aliases
`ar`	maintain a library archive
`cksum`	file checksum utility
`comm`	select/reject lines common to two files
`command`	execute a simple command
`ctags`	create a 'tags' file
`dd`	convert file format
`eval`	construct command by concatenating arguments
`exec`	execute command by replacing shell process
`expand`	replace tabs by spaces
`getconf`	get configuration variables
`join`	relational database operator
`locale`	display information about the 'locale'
`localedef`	define the 'locale'
`logger`	log message for the System Administrator
`make`	maintain and update groups of programs
`mkfifo`	create a FIFO file
`nm`	display name list of an object file
`pathchk`	check pathname is valid
`return`	return from a function
`split`	split a file into pieces
`strip`	remove unnecessary data from executable files
`stty`	set terminal options
`trap`	intercept a signal
`unalias`	remove alias definition
`unexpand`	replace spaces by tabs
`uudecode`	decode a file which was coded with `uuencode`
`uuencode`	encode a binary file
`xargs`	construct argument list and execute command

Problems

7.1 Write a *function* `thisyear` which will cause the message `This year is` to be displayed followed by the current year.

7.2 Write a *function* `changedir` which will prompt you for a directory name and `cd` to that directory. Why must you use a function, and not a script?

7.3 Write a *function* called `addtopath` which will request you to type the name of a directory, and if that directory exists and you can read it, will add it to the end of your `PATH`.

7.4 Write a script which will prompt you for the name of a directory, and the email address of a user, and will mail the contents of that directory to that user.

7.5 Define an alias `debugsh` which will have the effect of `sh` with option `-x`.

7.6 Write a script which will every minute display the date and time, but when run in the foreground will terminate if it receives *ctrl-C* 3 times.

7.7 Write a script which will request you to type in the name of a shell environment variable, and display its value.

Chapter 8

Regular expressions and filters

OBJECTIVES

In this chapter you will learn about:

- □ regular expressions;

- □ simple use of the commands `grep`, `sed` and `tr`.

The purpose of this chapter is to consider in detail three powerful UNIX utilities which are usually used as filters (components of a pipeline).

Using filters

Any command which reads data from standard input, and writes data to the standard output stream, is known as a **filter**. Most UNIX utilities are filters, or can be used as such. Most utilities are also simple in their functionality.

Much UNIX programming involves transforming input, which is of a known form, to output, also of a known form. This output depends on the input in a specified manner, and often involves creating a pipeline. In order to use UNIX effectively, you must develop the skill of being able to choose utilities to pipe together. It is not always obvious why the filters which are 'standard' for UNIX have been developed, but they have been found to be very powerful 'building blocks'. We now examine three filters, all significantly more complex than those we have met before, but whose relevance will be striking.

The editor `vi` is an interactive tool, and is one of the few UNIX utilities which cannot be used as a filter. The commands we now look at perform tasks which you might consider suitable for an editor such as `vi`, but are designed so that they can work as filters.

You may be wondering why, having discussed detailed syntax for the shell, we now need to introduce further commands. After all, we did claim that the shell was a 'full programming language'. In UNIX there are rarely unique solutions to problems. Most tasks have many possible ways a UNIX programmer can solve them, but an experienced programmer will be able to chose a solution which can be implemented fast and efficiently. The purpose of commands such as `grep`, `sed`, `tr` and `awk` is to provide speedy solutions for tasks which are frequently encountered, and which are difficult to program using the shell alone.

Whenever you write a shell script which takes more than a few lines, stand back from the problem for a moment and ask yourself whether some utility will do the job for you.

Although some techniques are arguably better than others ...

awk is discussed in the next chapter

Maybe there isn't, but often you will be able to save yourself time and trouble by recalling a utility you'd almost forgotten about. When you have finished reading this book, go back to the earlier chapters and remind yourself of the commands — such as comm and uniq — whose usefulness may not then have been apparent.

Collating sequence

Before considering these filters we must digress with some remarks about *characters*. Specifically, we must ask the question: 'how are they ordered?' We have already remarked that to each character is assigned a *code* which is normally the ASCII representation, and the ordering of characters corresponds with the numerical order of the codes. So, for instance, the code for b is one greater than the code for a. There are two possible problems with this: first, it is not necessarily the case that ASCII is being used, and secondly, the code representation — and ordering of characters — is different depending which native language you speak. Although most UNIX systems use standard English/American, and a standard keyboard, POSIX allows for user interfaces consistent with other languages and equipment. Where, for instance, do accented letters fit in the alphabet, or completely different letters such as Greek? We therefore have a concept called a **collating sequence** which is a specification of the *logical* ordering for the character set you are using. In practice, this ordering will apply just to letters and to digits, although it is defined for the whole character set. The collating sequence can be changed in POSIX by amending the **locale**, which was mentioned in Chapter 7 and discussed in further detail in Chapter 10.

In the following discussion we will refer to **ranges**, which are collections of characters which are consecutive within the collating sequence. A range is specified by a *first* and by a *last* character, separated by a hyphen. For instance,

```
b-z
```

will refer to the characters between b and z inclusive in the current collating sequence.

Characters come in various familiar flavours: there are letters, numbers, punctuation marks, and so on. These are **character classes**, and there is a notation for referring to these classes which is used by some utilities. The form this takes is a name of a class enclosed between [: and :] as shown in Figure 8.1.

Character-to-character transformation

The command tr can only be used as a pipe — it cannot take a filename as an argument

The length of a range or of a character class is the total number of characters it contains

Translating a file so that specific characters are replaced by others can be accomplished with tr. This command takes as arguments two strings, which may consist of any number of individual characters, ranges and character classes. If both strings are the same length instances of characters in the first string are replaced by the corresponding character in the second. For example, to capitalise all the lower-case letters in the input we would have:

```
tr "a-z" "A-Z"
```

or alternatively

```
tr "[:lower:]" "[:upper:]"
```

[:alnum:]	letters and digits
[:alpha:]	letters
[:blank:]	usually *SPACE* and *TAB*
[:cntrl:]	all control characters
[:digit:]	digits
[:graph:]	printable characters excluding *SPACE*
[:lower:]	lower-case letters
[:print:]	all printable characters
[:punct:]	punctuation marks
[:space:]	whitespace characters
[:upper:]	upper-case letters
[:xdigit:]	hexadecimal digits (0-9A-Fa-f)

Figure 8.1   *Character classes.*

Try this out using just standard input and standard output. To capitalise all the words in /usr/dict/words you would have:

```
tr "[:lower:]" "[:upper:]" < /usr/dict/words
```

Write a filter which will replace all digits by blank spaces.   **Worked example 8.1**
Solution: Use [:digit:] to represent digits as the first argument to tr.

```
tr "[:digit:]" "            "
```

The second argument to tr must not be shorter than the first. If the second argument is longer than the first, the excess characters in the second argument will be disregarded, so that in the pipe

```
tr "a-z" "A-Z123"
```

the characters 1, 2 and 3 will be unaffected.

The two arguments to tr are strings; as usual, if the strings contain whitespace they must be quoted, and the standard conventions for quoted strings are used. So for a filter to replace all blanks in the input with a B you could have:

```
tr ' ' 'B'
```

Remember that between double quotes the characters $, * and @ have special meanings and that certain characters must be escaped. If neither string argument to tr includes characters which require quoting, then the quotes are not needed. The following three filters are equivalent:

See the section on positional parameters in Chapter 5

```
tr a-z A-Z
tr "a-z" "A-Z"
tr 'a-z' 'A-Z'
```

Although the strings which `tr` is given as arguments do not always require quoting, when the strings contain no characters which will be interpreted by the shell in an undesired fashion, it may be helpful to quote them anyway. This has two benefits — firstly, it reminds you to be careful that some characters may need to be escaped in the strings, and secondly it may make it easier to see where the two strings start and finish.

We will from now on always quote strings

Worked example 8.2

Write a filter which will replace all double quotes by single quotes.
Solution: The tricky part of this example is to specify the strings correctly. The first string is a double quote, but in order for it not to be interpreted by the shell, it must either be preceded by a \ or enclosed by single quotes. The second must also either be escaped with a \ or enclosed in *double* quotes. Either of the following two filters will solve the problem.

At this point you may wish to re-read the section of Chapter 4 that deals with quotes

```
tr '"' "'"
tr \" \'
```

This notation is used by `tr` only

We can specify a string which is a number of instances of a single character: `"[X*5]"` is the same as `"XXXXX"`. The notation `"[X*]"` will yield a string containing sufficient numbers of the character X so that if used as a component of the second string the second string will be long enough to match the first one. For instance, to replace all digits with a question mark, you could use either of the following:

```
tr "0-9" "[?*10]"
tr "0-9" "[?*]"
```

Worked example 8.3

Write a filter which will replace all letters in the first half of the alphabet by A and all in the second half by Z.
Solution: Use `tr`, and note that there are 13 letters in the first half of the alphabet, each having an upper- and a lower-case character. Thus the first half of the alphabet is represented by a set of 26 characters.

```
tr "A-Ma-mN-Zn-z" "[A*26][Z*26]"
```

---

d = 'delete'
c = 'complement'

There are also options available to `tr`; with option `-d` and only one string as argument all occurrences of characters specified by that string will be deleted. With option `-c` as well as `-d` all characters not occurring within the string will be deleted.

Write a filter to delete all characters from the input which are not letters.
Solution: Use `tr` with option `-c` to specify all *non*-alphabetic characters, and `-d` to delete them.

```
tr -cd "A-Za-z"
```

Alternatively, use character classes:

```
tr -cd "[:alpha:]"
```

Worked example 8.4

After all other changes have been performed, repeated instances of a character which is specified in the final string argument can be replaced by single instances of the same character using option `-s`. In this case, the string passed to `tr` represents those characters which this operation will be performed upon. So to replace multiple spaces by single ones:

s = 'squash'

```
$ echo "hello     there    Chris" | tr -s " "
hello there Chris
```

Basic regular expressions

The *pattern matching* described in Chapter 6 is a very simple means of associating many strings which have a common pattern with a single string that describes that pattern. It is fine for matching filenames, and for the use of a `case` statement. A more powerful mechanism, known as **regular expressions** or **RE**s, is available for use in certain UNIX utilities.

There are different types of regular expression, and regular expressions can be defined in a variety of ways. UNIX specifies two sorts – a **basic regular expression** (or **BRE**), and an **extended regular expression** (or **ERE**). We commence by defining a basic regular expression.

The general idea is just like pattern matching – a BRE consists of a sequence of characters, some of which have a special meaning. The BRE is said to **match** a string if

- each part of the BRE with special meaning corresponds to a part of the other string, and

- the other individual characters in the BRE and the string correspond.

In order to check whether a BRE matches a string, the two strings are looked at working from left to right. Each time a match is found the corresponding parts of the BRE and the string are discarded and the process continues immediately after.

First of all we consider how to specify a match for a *single character*. For this we use a BRE called a a **bracket expression**, which is an expression enclosed in square brackets ([]). The expression enclosed by the brackets is either a **matching list** or a **nonmatching list**. A matching list consists of a sequence of:

- single characters (escaped, if necessary),

- ranges (as described above for `tr`),

- character classes (as for `tr`)

and a character matches a matching list if it matches any of the patterns which make up that sequence. The following BRE matches the letters a, x, y, z and any digit.

```
[ax-z[:digit:]]
```

Corresponds to `!` in pattern matching

If a matching list is preceded by a circumflex (^) it becomes a nonmatching list, and matches any character not specified in that list.

```
[^[:upper:]#]
```

will match any character which is neither an upper-case letter nor the symbol #. If you wish to specify the hyphen character in a range you must have it as either the first or the last character in the bracket expression, so

```
[-xyz]
```

will match x, y, z or -. A dot (.), when not enclosed in square brackets, matches any single character. To match a string containing more than one character, you can concatenate characters which you wish to match, dots and bracket expressions. So

```
[Cc]hris
```

will match Chris or chris, and no other string;

```
[[:alpha:]]..
```

will match any 3-character string commencing with a letter. More generally, if you follow a bracket expression (or a single character or a dot) with an asterisk (*), that expression together with the * will match zero or more consecutive occurrences of the expression. So

```
[[:digit:]][[:digit:]][[:digit:]]*
```

will match any string consisting of two or more digits. The two characters ^ and $ are used to indicate the start and end of a string respectively, so

```
^A.*E$
```

will match any string commencing with A and terminating with E, so will match ANGLE and AbbreviatE but not DALE or Alpha.

Worked example 8.5

What BRE will match a string which is just a sequence of digits?
Solution: One digit is matched by `[[:digit:]]`, zero or more digits are matched by `[[:digit:]]*`, and so `[[:digit:]][[:digit:]]*` will match one or more. The BRE will commence with ^ and end with $, to indicate that this is *exactly* what the string will contain, and will not have other characters at the start or at the end. The answer is therefore

```
^[[:digit:]][[:digit:]]*$
```

Extended regular expressions

Basic regular expressions are sufficient for most purposes, but a more sophisticated form of regular expression is available known as an **extended regular expression** or **ERE**. There are a couple of principal extra features available using EREs which are unavailable to BREs.

    The symbol +, following a bracket expression (or single character or dot) indicates one or more consecutive occurrences of the expression, in the same way that * indicates zero or more. The symbol ?, in the same context, indicates zero or one occurrences of that expression, so

```
[[:alpha:]]+[[:digit:]]?
```

matches any string commencing with a letter, consisting only of letters, and terminated optionally by a single digit.

    If two EREs are separated by a | (vertical bar), the result matches either of those two EREs. Parentheses may be used to group subexpressions together:

```
(xyz|ab)\.c
```

will match either `xyz.c` or `ab.c`, and no other string. If you need a parenthesis to be a matched character in an ERE you must escape it.

Write an ERE which will match any string which consists either of only upper-case letters or only lower-case letters.
Solution: As in the previous worked example, the expression will commence with ^ and end with $. By taking advantage of the symbol + a match for upper-case letters would be `[[:upper:]]+` and `[[:lower:]]+` for lower-case letters. A sequence of letters of the same case will be matched by `([[:upper:]]+|[[:lower:]]+))` and a solution is therefore

```
^[[:lower:]]+|[[:upper:]]+$
```

Worked example 8.6

Selecting lines according to their content

We have defined regular expressions; in order to use them, we begin with a utility called `grep`. The function of `grep` is to select lines from its input (either standard input or named files given as arguments) which match a BRE normally given as first argument to `grep`. The BRE is known as a **script**. Those lines of input which match the BRE are then copied to standard output. For instance, to print out all words ending in `ise` or `ize` from `/usr/dict/words`, you could have:

```
$ grep 'i[sz]e$' /usr/dict/words
```

With option `-E`, `grep` will use EREs instead of BREs. With option `-F`, `grep` uses only *fixed* strings – there are no regular expressions, the string given as argument to `grep` is matched against the input exactly as it appears. With option `-c` instead of copying matched

This section may be omitted at first reading

Not to be confused with the ? in pattern matching

grep refers to the ex command g/RE/p
On some non-POSIX systems separate commands egrep ('Extended GREP') and fgrep ('Fixed GREP') are used instead of grep -E and grep -F
Single quotes needed here as $ is in the BRE

lines to standard output, a count of the number of matched lines is output instead.

Worked example 8.7

How many words in /usr/dict/words commence with a vowel?

Solution: Use grep with option -c, to select and then count lines which begin with upper- or lower-case vowels. The BRE contains a list of all such vowels, preceded with a ^ to indicate the vowel must be at the start of each word:

```
$ grep -c '^[AEIOUaeiou]' /usr/dict/words
```

---

i = 'insensitive'

Option -i causes grep to ignore the case of letters when checking for matches, and overrides any explicit specification regarding upper- and lower-case letters in the regular expression. Thus a solution to the previous worked example could be:

```
$ grep -ci '^[aeiou]' /usr/dict/words
```

f = 'file'

With option -f followed by a filename, regular expressions contained in that file will be used instead of being given as an argument to grep. If the file contains more than one regular expression, then grep will select lines which match any of the REs in the file. This is the preferred method by which grep can select lines where there is a choice of matching specifications.

v = 'inVert'

The 'reverse behaviour' — namely outputting those lines which do not match the RE specified — can be enabled with option -v. This is often simpler than constructing a new regular expression. An example of this being useful might be to a FORTRAN programmer. A program written in the computer language FORTRAN treats any line commencing with a C as a comment; if you were examining such a program, and wished to search for lines of code containing some identifier, and were not interested in the lines of comments, you might wish to use

```
grep -v '^C'
```

to strip out the comments to begin with.

l = 'list'

If grep is given several files as arguments, option -l will output a list of those files which contain a matching line, rather than those lines themselves.

Worked example 8.8

Suppose you have saved many mail messages in files in the current directory, and you wanted to check which file or files contained messages whose subject was something to do with 'examinations'. Each mail message contains a line which begins with the string Subject: followed by the subject of the message (if any).

Solution: We require grep -l followed by a BRE followed by * to list the filenames. The following lines might occur as the 'subject' lines of the messages:

```
Subject: Examinations
Subject: examinations
Subject: NEXT MONTH'S EXAMS
Subject: Exams
```

These all have a common string, namely `exam`, in upper- or lower-case (or a mixture of cases). So to match these lines a BRE is required which recognises `Subject:` at the start of the line, followed by some characters (possibly none), followed by `exam` in any mixture of cases. The `Subject:` at the start of the line is matched by `^Subject` and `.*` matches the characters between that and `exam`. In order to ensure that the cases of the letters in `exam` do not matter, you can either explicitly match them with `[Ee][Xx][Aa][Mm]`, or you can instruct `grep` to be 'case-insensitive' with option `-i`. The following two solutions would be acceptable:

```
grep -l '^Subject: .*[Ee][Xx][Aa][Mm]' *
grep -li '^Subject: .*exam' *
```

Note that this is not an infallible solution. It will also select files with subjects related to `counterexamples` and `hexameters`, and will not find a file with subject `exminations`. When using UNIX tools to process data from electronic mail or other documents which contain English text, you must be conscious of human fallibility. Some solutions will of necessity be approximate.

Stream editor

Whereas `grep` will select lines from input and copy those lines to standard output, `sed` will in addition change those lines if required. Just as with `grep`, `sed` will take a **script** either as an argument, or from a file by using option `-f`, and will filter its input according to the instructions in that script. For `grep`, the script consists simply of one or more BREs, and the output is formed of those lines of input matching one or more of those BREs. For `sed` the behaviour is more complex. Each `sed` instruction is of the form

address command arguments

where *address* and/or *arguments* are optional. The *address* indicates which lines of the input *command* is to be performed on.

Actually, we need to be slightly more precise than this. Each time a line of input is read in, it is first of all stored in an area called the **pattern space**. The instructions forming the script are then examined one-by-one, in order, and each instruction whose *address* matches the address of the input line has its command applied to whatever is currently in the pattern space. When all the instructions in the script have been examined, the contents of the pattern space are copied to the standard output, and the pattern space emptied ready for the next input line. This is repeated for the next line of input until the input is exhausted.

The simplest `sed` script is the script containing nothing; since there are no instructions, an input line will be copied to the pattern space which will then immediately be copied to the standard output. Try it:

sed = 'stream editor'

You may wish to re-read this paragraph after you have completed this section

```
$ sed ''
```

Addresses for sed come in several forms:

- *empty* – which matches *all* lines,

- a *number* – which matches input line *number*,

- *number1* , *number2* – which matches all lines in the range from *number1* to *number2* inclusive,

- $ – which matches the *last* input line, and can also be used in place of *number2* in the previous type of address,

- /*BRE*/ – which matches any line matched by BRE.

Both ^ and $ can be used. To try some of these addresses, the easiest command we can use is probably d to *delete* the contents of the pattern space. So

```
sed '1,4d'
```

will delete lines 1 to 4 inclusive from the input. Try the following using the standard input:

```
            sed 'd'        deletes all the input
            sed '3d'       deletes line 3 only
            sed '2,$d'     deletes all lines except the first
            sed '/^A/d'    deletes all lines commencing A
```

s = 'substitute'   An often used command is s, which is used to exchange part of a line (specified by a BRE) by another string. This command is used so:

s/*BRE*/*replacement*/

The pattern space is searched from left to right to find an instance of the BRE. If none is found, no change is made, otherwise the string which matches the BRE is replaced by the *replacement*. Normally only the first occurrence of the BRE is altered, but if you follow the command with g then *all* matches for the BRE in the pattern space will be changed. Note that after the change, the altered string stays in the pattern space and can then be changed by later sed commands in the same script. So, for example,

g = 'global'

```
$ sed 's/Chris/Sam/g'
```

will change all occurrences of Chris to Sam,

```
$ sed 's/^= /?/'
```

will change each equals symbol at the start of a line to a question-mark,

```
$ sed 's/[:punct:]//g'
```

removes all punctuation (equivalent to tr -d "[:punct:]").

Write a `sed` command that will remove all whitespace which terminates lines.

Worked example 8.9

Solution: The BRE `[:blank:]` matches a single whitespace character, `[:blank:]*` matches any number of them, and `[:blank:]*$` when they occur at the end of a line. To delete them we replace them by nothing.

```
sed 's/[:blank:]*$//'
```

Although it is most common for simple `sed` commands to be applied to all lines of the input, you should be familiar with being able to specify addresses of lines also. Sometimes an editing problem can be solved either by a complex edit on every line of input or by a simple edit on only some of the input lines – the latter approach is preferable.

Write a filter which will precede each word in `/usr/dict/words` which contains a capital letter by an asterisk.

Worked example 8.10

Solution: Using `sed` we can match lines containing such words by the BRE `[A-Z]`. Using this BRE to specify addresses, on those lines we can use `s` to substitute the start of each line (`^`) by a `*`:

```
$ sed '/[A-Z]/s/^/*/' </usr/dict/words
```

It is usual for `sed` to be an element of a pipeline, but `sed` can – unlike `tr` – take a filename as argument, in which case the input will come from that file. So another solution would be

```
$ sed '/[A-Z]/s/^/*/' /usr/dict/words
```

If an ampersand (`&`) is met as part of the replacement string, it is replaced by the string which has been matched; the following will enclose each capital letter in the input by square brackets:

```
$ sed 's/[A-Z]/[&]/g'
```

If you want an actual ampersand to occur in the replacement string it must be escaped by preceding it with a backslash.

If you give `sed` option `-n` then the pattern space will not automatically be sent to standard output; so `sed -n ''` will not give any output at all. We can use command `p` to copy the pattern space explicitly to standard output; so the following two commands are equivalent:

n = 'noprint'

p = 'print'

```
sed ''
sed -n 'p'
```

See what happens if you have just:

```
sed 'p'
```

We can use p to good effect if we wish to select only part of the input, so

```
sed '15p'
```

will output line 15 of the input only, and

```
sed '1,10s/[:alpha:]//g'
```

will output the first ten lines only with all letters deleted. By using option -n, we can simulate simple use of grep using sed, since the following are equivalent:

```
grep 'BRE'
sed -n '/BRE/p'
```

Worked example 8.11

Write a filter which will output the last line of the input prepended by The last line is.

Solution: Use $ to match the last line of input, option -n of sed to ignore other lines in the input, and command p to print it out after substituting The last line is for the beginning of the line:

```
sed -n '$s/^/The last line is /p'
```

Choosing between these three filters

It is good practice to use the simplest filter available to you, if a choice exists

It will be apparent that anything grep or tr can do, sed can also do (though possibly not as elegantly). Why do we need grep and tr?

Speed may be important if the data you wish to filter is large, or your UNIX system is small and not very powerful. Since sed does more than the other two utilities, it is almost certainly slower. Unless you really need the facilities offered by sed, then it will be easier to remember how to use the other two utilities. Extended regular expressions are only available to grep. Finally, some operations are not easy to perform using sed – try coding the following using only sed:

```
tr A-Z a-z
grep -l abc *
```

Splitting a file according to context

We have already met split as a method of splitting a file into smaller units, and have indicated its use when mailing large text files. Another reason for splitting a file is where you know that the file contains separate identifiable portions. For instance, suppose you had a simple text file consisting of paragraphs of English separated by blank lines, and you wanted the paragraphs to be in separate files. The blank lines would identify where to break the file, and you can specify a blank line by means of the BRE which is ^$. The command csplit will split a file into sections where the sections either contain specified numbers of lines or are delimited by text which can be described by a basic regular expression. To start with a simple example,

```
$ csplit data 10
```

will take file data, and create two new files called xx00 and xx01. File xx00 will contain lines 1 through 9 of file data, and xx01 will contain line 10 up to the end of file data. File data remains unaltered. When each new file is created, csplit will print the size (in bytes) of that file, on the standard error stream (this can be suppressed with option -s).

The first argument to csplit is the name of a file (or - (hyphen) if standard input) and the following one or more arguments indicate where the file is to be split. An argument which is a line number instructs a break to be made at the beginning of that line (hence in the previous example line 10 is sent to the second file). The new, smaller, files are named xx*nn*, where *nn* starts at 00 and counts upwards. With option -f followed by a string that string will be used as the **prefix** instead of xx. Any number of arguments can follow the filename.

Worked example 8.12

Split /usr/dict/words into three files called words00, words01 and words02, the first two containing 10000 lines, the final one containing the rest of /usr/dict/words. **Solution**: Use csplit to split the file with option -f to specify that the prefix is words. The next argument is /usr/dict/words, and this is to be split at lines 10001 and 20001.

```
$ csplit -f words /usr/dict/words 10001 20001
```

Now use wc to check that the files you have created are of the specified length:

```
$ wc words??
```

The three files you have created are fairly big, so don't forget to delete them.

If an argument to csplit is a number *n* and is then followed immediately by an argument of the form {*count*}, then it will be split at line *n* and then repeatedly every **n** lines up to a maximum of *count* times. Delete any previous xx files you have created, and try the following:

```
$ csplit -s /usr/dict/words 1000 {2}
$ wc -l xx??
```

You will see that /usr/dict/words has been split into four files. The first split is at the start of line 1000, so the first file is 999 lines long, then the subsequent two splits are each 1000 lines longer. The final file xx03 contains the rest of /usr/dict/words.

csplit = 'context split'

s = 'silent'

If you specify that the file be split at too many places, no split files will be created and an error message will be generated. For instance, to try to split /usr/dict/words into 5000 files of 10000 lines each (which we clearly cannot do):

```
$ csplit /usr/dict/words 10000 {5000}
82985
82982
csplit: '10000': line number out of range on repetition 2
40695
```

82985 is the number of bytes in xx01, etc.

Delete xx files which have been created by csplit when they are no longer needed — they may take up a substantial amount of storage space

The reason for this behaviour is to encourage you to be aware of how you are splitting your files, and csplit errs on the side of caution. Mistakes when specifying the arguments to csplit would otherwise be prone to causing large volumes of unwanted split files to be generated, thus wasting valuable storage space. There are some instances, however, when this behaviour is undesirable, especially when the length of a file is not initially known. If you give csplit option -k it will warn you if you try to split the input file too many times, but it will create the xx files anyway. So, to split /usr/dict/words into as many files as possible each containing (roughly) 5000 lines:

```
$ csplit -k /usr/dict/words 5000 {10000}
```

Worked example 8.13

Split /usr/dict/words into three files called w0, w1 and w2, each containing a roughly equal number of lines.
Solution: Use wc to count the lines in /usr/dict/words, then arithmetic expansion to calculate one-third and two-thirds of that number.

```
$ LINES=$( wc -l < /usr/dict/words )
$ ONETHIRD=$(( $LINES / 3 ))
$ TWOTHIRDS=$(( $ONETHIRD + $ONETHIRD ))
$ csplit -f w -n 1 /usr/dict/words $ONETHIRD $TWOTHIRDS
```

When performing wc we redirected the standard input from the file /usr/dict/words; by doing that, wc does not include the filename on its output. Had we used wc -l /usr/dict/words it would have been necessary to pipe the output to cut in order to isolate the first field, as the output from wc would have included the filename /usr/dict/words.

An argument to csplit can be a basic regular expression enclosed between two / (slash) symbols, in which case the file which is being split will be broken at the start of the next line matching that expression.

Split /usr/dict/words into two files, the first containing all words commencing with characters up to and including m, the second containing words commencing n through z. **Solution**: Use csplit with argument '/^[Nn]/' indicating that /usr/dict/words should be split at the start of the first line commencing either N or n.

```
$ csplit /usr/dict/words '/^[Nn]/'
```

Consider the problem posed at the start of the section, namely splitting a text file into paragraphs. The BRE which denotes a blank line is ^$ and so if we have in file X some such text we might have:

```
$ csplit X '/^$/'
```

This will not work; it will split the file at the first blank line only. Just as with number arguments we can follow a BRE argument to csplit by a number in braces, to indicate that the split should occur multiple times. If we don't know how big X is, we must use option -k as above:

```
$ csplit -k X '/^$/' {10000}
```

Create a small file containing a few paragraphs of text and try this command.

File book contains the text for a book, with each of 10 chapters commencing with a line starting Chapter ... so:

```
Title: ...
    ...
Chapter 1: Introduction
    ...
Chapter 2: Getting started
    ...
```

Split this file into several files, called chapter00, etc., one for each chapter. **Solution**: Use csplit with option -f (to denote the names of the split files), and split at the start of each line commencing Chapter. The split will need to be repeated an extra 9 times:

```
$ csplit -f chapter book '/^Chapter/' {9}
```

More on 'vi'

At this point mention should be made of `vi` commands which are almost identical to those of `sed`, and which rely on BREs. First of all, `/` and `?` are used for searching for strings. Followed by a BRE, each will locate the next (or previous) string which matches that BRE. So, to move the cursor to the next blank line, and assuming you are in command-mode, type

`/^$`

or, if the apparently blank lines in your file may contain spaces also,

`/^ *$`

In colon-mode the commands available are, like `sed`, of the form

address command arguments

Addresses constructed are the same as for `sed`, with the addition of two extra symbols. These are `^`, which means the first line of the file, and `.` (*dot*), denoting the current line as indicated by the cursor.

s = 'substitute'

There is a command `s` which can be used to exchange occurrences of a string (denoted by a BRE) for another string. Suppose in the file you are editing the cursor is on a line containing

`Jack and Jill went up the hill`

you could swap `up` for `down` by

`:s/up/down/`

The `:` gets you into colon-mode, `s` is the command to perform a substitution, and following `s` are three slashes. Between the first two is the BRE you wish to be changed. Between the final two is the string (just a string, not a BRE) it is to be changed to.

Normally a substitution will happen once on the current line. That is, the address `.` is assumed by default. If the BRE which is to be substituted does not exist then no change will happen. If you follow the command by a `g` the substitution will be made for all occurrences of the BRE on that line. So to change all words on the current line commencing `J` to the string `someone`, you would type

`:s/J[a-zA-Z]*/someone/g`

g = 'global'

Before a substitution command you can indicate which lines it is to be performed on by indicating an address explicitly. Preceding the command `%` (percent) will cause it to be performed on every line in the file, preceding it by a single line number will do the substitution on that line only. A pair of line numbers, separated by a comma, will apply the substitution to that range of lines. The start of the file is denoted by `^` and the end by `$`. Thus

`:10,20s/Hello/Bonjour/`

will substitute the first occurrence of `Hello` for `Bonjour` on lines 10 through 20 inclusive.

You are using `vi` to edit a file, and wish to change all occurrences of `Chris` to `Sam` on all lines.

  Solution: Use the substitution command in colon-mode, apply it from the start of the file to the end, and globally on every line:

```
:^,$s/Chris/Sam/g
```

The symbol `%` can be used instead of `^ , $` to mean the whole of the file.

Worked example 8.16

Be careful if your file contains (say) `Christine` — this solution changes it to `Samtine`

The `vi` colon-mode commands which were discussed in Chapter 2 can be preceded by an address and/or followed by arguments. The command `w` assumes the address `%`, and so will normally write the whole file; if a filename follows the `w` as an argument to the command, it will be that file which is written to and the original file will remain unchanged. The command

```
:1,10w xyz
```

will write the first ten lines of the file to the file named `xyz`.

  Often you will wish to perform an action on many lines, and the same action on each. The colon mode command `g` is used to apply a command to all lines which match a regular expression. The command is used in the following way:

`g` = 'global'

```
:g/BRE/action
```

For instance, to delete all completely empty lines,

```
:g/^$/d
```

or to insert an asterisk at the start of each line containing `Chris`

```
:g/Chris/s/^/*/
```

Summary of utilities

`csplit`	split a file according to context
`grep`	select lines matching regular expression
`sed`	stream editor
`tr`	translate characters

Problems

8.1 Write a filter which will extract from /usr/dict/words all words containing all five vowels in alphabetical order.

8.2 A utility known as *rot13* is a very simple encryption mechanism which replaces every letter by the letter 13 further on (or previous to it) in the alphabet. Thus

```
The quick brown fox jumped over the lazy dog
```

would be changed to

```
Gur dhvpx oebja sbk whzcrq bire gur ynml qbt
```

Write a script which will encrypt standard input using the *rot13* algorithm.

8.3 List the names of all files (excluding directories) in the current directory which contain the string program (or some other string).

8.4 The file /etc/group contains lines of the form
group-name:*GID*:*list-of-members*
for instance, a line defining group ateam, with group ID 99, and consisting of users chris, jo and sam, would be

```
ateam:99:chris,jo,sam
```

Write a script to list the names of all the groups of which jo is a member.

8.5 Write a filter numbers which considers its input as consisting of whole numbers (containing only digits), together with other text, and outputs a list of those numbers, one per line, sorted into numerical order with duplicates removed, so:

```
$ numbers <<END
1st Blankshire Bank Ltd.,
17-19 High Street,
Anytown,
Blanks.,
AN1 4GQ.
END
1
4
17
19
```

8.6 How many words in /usr/dict/words contain at least three vowels?

8.7 Split the file /usr/dict/words into two halves, the first containing all words up to (but not including) middle, the second containing the rest.

Chapter 9

Awk

OBJECTIVES

In this chapter you will learn:

  □ simple use of awk.

The utility known as awk, and described as a 'pattern scanning and processing language', is a complete programming language, with a syntax resembling that of C. Its name is an acronym of its inventors' names. It can be studied as a language in its own right, or can be integrated into shell programming when other utilities are found to lack sufficient power or flexibility.

Aho, Weinberger and Kernighan

What is 'awk'?

If you are familiar with high-level programming languages, you will recognise the need for such constructs as loops, variables, conditional statements, input and output facilities, and a library of predefined procedures. In other words, a rich syntax allowing many complex tasks to be performed easily and efficiently by an experienced programmer. The shell is a high-level language, although its features are tailored to a very special task, namely managing UNIX processes, and many high-level constructs are not present in the shell.

Procedural languages, not declarative languages

If you need to write a program which is not clearly suited to writing in the shell, you would normally choose a language such as C or Pascal in which to write it. There is a grey area, though, where the application does seem to fit in well with the ideas and methods underlying shell programming, yet the power of a full high-level language would be advantageous. A typical situation would be where the contents of a file (or output from a pipe) contained complex (numerical or textual) data, organised into records (e.g. lines) and fields (e.g. columns), and calculations are required to be performed on the data.

To illustrate this, consider data which has as its columns a person's name, followed by numbers representing that person's marks in a number of examinations. You require to process that data to determine each person's overall mark, possibly converting it to a grade, and to calculate overall statistical data for the individual examinations. Perhaps you would like a graphical display of the mark distribution. These tasks could be performed with the shell (with some difficulty), but they can be programmed naturally using awk.

Mention has been made before of the language C – if you can program in C then awk will look familiar to you, and vice versa. There are features of awk – such as pattern matching and associative arrays — which are not available with C, and vice versa. If you write a program in C, then it will probably execute faster than an equivalent program in awk. You should therefore bear in mind that significant differences do exist, and take care not to confuse the two. There is insufficient space in this book to examine awk in great detail, so we shall concentrate on those features of awk which complement the other shell utilities.

Invoking 'awk'

Just as with grep and sed, simple use of awk involves a **script** containing the commands which awk uses. This script can either be a string which is an argument to awk, or can be contained in a file which is named by option -f.

As is standard with many utilities

The data which the awk script will process is either piped from standard input, or is contained in one or more files given as arguments to the command. The data is divided into **records** each of which is subdivided into **fields**. Unless otherwise stated, each record is a single line of the data, and fields will be separated by whitespace. For instance, to represent students with their marks, a dataset might look like:

```
Cringle Chris 14 75 33
Smith Sam 56 58 45
Jones Jo 9 63 51
```

This data contains three records (lines), each record containing five fields (columns of text). An awk script consists of a sequence of pairs

pattern { *action* }

where either the *pattern* or the *action* can be omitted. The data will be read, record by record, and each record which *matches* a pattern in the script will cause the corresponding action to be performed. If the pattern is omitted the action will be performed on every single line of input data. For the rest of this chapter we shall concentrate on the format of the script, and assume that data is piped from standard input. The simplest awk script is

```
{ }
```

which will do precisely nothing for each line of data — the effect will be indistinguishable from cat >/dev/null. This can be invoked either by creating a file (say awkfile) containing a single line, namely the pair of braces, and

```
awk -f awkfile
```

or by

Recall the conventions for double and single quotes

```
awk '{ }'
```

where the script is a string following awk. For the rest of this chapter, the word *script* will refer to an awk script (not a shell script), unless otherwise stated.

Naming the fields

In a shell script, $1 , $2, etc., name the arguments of the script, but in an awk script $1, $2, etc., name the fields of each record of data. The whole record is referred to as $0. To cause awk to print something on standard output the command print can be used. Whenever the action print is performed, a *NEWLINE* character is always output afterwards, just like the shell command echo. The following script will copy standard input to standard output:

```
{ print $0 }
```

Write a shell script which runs awk to print out the first field of each line of standard input. **Solution**: The awk script will be simple for this task, so we can enclose it within single quotes in the shell script. The awk action will be print $1 performed on each line. The awk pattern which matches every line is the null pattern, so that the awk script becomes

```
{ print $1 }
```

To run awk from a shell script, we require the utility awk, followed by this script (enclosed in quotes).

```
# This shell script prints the first field of each
#    line of standard input
awk '{ print $1 }'
```

Worked example 9.1

Don't forget to comment your shell scripts!

If you give print several arguments, it will concatenate their values before printing them out. The following awk script will output each line of input enclosed in parentheses:

```
{ print "(" $0 ")" }
```

so for input

```
hello there
Chris
```

the output would be:

```
(hello there)
(Chris)
```

Formatted output

You will recall the use of printf as a shell utility for displaying information on standard output in a format which you specify. For instance

```
$ printf "Hello %s!\n" $LOGNAME
```

will print on your screen

printf never outputs a *NEWLINE* unless explicitly instructed to do so

```
Hello chris!
```

The *shell* utility `printf` takes a number of arguments: the first is a string specifying the *format* of the output, the second and subsequent arguments are data (such as values of variables) to be output according to the specification given by the format string.

In `awk` there is also a command called `printf`, which is almost identical to that used by the shell. The only major difference is that the arguments are separated by commas, not by whitespace. Try the following `awk` script:

```
{ printf "The first field is %s\n", $1 }
```

Worked example 9.2

Write an `awk` script which when given input in two columns, representing a person's first name followed by their family name, such as

```
Abraham Lincoln
John Kennedy
Benjamin Disraeli
```

will reverse the order of the names, and separate them with a comma:

```
Lincoln, Abraham
Kennedy, John
Disraeli, Benjamin
```

Solution: Using `$1` and `$2` to represent the first name and the family name of each person, print them out using `printf` thus:

```
{ printf "%s, %s\n", $2, $1 }
```

Alternatively, using `print`, this would be

```
{ print $2 ", " $1 }
```

Before we can experiment much further with `awk`, we need some data. Consider the problem of a grocery bill – you have purchased some vegetables which are priced in £ per kilogram, and you buy a number of kilograms of various different vegetables. Create a file containing in column 1 the names of vegetables, in column 2 the price (in £) per kilogram, and in column 3 the number of kilograms purchased, something like:

```
potatoes 0.50 5
carrots 0.80 2.5
peas 2.20 1
beans 2.10 2
artichokes 8.50 0.5
sweetcorn 0.90 3
```

Name this file `vegetables`. We shall use this file, and `awk`, to perform tasks such as totalling the cost for each vegetable, and evaluating the total bill. Recall that when using

+	addition
-	subtraction
*	multiplication
/	division
%	integer remainder
^	'to the power of'
==	is equal to
!=	is not equal to
>	is greater than
>=	is greater than or equal to
<	is less than
<=	is less than or equal to
&&	'and'
||	'or'

Figure 9.1   *Operators used by* awk.

printf to format an integer you use the format specifier %d; for a **floating-point** number the specifier is %f. You can also require a floating-point number to be printed to a specific accuracy — if you include between the % symbol and the f a dot followed by a number, the floating-point number will be output with that number of digits after the decimal place. So we could copy the file vegetables using

```
{ printf "%s %.2f %.1f\n", $1, $2, $3 }
```

Try this, using

```
$ awk '{ printf "%s %.2f %.1f\n", $1, $2, $3 }' <vegetables
```

Note what happens when you have a whole number as one of the last two columns — it is printed with the relevant number of decimal places containing zeroes:

```
potatoes 0.50 5.0
carrots 0.80 2.5
peas 2.20 1.0
beans 2.10 2.0
artichokes 8.50 0.5
sweetcorn 0.90 3.0
```

Simple arithmetic can be performed by awk, with the same operators and conventions as bc. These are listed in Figure 9.1. To evaluate the number of seconds in a day and print it out, the following would suffice:

```
$ awk '{ print 24*60*60 }'
```

Try it—but remember that this will be done for each line of input, so if you pipe the contents of a file to this command, the output will have the same number of lines as the input, each line being the number `86400`. If you just wish to do an arithmetic calculation, use `bc`.

Worked example 9.3

Write an `awk` script which will reformat the data in `vegetables` in the following format:

```
I bought 5.0 kilos of potatoes at 50p per kilo
I bought 2.5 kilos of carrots at 80p per kilo
 ...
```

Solution: Use `printf` with the `%f` specifier to output the 'number of kilos' field to one decimal place accuracy, and calculating the number of pence per kilo as 100 times the price in £. Since the pence per kilo is an integer, use the `%d` format specifier.

```
{ printf "I bought %.1f kilos of %s at %dp per kilo\n",
         $3, $1, 100*$2 }
```

If you wish to do floating-point arithmetic in `awk`, and your script contains some whole numbers, then `awk` will automatically convert those integers to floating-point numbers when it is sensible to do so. Thus `1/2` will evaluate to `0.5`. Similarly, if `awk` is expecting a field to be a string, and receives a number as input instead, that number will be treated as a string of digits (together with decimal point or minus sign, if appropriate).

Worked example 9.4

Write an `awk` script which uses the data in `vegetables` to calculate the total amount of money spent on each vegetable, printing it in the following format:

```
potatoes cost 2.50
carrots cost 2.00
 ...
```

Solution: We can calculate the total cost for each vegetable by multiplying the second and third fields together.

```
{ printf "%s cost %.2f\n", $1, $2*$3 }
```

Earlier on we used `cut` to extract fields from lines of input. You may find it easier to use `awk` in some instances.

Display the current year.

Solution: We could use date and pipe the output to cut, as before, or we could use a format argument to date. Another method is to pipe the output of date to awk, using awk to print out the sixth field.

```
$ date | awk '{ print $6 }'
```

For comparison, the other two methods would be written:

```
$ date | cut -d' ' -f6
$ date +"%Y"
```

It is up to you to decide which one you think is most clear.

Worked example 9.5

Patterns

In the previous examples we have performed a task on every line of the standard input, by using a null pattern. There are two simple patterns which are very useful – they are called BEGIN and END. An action associated with pattern BEGIN will be executed once, when the awk script starts and before any lines are read from the standard input. The action associated with END is performed after all other actions, and immediately prior to awk terminating. The following awk script will copy its standard input to the standard output, but also write Start of file at the beginning of the output, and End of file at the end:

```
BEGIN { print "Start of file" } # Done at the start
{ print $0 }                     # for each line of input
END { print "End of file" }      # done at the end
```

Just as in shell scripts, comments can be inserted into awk scripts

Try it with the input coming from vegetables. More generally, many sorts of pattern are available. An ERE enclosed between slashes (/) is a pattern which will match any line of input matched by that ERE. So to print the cost per kilo of every vegetable whose name commences with a vowel, we could have

See Chapter 8 for a detailed discussion of regular expressions

```
/^[aeiou]/ { printf "%s costs %.2f per kilo\n", $1, $2 }
```

The pattern specified by the ERE will normally apply to the whole record. It can be restricted to a single field by preceding the ERE by the field number and a tilde. So in the above example we are interested in the first field commencing with a vowel, so we could restrict the pattern match to the first field thus:

```
$1 ~ /^[aeiou]/ { printf "%s costs %.2f per kilo\n", $1,$2 }
```

The behaviour of grep can be mimicked by awk – the following two shell commands will have the same effect:

```
grep -E 'ERE'
awk '/ERE/ { print $0 }'
```

The pattern can also be an expression which evaluates to true or to false. The following will print out the cost per kilo of all expensive (more than £1 per kilo) vegetables:

```
$2 > 1.00 { printf "%s costs %.2f per kilo\n", $1, $2 }
```

Worked example 9.6

Print out the total costs for vegetables only if that cost is at least 2.50.
Solution: For each line, evaluate the total cost (`$2*$3`), and perform `printf` if that value is greater than or equal to `2.50`:

```
$2*$3 >= 2.50 { printf "%s cost %.2f\n", $1, $2*$3 }
```

More complicated patterns can be constructed using `&&` ('and') and `||` ('or'). These are *boolean* operators:

expression1 `&&` *expression2*

is true if both *expression1* and *expression2* are true, whereas

expression1 `||` *expression2*

is true if either *expression1* or *expression2* is true, or if both are true.

Worked example 9.7

Print out the names of each vegetable purchased which either cost at most £1 per kilo, or for which less than 1 kilo was purchased.
Solution:

```
$2 <= 1 || $3 < 1 { printf "%s\n", $1 }
```

Variables

In the shell, we use variables, which we give names to, and access their values by placing a dollar before their names. In awk we also have variables, which we can assign values to in the same way as the shell, but to use a variable we do not need the dollar. The reason that the shell needs the dollar is a technical reason, which relates to ensuring that each shell statement is unambiguous. The ambiguities that might arise in the shell do not happen in awk.

Suppose we require a total grocery bill. We could use a variable (`total`, say) to keep a 'running total' of the cost of each vegetable and print it out at the end:

```
# Initialise total to 0
BEGIN { total = 0 }

# For each line of input, that is, each vegetable, add
# the total cost to variable total
{ total = total + $2*$3 }

# At the end, print out the total
END { printf "Total cost is %.2f\n", total}
```

Some explanation is required for the action $total = total + \$2*\$3$: the *current* value stored in the variable total has the values of $\$2*\$3$ added to it, and the resulting number is stored back in total. So the value of the variable total has been updated. Another way of stating this action is to use the symbol +=, so:

```
total += $2*$3
```

So total += ... is just shorthand for total = total + ...
Analogous to += are -=, *=, /=, %= and ^= .

Work out the average price per kilo of the vegetables you have purchased.   **Worked example 9.8**
Solution: We need to total the amount of money spent, and also the number of kilograms. The final answer is calculated by dividing one by the other.

```
# Use variable totalcost for the money spent
# Use variable totalweight for the total kilos
# Initialise totalcost and totalweight to 0
BEGIN { totalcost = 0
        totalweight = 0 }

# For each line of input update the running totals
{ totalcost = totalcost + $2*$3 }    # Cost
{ totalweight = totalweight + $3 }   # Weight

# At the end, print out the average
END { printf "Average cost is %.2f pounds per kilo\n",
      totalcost/totalweight}
```

Special variables

Just as the shell can use predefined variables such as HOME, so also can awk. There are many of these, all of which use capital letters only (so variable names you choose yourself should use lower-case letters). Some of these, which we discuss here, are listed in Figure 9.2.

FILENAME	The pathname of the current input file
FS	Input field separator, usually *SPACE*
NF	Number of fields in current record
NR	Number of current record from start of input
FNR	Number of current record from start of current input file
OFS	Output field separator used by print, usually *SPACE*
ORS	Output record separator used by print, usually *NEWLINE*

Figure 9.2   *Predefined* awk *variables.*

NR = 'number of record'

Each input record is counted, starting at 1. The variable NR contains the number of the current record. The following script will prepend each input line with the line number (unless otherwise specified, a record is assumed to be a single line). The format is that of cat -n, where six spaces are allowed for the line numbers, which are separated from the line contents by two blanks. The format specification %6d indicates an integer right-justified within six spaces.

```
{ printf "%6d  %s\n", NR, $0 }
```

Try this awk script, and also cat -n, with a file such as vegetables.

Worked example 9.9

Using awk, select the first three lines of standard input, in the manner of head -3.
Solution: Print out only those lines whose number, as given by NR, is at most three. When NR is equal to three, the program should finish – otherwise it will continue reading input until the input terminates. The action exit causes awk to terminate.

```
NR <= 3 { print $0 }
NR == 3 { exit }
```

FNR = 'File Number of Record'

The variable NR starts off with value 1 on the first line of input, and continues counting however many files you have given as argument to awk. There is another variable FNR which is similar to NR, but is reset to 1 each time a new file is read as input. The variable FILENAME holds the name of the current data file being read in.

Worked example 9.10

Write an awk script firstlines which will read from a number of files and print out the first line of each file preceded by the message The first line of *filename* is: in the following manner:

```
$ awk -f firstlines vegetables /usr/dict/words
The first line of vegetables is:
potatoes 0.50 5
The first line of /usr/dict/words is:
AAAA
```

Solution: Use variable FNR to form the pattern to find the first line of each input file, then printf to display that line ($0).

```
FNR == 1 { printf "The first line of %s is:\n%s\n",
                              FILENAME, $0 }
```

Each record consists of a number of fields. The variable NF is the number of fields contained in the current record. Try the following:

NF = 'number of fields'

```
$ awk '{ print NF }'
hello there
2
A B C D E
5
(blank line)
0
ctrl-D
```

If some data in vegetables had been mistyped, there might be lines in the file which contain either less than or more than three fields. Such lines cannot be processed correctly by the previous awk scripts. Write an awk script which will read a file and print out a list of which lines contain a number of fields different to three.

Worked example 9.11

Solution: Use the pattern NF != 3 to choose those lines, and the value of NR to indicate which lines they are:

```
NF != 3 { printf "Line %d has %d fields\n", NR, NF }
```

Use this script to check that your file vegetables is indeed of the correct format. Try it on some other files you own and see what happens.

Arguments to 'awk' scripts

Suppose we wished to write a shell script called price which would take one argument, representing a vegetable name, and interrogate the file vegetables as before to print out the total price paid for that vegetable. One solution would be to get awk to evaluate the total cost for all vegetables, and then use grep to filter out the single line of output from awk:

```
awk '{ printf "%s %.2f\n", $1, $2*$3 }' vegetables | grep $1
```

In grep $1 the $1 refers to the first argument of the shell script

This is a perfectly acceptable solution. Another would be to use a pattern for awk so that only that single line would be processed by awk. But here is a problem — we cannot use the following:

```
awk '/$1/ { printf "%s %.2f\n", $1, $2*$3 }' vegetables
```

The pattern /$1/ is an ERE pattern. The character $ in an ERE matches the end of a string, and since each record which awk processes is a line, $ matches the end of an input line. The ERE $1, and thus the awk pattern /$1/, will match all lines containing the digit 1 as the character after the end of that line. This an impossible pattern, so it will not be matched by any line. Try it — you should expect not to get any output. The point to remember is that the $1 has nothing to do with the $1 which would represent the first argument to a shell script.

There is, fortunately, a way around this problem. When invoking awk you can preset awk variables by specifying their initial value on the command line. So, we could assign an awk variable called veg (say) which would start off with the value which was the first argument to the script:

```
awk '{ if (veg == $1)
          printf "%s %.2f\n", $1, $2*$3 }' veg=$1 vegetables
```

By placing veg=$1 immediately after the awk script, this will set the value of veg to $1 — the first argument to the shell script — as soon as awk starts up. Another method would be to use veg as part of a pattern:

```
awk ' veg == $1
          { printf "%s %.2f\n", $1, $2*$3 }' veg=$1 vegetables
```

Worked example 9.12

Write a shell script which will take a single argument, representing a cost in pence, and print out the names of all vegetables listed in file vegetables which cost more than that number of pence per kilo.

Solution: Use awk, but pass a variable cost to it which is set to the first argument of the shell script.

```
# First, check the shell script has one argument
if   [ $# -ne 1 ]
then echo "One argument needed"
     exit 1
fi

# Now fire awk ...
awk '{ if ($2 * 100 >= cost)
          printf "%s\n", $1 }' cost=$1 vegetables

# Exit cleanly
exit 0
```

Arrays

Most high-level languages include **arrays**. An array (or **associative array**) is a collection of variables which has a **name**, and each variable in that array has an **index**. An array index can be a string or a number. For example, we might have an array called `daysin` consisting of 12 variables, indexed by the names of the months of the year. These 12 variables would have names `daysin["January"]`, `daysin["February"]`, and so on up to `daysin["December"]`.

Write an `awk` script which will read as input a sequence of lines each containing the name of a month. Output should be the name of the month read in followed by the number of days in it, for instance for input

```
March
November
```

we would have as output

```
March has 31 days
November has 30 days
```

Worked example 9.13

Solution: Use an array indexed by the names of the months, and each array element has as its value the number of days in the month which is its index. At the start of the script the array must be initialised.

```
BEGIN {   # Initialise the array daysin
    daysin["January"] = 31;   daysin["February"] = 28
    daysin["March"] = 31;     daysin["April"] = 30
    daysin["May"] = 31;       daysin["June"] = 30
    daysin["July"] = 31;      daysin["August"] = 31
    daysin["September"] = 30; daysin["October"] = 31
    daysin["November"] = 30;  daysin["December"] = 31
    }
# For each input line, output month name and no. of days
    { printf "%s has %d days\n", $1, daysin[$1] }
```

Note that we can place multiple `awk` commands on a single line by separating them with semicolons. Try this example. If you enter a month name which is incorrectly spelled, `awk` will see that the element of the array with that index has not been assigned a value, and will assume it is therefore 0.

Returning to our shopping expedition, we may wish to store the data on each vegetable to be used later on. For example, if we purchased several bags of potatoes at different shops, we would need to enter several lines commencing `potatoes`. The scripts we have written already will not be able to total the costs for potatoes, they will just total the cost of each item on each line of input, that is for each separate purchase. What we could do is to have an array `costs` indexed by the names of the vegetables, which we can update each time a new line of data is read in:

```
{ costs[$1] += $2*$3 }
```

The symbol `+=` indicates that the variable on the left of the symbol has its value updated by adding to it the number on the right of the symbol. At the start of the script, we would not initialise `costs`, since we do not at that point know the names of the vegetables to be mentioned in the input. When the first line of `vegetables` is read in, which is

```
potatoes 0.50 5
```

the following action is performed:

```
costs["potatoes"] += 0.50*5
```

The value of `costs["potatoes"]` starts off at 0, since it begins uninitialised, and its value is increased by 2.50.

Just as in the shell, `awk` contains `for` loops. In fact, `awk` allows several types of `for` loop. One of these allows you to loop through arrays and pick out those indices which have been used. The `for` statement looks like:

```
for (variable in array) statement
```

So we could examine the values of the elements of `costs` for all indices by using

```
for (veg in costs) printf "%s costs %.2f\n",
            veg, costs[veg]
```

So a complete `awk` script for totalling the costs for all vegetables would be

```
{ costs[$1] += $2*$3 }
END  { for (veg in costs)
                printf "%s costs %.2f\n", veg, costs[veg] }
```

Worked example 9.14

Calculate the average cost per kilo for each vegetable.
Solution: The *total cost* and the *total weight* for each vegetable must be calculated.

```
# Use arrays costs and weights to store the total costs
#   and total weight for each vegetable.
{ costs[$1] += $2*$3; weights[$1] += $3 }

# At the end, for each vegetable, divide its total costs
#   by the total weight, and output the value
END { for (veg in costs)
        printf "%s: %.2f pence per kilo\n",
            veg, costs[veg]/weights[veg] }
```

There is a special array `ENVIRON` which contains all the (exported) shell environment variables. To print out the value of your `PATH`, the following `awk` statement could be used:

```
printf "%s\n", ENVIRON["PATH"];
```

Field and record separators

The fields in a record are normally separated by whitespace. This is not always convenient. Suppose a file (`ages`, say) contains a list of people's names and their ages:

```
John 13
Sue 12
James Smith 15
James Jones 14
```

The number of fields on each line varies. This is a potential problem. Let us suppose we wish to write a simple awk script which will output

```
John is 13 years old
Sue is 12 years old
James Smith is 15 years old
James Jones is 14 years old
```

There are several possible solutions. One which you will already be able to find is one which checks the number of fields and performs a separate action each time:

```
NF == 2 { printf "%s is %d years old\n", $1, $2 }
NF == 3 { printf "%s %s is %d years old\n", $1, $2, $3 }
```

This solution is fine if you know how many names a person is likely to have – but it is not elegant since there is a lot of duplication in the awk script. If you were to allow persons with many forenames to appear in the list the awk script would become unmanageable. Loops, such as `for` and `while` loops, are provided in awk, and although we do not discuss them here they could be used to 'count over' the first few fields. However, the solution begins to get moderately complex if that method is adopted.

The reason that the awk scripts to perform this apparently simple task are less straightforward than you might expect is that the data has been coded unwisely. The fields are separated by characters which themselves appear in one of the fields, namely blanks. If the data had been

```
John:13
Sue:12
James Smith:15
James Jones:14
```

so that a colon (say) was used to separate the names from the numbers, then each line would have precisely two fields, and the spaces in the names would not matter. We can instruct awk to use a different **field separator** to the usual whitespace by resetting the value of the variable FS; this should be done at the very start of the awk script. Create a file called `ages` with the above names and ages in the 'colon-separated' format, and run the following awk script:

FS = 'field separator'

```
BEGIN { FS=":" }
{ printf "%s is %d years old\n", $1, $2 }
```

The field separator can be any ERE, and can also be changed by giving awk the option -F followed by that ERE. For instance, to allow a sequence of one or more blanks, commas and colons to separate fields, you might have

```
awk -F "[ ,:]+"
```

On your UNIX system there should be a file called /etc/passwd which contains information about users on your system. This file consists of a sequence of lines which look like:

```
chris:hi64MH4uhJiq2:1623:103:Chris Cringle:/cs/ugrad/chris:
sam:a8PyPVSiPVXT6:1628:103:Sam Smith:/cs/ugrad/sam:/bin/sh
jo:9gqrX4IOig7qs:1631:103:Jo Jones:/cs/ugrad/jo:/bin/sh
geo:58esMw4xFsZ9I:1422:97:George Green:/cs/staff/geo:/bin/sh
    ...
```

Each line contains seven colon-separated fields; these represent:

1 A user's username (e.g. chris)

2 That user's *encrypted* password (e.g. hi64MH4uhJiq2). Passwords are usually stored in a coded form; if you know a password it's easy to encrypt it, but virtually impossible to take an encrypted password and *de*code it. So it's safe for the encrypted passwords to be accessible by everyone. Having said this, some UNIX implementations – especially networked systems – impose a higher degree of security and do not allow the encrypted passwords to be accessed. In that case, the second field will be replaced by some other value.

3 The user's user-id (see Chapter 3).

4 The user's group-id (see Chapter 3).

5 The user's 'real' name; sometimes this field will also include other information, such as the user's office phone number or course of study.

6 The user's home directory.

7 The user's login shell (if empty, defaults to /bin/sh).

Some systems which 'hide' the encrypted passwords will also have another mechanism for storing the data normally in /etc/passwd. If you find that this file either does not exist, or does not contain the information just described, then it is likely to be available using a special command. A common method of organising users' data over a network uses a system called **NIS**, which will be discussed in Chapter 10. To display the password file using NIS you should type

Network Information Service

yp = 'yellow pages'

```
ypcat passwd
```

and the data will be sent to standard output.

Worked example 9.15

Using awk and /etc/passwd write a shell script findname which takes an argument, which is a usercode, and displays the name of the user who owns that usercode.
Solution: We need to look at fields 1 and 5 of the password file; if field 1 is the shell script argument we print out field 5.

```
# As usual, make sure the script has one argument ...
if   [ $# -ne 1 ]
then echo "findname requires one argument"
     exit 1
fi

awk '
      # Set field separator to :
      BEGIN { FS=":" }
      {
        # Is the first field the usercode?
        if ($1 == usercode)

          # If yes, print out field 5, the user's name
          printf "%s\n", $5 }

    ' usercode=$1 </etc/passwd
    # Run awk with usercode set to the value of the
    #    first argument of the shell script, and read
    #    the data from /etc/passwd
```

Just as we can specify what should separate fields within a record, so we can specify what should separate records. Unless otherwise specified, a record is a line of input, so the **record separator** is the *NEWLINE* character. The special variable which is used to change this is RS.

RS = 'record separator'

Write an awk script which will read standard input containing a list of company names and phone numbers, together with other information. All companies in the input which have the keyword Anytown as part of their data should be printed out. The data for each company should be separated by a single line containing a single % symbol:

Worked example 9.16

```
Toytown Telecom
Birmingham
021-123 4567
Sells phones and answering machines
%
Sue, Grabbit and Runne
Solicitors
London
071-999 9999
%
Chopham, Sliceham and Son
Anytown 234
family butchers
```

So with this data the output would be

```
Chopham, Sliceham and Son
Anytown 234
family butchers
```

Solution: Set the record separator to a %.

```
BEGIN      { RS="%" }      # Set RS
/Anytown/ { print $0 }'  # Print records matching "Anytown"
```

WARNING!

You must be *very* careful if you reset the record separator. If the *NEWLINE* character is no longer the record separator, any *NEWLINE*s will be a part of the record. Unless the field separator is an ERE which allows a *NEWLINE*, it will also be part of one of the fields. You will seldom need to reset the record separator.

Although the function `print` has been mentioned briefly, we have so far used the function `printf` as the usual means of displaying output from awk. This is because `printf` is very flexible. For simple output, `print` can be 'tailored' to individual requirements by use of the **output field** and **output record** separators OFS and ORS. When `print` takes several arguments, they will be printed out separated by the value of OFS (normally *SPACE*), and each record will be terminated by ORS (normally *NEWLINE*).

Worked example 9.17

Write an awk script which will read in the password file and output users' names and home directories, in the following format:

```
Chris Cringle has home directory /cs/ugrad/chris.
Sam Smith has home directory /cs/ugrad/sam.
    . . .
```

Solution: Use `print` to display the fifth and sixth fields of `/etc/passwd`. Set the input field separator to a colon, the output field separator to

```
has home directory
```

and the output record separator to *NEWLINE*.

```
awk ' BEGIN { FS=":"
              OFS=" has home directory "
              ORS=".\n" }
  { print $5,$6 }' </etc/passwd
```

Functions

Just as bc and expr have functions defined that you can use with them (such as exp), so also awk. Some of these are listed in Figures 9.3 and 9.4.

`sin(x)`	returns the sine of x
`cos(x)`	returns the cosine of x
`atan2(x,y)`	returns the inverse tangent of x/y
`exp(x)`	returns the exponential of x, viz. ϵ^x
`log(x)`	returns the natural logarithm of x
`sqrt(x)`	returns the square root of x
`int(x)`	truncates x to the nearest integer to 0
`rand()`	returns a random number x with $0 \leq x \leq 1$

Figure 9.3   *Arithmetic functions used by* awk.

`tolower(s)`	returns the string s with all upper-case letters in s replaced by their lower-case equivalent
`toupper(s)`	returns the string s with all lower-case letters in s replaced by their upper-case equivalent
`split(s, a, fs)`	splits the string s into array elements $a[1]$, $a[2]$, ..., $a[n]$, and returns n; separation is done with the regular expression *fs*
`length(s)`	returns the length in characters of string s
`getline`	moves on to the next input record; `$0`, `NF`, etc., are reset to their new values
`match(s, ERE)`	returns the position in string s, starting at 1, where *ERE* occurs; 0 is returned if *ERE does not occur* in s
`sub(ERE, rep)`	substitutes string *rep* for the first occurrence of *ERE* in the current record
`sub(ERE, rep, in)`	substitutes string *rep* for the first occurrence of *ERE* in the string *in*
`substr(s,m)`	returns the substring of s beginning at character position m
`substr(s,m,n)`	returns the substring of s beginning at character position m of length n (or up to the end of the string, if sooner)
`system(expression)`	evaluates *expression* as a *shell* command and returns its exit status

Figure 9.4   *Other functions used by* awk.

Worked example 9.18   Write a script which will 'roll a die'. Each time a line of input is entered the script will
print out a number between 1 and 6 to mimic someone throwing a die.
Solution: Use awk. All the input should be discarded, but whenever a line is entered from
standard input the function `rand` is called to generate a number between 0 and 1 (but not
including 1). This is multiplied by 6 to get a number between 0 and 6 (but not including
6). Adding 1 to this produces a number between 1 and 7, and giving this as argument to
`int` will yield a whole number between 1 and 6 inclusive.

```
awk ' { printf "%d\n", int(rand()*6 + 1) }'
```

The trigonometric functions use radians, not degrees, and the number returned by `rand`
might be 0, but will be strictly less than 1.

Worked example 9.19   Write a shell script which will read the password file and display each user's name in
capitals.
Solution: Use awk to pass the fifth field of its input to the function `toupper`, the result
of which is then printed.

```
awk ' BEGIN { FS=":" }
  { print toupper($5) }' </etc/passwd
```

Where a function takes a string as argument, that string is not itself altered, so that if you
passed $0 to one of those functions, $0 would stay the same, but the function would return
a new string which is based on $0.

Worked example 9.20   A certain Birmingham electrical retail company offers free delivery of its products to
customers living in the Birmingham area, defined as having addresses with postcode commencing B followed by at least one digit. Delivery outside this area is charged at a flat rate
per delivery. It is company practice for the driver of its delivery van to collect that fee. The
company stores part of its customer data in the following format:

invoice number , customer , road , town , postcode

For example,

```
6152,J. Smith,1 High St.,Birmingham,B99 9ZZ
6183,F. Bloggs,5 Long Ave.,Dudley,DY1 1AA
```

The company requires a document to instruct the delivery driver which customers to visit
and which to collect a delivery fee from.
Solution: This is an exercise which could be accomplished using `sed`, although it would
be quite messy. Using `awk` we can use function `match` to examine the postcode. The
ERE which matches a Birmingham postcode is

```
^B[0-9]
```

namely a B at the start of the postcode followed by one digit. What follows the digit — if
anything — does not concern us. The awk script might be:

```
# Set the field separator to be a comma
BEGIN { FS="," }

# For each line, $5 is the postcode
# Check if it is a Birmingham one
{ if ( match($5, "^B[0-9]") > 0)
     fee = "no fee"
 else
     fee = "standard fee"
# Print out message for driver
printf "%s, %s, %s, %s: %s\n", $2, $3, $4, $5, fee
 }
```

Perl

There is a utility called perl which has many of the features of sed, awk, sh and the
programming language C. There are even translators to turn your sed and awk scripts
directly into perl. It is a very powerful tool allowing you, in a single script, to perform
tasks that might require several other utilities in combination. Although not supplied as
standard on many UNIX machines, many places have it installed.

perl = 'Practical Extraction and Report Language', not a POSIX utility

    Perl can be obtained free using FTP from ftp.perl.com and from many other FTP
sites worldwide.

FTP is discussed in Chapter 10

Problems

9.1 A railway company operates trains which travel between a number of cities. The
company offers three types of *service*: *local*, *fast* and *express*. Its fares are based on
10p per mile travelled per passenger for local trains, 12p for fast trains, and 15p for
express. The company keeps a log of all journeys made. For each year this data is
kept in a file (trainlog, say), which contains a number of fields. These are, in
order, the *departure* city, the *destination* city, the *distance* travelled (in kilometres),
the number of *passengers* carried, and the service (local, fast or express).
The final two fields represent the *day* and *month* that the journey took place. A
typical part of the log file might look like:

```
    . . .
Edinburgh Glasgow 71 23 local 14 5
Aberdeen London 805 675 express 14 5
Manchester Birmingham 128 534 fast 15 5
Exeter Exmouth 8 112 local 15 5
    . . .
```

The costs to the company of running trains are a fixed cost of £100 per journey made plus £5 per mile travelled. Write `awk` scripts which will take input from `trainlog` and output the following information:

9.1a The number of trains run.

9.1b The number of trains run in May.

9.1c The number of fast trains run in May.

9.1d The total number of passengers carried in the year.

9.1e The total fares collected in the year.

9.1f The percent of revenue which was generated by local trains.

9.1g For each train, the profit or loss made on the journey; the output should be a sequence of lines formatted so:

```
   ...
14/5 Edinburgh-Glasgow: loss 291.70
14/5 Aberdeen-London: profit 77381.25
15/5 Manchester-Birmingham: profit 7462.24
15/5 Exeter-Exmouth: loss 50.40
   ...
```

9.2 The Anytown and Blankshire Historical Society has decided to computerise its membership records. There are 3 classes of membership:

- *Annual*, renewable on the anniversary of joining and subject to a fee of £10.00 each year.

- *Life*, subject to a single payment of £250.00.

- *Honorary*, which gives the same rights and privileges as Life membership, but is awarded by the Committee and no fee is payable.

Its membership secretary proposes to store its membership records in a file containing single-line records. Each record contains a number of colon-separated fields, the number of fields dependent on the class of membership.

For annual members, the fields have the following meaning:

1 Surname

2 First name(s) or initials

3 Class of membership, the string 'annual'

4 Address

5 Home phone number

6 Date of first joining (dd/mm/yy)

7 Date renewal due

For life and honorary members, field 3 is 'life' and 'honorary' respectively, and there are only six fields. For example,

```
Bloggs:Fred:annual:1 High Street:1234:03/12/90:03/12/97
Smith:John J.:annual:2 High Street::13/01/97:13/01/98
Doe:Jane:life:3 High Street:123 4567:22/02/93
Jones:Cllr. A.:honorary:New House:123 2345:22/02/93
```

Write shell scripts which will read a membership file from standard input and produce the following information:

9.2a A list of members' names, sorted by category of membership, then alphabetically by surname.

9.2b A list of annual members whose membership has expired and is due for renewal.

9.2c The total number of annual members due to renew in the current year.

9.2d The total dues paid already by each member during their membership of the society.

9.2e A list of honorary members who will have been of 10 years' standing in the current year.

9.2f Combine (a–e) to produce a single shell script which will output a comprehensive report. Take care to include messages in the output so that the report is easy to read.

For each of these tasks, you should also ask how else you might solve the problem under UNIX, for instance with grep or sed. Is awk the most appropriate tool?

Chapter 10

Internet and multimedia

OBJECTIVES

In this chapter you will learn about:

☐ networks and graphical user interfaces;

☐ wordprocessing and text formatting utilities;

☐ legal requirements incumbent on using a computer system;

☐ the Internet and the World-Wide Web.

The first nine chapters of this book have concentrated on those aspects of UNIX, specified in the POSIX standard, which are relevant to someone meeting UNIX for the first time. POSIX.1 and POSIX.2 do not attempt to cover aspects of a computer system beyond those basic utilities which a shell and kernel might be expected to include. Further discussion of UNIX systems, and how they fit into the more general scheme of things, is therefore essential if you are to get the most benefit from use of your UNIX system.

Networks

Most general-purpose computers are parts of **networks**, that is, they are linked to other computers in some manner which allows them to communicate with each other. In an office, desk-top computers may be able to access a common filestore and exchange electronic mail. A company might use hand-held computers which use radio signals to talk to each other and to computers in the company's offices. Larger computers may be linked by high-capacity telephone lines. Some or all of those computers may also be connected to the Internet.

It is becoming increasingly difficult for a computer user to be aware of exactly where the physical communication links between the system they are using and 'the rest of the world' are situated, and what form they take. We can, however, broadly categorise the types of network which exist, and indicate their function from the user's point of view.

One method of classifying networks is by the geographical extent. A network is either a **local area network** or **LAN**, or is a **wide area network** or **WAN**. A LAN will typically connect machines in a single building, or similar area, whereas a WAN might connect machines in different buildings, or even different countries. The technologies used for these two types of network are different; communication over a distance of a few metres is virtually instantaneous, whereas sending a message across the world takes a significant fraction of a second.

Ethernet is a type of LAN, which originated from a packet radio broadcast system, developed at the University of Hawaii in 1970. This system worked by splitting the radio signals into individual units known as 'packets' which could be individually received and transmitted. Each radio receiver would receive *all* packets, but would only decode those packets destined for that specific receiver. The Xerox Corporation developed the system so that it would use cable rather than radio, and an experimental Ethernet came into being around 1975. Now an international standard, the Ethernet is one of the most widely-used LAN technologies today, and can handle up to 20Mbps. Other LAN technologies exist, including **token ring** and the **Cambridge Ring**, both contemporary with the Ethernet. From the user's point of view, a LAN is 'transparent' – the details of how the units within the network are interconnected are not of interest, and are the concern of the System Administrator and technical support staff.

A WAN will typically connect separate computer *systems*, rather than processors and devices within a single system. The technology typically used will consist of a **packet switching** mechanism. What this entails is that two computer systems will be connected by some physical communication line (a telephone wire, a radio link, a dedicated fibre optic cable, and so on) and will then exchange messages. Each message is known as a **packet**, and will contain the data together with information specifying which computer system the packet is destined for. This is analogous to a postal system where each written message is enclosed in an addressed envelope – the filled envelope corresponds to a packet, the message in the envelope to the data which the packet contains, and the envelope address to the electronic destination for the packet. The software running on the computer systems connected to the WAN is able to route the packets to their correct destinations. Thus a single physical network can support communication between many different systems at the same time. It will normally be possible to send a packet via different routes from its source to the destination, and so if part of the physical network is broken the data can still be transmitted successfully.

Unlike a LAN, when using a WAN you do have to be aware of the network. Although the infrastructure – the telephone lines, or whatever communication lines are used – are hidden from you, you do need know which system (or systems) is communicating to which other. If you wish to transfer a file from a remote system to your own system, you need to know which system you are transferring it from.

The boundary between what constitutes a LAN and what should be regarded as a WAN is blurred, and becoming increasingly so. A governing factor is the ability of the infrastructure to handle large volumes of data, the **bandwidth** of the communication lines. With the advent of fibre-optic cables and **FDDI** with the capability of over 100Mbps it is now possible to connect together large numbers of processors and devices in a LAN over a much larger area than before; an organisation spread over a whole city can link its equipment in a LAN.

The latest technology is **ATM**, which allows a single physical network (LAN or WAN) to simultaneously support differing types of signal at speeds of up to 2.5Gbps. For instance, a very high bandwidth video data signal can share the same network with a high-volume low-priority file transfer. With older technologies, this would be difficult and wasteful of resources.

Margin notes:

Ethernet is defined in the ANSI/IEEE standard ISO/-IEC 8802-3: 1993

Known as 'ALOHA'

bps = 'bits per second'
Developed at Cambridge University

A WAN packet is different to an Ethernet packet

FDDI = 'Fiber Distributed Data Interface'

ATM = 'Asynchronous Transfer Mode', not to be confused with 'Automatic Teller Machine'

Internet

The **Internet** is a world-wide WAN which links most institutions of higher education, together with many companies, research institutes, military establishments and individual computer users. Each computer linked to the Internet is assigned a unique identification, known as an **Internet number** or **IP address**, of the form $n.n.n.n$ where each n is a number in the range 0 to 255. For instance,

IP = 'Internet Protocol'
Internet numbers always
contain 4 elements

```
192.0.2.123
```

You will usually use the
Internet name rather than
the number of a computer

Each computer is also assigned a name. This is a sequence of alphanumeric components separated by dots, in the form of *computer-name*.*site-name*.*domain* where *domain* might typically be a country code (such as `fr` for France) and the *site-name* might be the institution. The number of components (or **sub-domains**) need not be three, as the site-name or domain can itself be subdivided. For example,

```
spod.cs.nantucket.edu
```

might refer to a computer named `spod` in the Computer Science department (`cs`) at Nantucket University which is in domain `edu`.

As defined in ISO 3166

Strictly speaking, the *top-level* domain, namely the sub-domain right-most in the Internet name, should be the 'official' two-letter country code, but in practice the Internet has developed several other top-level domains. For most countries, they are the country code, with a number of exceptions, including:

- `uk` is the top-level domain for Great Britain (not `gb`);

- `edu` serves as a top-level domain for educational institutions in the United States, but some other institutions elsewhere in the world use `edu`;

- `mil` is the top-level domain for all US military establishments;

`com` = 'commercial'

- `com` is similar to `edu`, but for companies rather than educational institutions;

- `org` is similar to `edu`, but for private organisations which do not come under `edu` or `com`;

- `gov` is for civilian US government establishments;

- `net` is for Internet service providers.

Although some top-level domains, like `edu`, have no sub-domains between them and the institution name, other top-level domains may do. For example, the UK top-level domain `uk` is subdivided into `co` (for companies), `ac` for academic institutions and `gov` for government institutions, so that machine `bubbles` in the Engineering department at Newtown University might be referred to as:

A single machine with a
specific IP address may
have several names

```
bubbles.engineering.newtown.ac.uk
```

Domain names sometimes have abbreviations which the Internet recognises, and `bubbles` might also be

```
bubbles.eng.newt.ac.uk
```

You may be allowed access to the Internet, though some institutions restrict access. Your System Administrator will advise you. Assuming that no restrictions have been placed upon you, there are several ways in which the Internet may become useful.

As an individual, you can also access the Internet via a **service provider**, a company with network connections into the Internet which sells connection time to subscribers. You would typically connect to the Internet using a home computer, a modem and a telephone line provided by your local phone company. The scales of charges levied by such companies vary enormously, and if you decide to use the Internet from home you should be aware of the costs involved, not forgetting that a substantial phone bill may be incurred.

Since the Internet is a WAN, a major use is to enable you to login to remote machines. Suppose you have been allowed access to `bubbles` at Newtown, then to connect from your machine to `bubbles` you would use:

> Only if you have permission to do so

```
$ telnet bubbles.eng.newt.ac.uk
Trying 192.0.2.123
Connected to bubbles.
Escape character is '^]'
StarOS UNIX (bubbles)
login:
```

> `tel` comes from the Greek word $\tau\eta\lambda\epsilon$ meaning 'far'

You can then conduct a dialogue with `bubbles` just as you would with your normal system. You could use the IP address rather than the Internet name, if you wished, and

```
$ telnet 192.0.2.123
```

The line which `telnet` prints out relating to **escape characters** indicates that if you type *ctrl-]* then the connection with `bubbles` will be suspended. Suppose you are communicating with `bubbles`, and you type *ctrl-]*, then several commands will be available to you:

>] is square right bracket

```
$ ctrl-]
telnet> ?
Commands may be abbreviated.    Commands are:
close            close current connection
```
(several more lines of telnet commands)
```
quit             exit telnet
?                print help information
telnet> close
Connection closed
```

Thus if a problem arises with the connection (like computers, networks do sometimes go wrong) you can disconnect from the remote machine (and you will automatically be logged off that machine). The other commands which `telnet` allows if you escape using *ctrl-]* during a session are principally concerned with tailoring the connection should you have an unusual terminal or connection into the network, and should not concern you at this stage.

After the `telnet>` prompt, you can continue the session with the remote system by just pressing *RETURN* instead of typing in a specific command.

If you wish to experiment with `telnet`, use the address either `localhost` or `127.0.0.1`, each of which refers to the machine you are currently logged in to. This is safe, and will use minimal extra resources.

Also known as RFC 854

The word *telnet* also refers to the **protocol** which telnet uses. A protocol is a set of rules defining how messages sent across a network are to be understood by the software connected to the network. In other words, messages sent across the Internet by the `telnet` command must all be structured in a specific way.

World-Wide Web

Referred to as WWW or just as the Web

The **World-Wide Web** and the Internet are almost – but not quite – synonymous. When referring to the Internet, we tend to think of a physical network capable of supporting various types of communication, including telnet, FTP and HTTP. The WWW in contrast is a phrase used to name the information network whose physical implementation is almost wholly hidden from the user. The Web is an *environment* allowing access to the Internet. Thus a lawyer interested in (say) issues of libellous messages sent across the Internet will probably not use the phrase WWW, since it will be important to him or her *where* the messages have been distributed to and from. An individual connected to the Internet via a computer at home, and who just **surfs** the network looking for interesting information or entertainment, will probably refer to the WWW as they are interested in the content of the messages only.

Such as Netscape, Mosaic and Lynx

The WWW is evolving rapidly. Use of the WWW is at present mainly via **Web browsers** which display **hypertext** pages that allow the user to select other pages by clicking on highlighted text or images on the displayed page. Full multimedia interfaces to the WWW will be available soon, allowing high-quality audio and video capabilities. Hypertext

HTTP = 'Hypertext Transfer Protocol'

messages are transmitted across the Internet using a protocol known as **HTTP**. A **Web server** is a computer running software which will receive HTTP **requests** and transmit data to the computer which sent the request. A **Web client** is a program which sends requests to a Web server and processes the data returned. A Web browser is an example of a typical client program.

The WWW and the Internet are important to the UNIX programmer. Not only do they allow easy transfer of data and programs, but also the sophisticated communication facilities desirable in the modern business and academic environments.

Usenet news

News is also propagated to systems on networks other than the Internet

When you use electronic mail, you would normally send messages to specific users or groups of users. A system exists called **news** – or **Usenet news** – which runs on the Internet, which resembles electronic mail. The difference between news and mail is that a message (called an **article**) will, instead of being received by a user, be received by a

NNTP = 'Network News Transfer Protocol'

site, and be made available to all users of that site. News messages use the protocol called **NNTP**.

Messages sent via news are structured in a tree-like hierarchy, in a similar fashion to Internet site names. Some examples are presented in Figure 10.1.

Newsgroup	Description	
alt.food	Discussions about food	alt = 'alternative'
comp.lang.pascal	Discussion about the computer language Pascal	comp = 'computing'
comp.unix	UNIX	
rec.arts.movies	Discussions of movies and movie making	rec = 'recreation'
soc.misc	Socially-oriented topics not in other groups	soc = 'society'
talk.religion.misc	Miscellaneous chat about religion	
uk.general	General topics of interest to UK users	
uk.telecom	Discussion of UK telecommunications	
uk.transport	Transport related UK issues	

Figure 10.1   *Some typical newsgroups.*

There are several thousand newsgroups. Most sites do now receive news, although some restrict the number of newsgroups which they make available. The number of articles sent via news each day is immense, and any system with limited storage may be unable to store them all. Additionally, each system receiving news will assign to each article an **expiry date** after which that article will be removed from the system. This is a mechanism for controlling the storage occupied by news articles, and the individual expiry dates – which are usually set up on a per-newsgroup basis – are determined by the System Administrator. In order to read news articles, you should use a **newsreader**. This is a program which is similar to a mail reader, but is specifically tailored to reading (or inspecting) a large number of messages quickly. A good newsreader allows you to select which newsgroups you wish to read, and to filter out articles whose subject is not of interest to you. This is important, since the number of articles in some newsgroups can be very large. You may have access to newsreaders such as rn, trn or nn. Most Web browsers also have the facility to act as newsreaders.

rn = 'read news'
trn = 'threaded rn'
nn = 'network news'

Encryption and data security

One of the obstacles in the path of the Internet being used outside the academic community has been the problem of data security. If a confidential message is sent, both the sender and the recipient need to be sure that the message has been received intact, and that the message has not been intercepted and read by a third party. This is a serious issue. For instance, if a company wishes to trade using the Internet, financial transactions between itself and clients must remain confidential; without encryption, messages can be intercepted. Private networks, which have been used by financial institutions for many years, have used encryption as a matter of course.

A commonly used method for encryption is known as **public key encryption**, which relies on the recipient of a message possessing two **keys**. A key is a secret password, except it is very big (typically at least 256 bytes), and is normally generated automatically (and randomly) by the encryption software. The first key, the **private key** is known only to the sender; the second, the **public key**, is made publicly available (perhaps via a Web page). The sender encrypts their message using the recipient's public key, which can *only* be decrypted using the recipient's private key.

Various algorithms for performing public key encryption are known. The first was invented by Rivest, Shamir and Aldeman, and has mathematical foundations based on the factorisation of large numbers. Now licensed by **RSA Data Security**, it is used in many applications, including Web browsers, and with the support of credit card issuers some companies do now allow credit card transactions to take place across the Internet.

Encryption is generally classified as either **strong** or **weak**. A weakly encrypted message can be decoded reasonably quickly if you have access to sufficiently powerful computing resources. Strong encryption prevents this, not by making decoding impossible, but by making the time necessary to do it so long that it is pointless trying. A difference lies in the size of the keys – the bigger the key, the stronger the encryption. In 1991 Phil Zimmermann wrote a program called **PGP** which uses a strong RSA algorithm to encrypt data and which he distributed on the Internet.

Unfortunately encryption generates strong feelings – law enforcers fear it can be used by criminals, and governments are apprehensive about being unable to control and intercept communications. For several years the US authorities tried (unsuccessfully) to prosecute Zimmermann under legislation forbidding the unauthorised export of munitions. In some countries, including France and Russia, encryption is prohibited. Another approach to controlling the spread of encryption which some countries are attempting to legislate on is **key escrow**, in which there are *three* keys, the third held by a third party such as a government agency. A message can be decoded using the third key alone.

FTP

A utility which allows you to transfer files between systems is known as **FTP**, for which command `ftp` is provided. Supposing you are authorised to use `bubbles`, and your usercode on `bubbles` is `chris`, then a dialogue may look like:

```
$ ftp bubbles.eng.newt.ac.uk
Connected to bubbles.eng.newt.ac.uk.
220 box FTP server (Version 5.60) ready.
Name (bubbles.eng.newt.ac.uk:chris):chris
331 Password required for chris.
Password:(password)
230 User chris logged in.
ftp>
```

You then have available commands enabling you to transfer and to manipulate files; many of these are similar to their UNIX counterparts, and include `ls` and `cd`. The *prompt*

Also called the 'secret key'

Including Mastercard and Visa

Billions of years

PGP = 'Pretty Good Privacy'

Strong encryption software in the US is classed as a munition

FTP = 'file transfer protocol'

is `ftp>`, and you can respond with the command `help` to obtain brief help on which commands `ftp` has available. Commonly used commands are `get` which allows you to receive a file from the remote system, and `put`, with which you can transmit a file to the remote system. For example, to get file `junk` from `bubbles` (the received file will be copied to the current directory):

```
ftp> get junk
200 PORT command successful.
150 Opening ASCII mode data connection for junk (659 bytes).
226 Transfer complete.
local: junk remote: junk
701 bytes received in 0.061 seconds (11 Kbytes/s)
```

If – as is likely – you do not have an account on any remote system, you can still use `ftp`. A number of institutions maintain a 'library' of files which are made available to the Internet community using **anonymous FTP**. This is a mechanism with which you can connect to a system using `ftp` as the account name; you provide your e-mail address as the password for the remote system's information. You can then retrieve files from the remote system. For example, suppose Newtown had set up an anonymous FTP 'server' called `ftp.newt.ac.uk`, then

```
$ ftp ftp.newt.ac.uk
Connected to squiggles.newt.ac.uk.
220 squiggles FTP server (Version 5.60) ready.
Name (ftp.newt.ac.uk:chris):ftp
331 Guest login ok, send ident as password.
Password:chris@bubbles.eng.newt.ac.uk
230 Guest login ok, access restrictions apply.
ftp>
```

In this example, machine 'ftp' is a synonym for a machine which is also called 'squiggles'

If you have access to news, you will quickly discover FTP sites which have files that will interest you, and which you can use to practise using `ftp`. One word of warning – the Internet can only carry a certain amount of data at any one time. If a lot of people are attempting to move data or send messages between systems at once, the speed at which the transfers happen will decrease. If you use FTP at 'peak' times it will be much slower than 'off-peak'. Therefore if at all possible you should avoid normal office hours, and if a site you are accessing is abroad, remember that there is probably a time difference, and time your work accordingly. FTP sites in the United States, for instance, should be accessed from the UK early in the morning.

The time in New York is 5 hours in advance of GMT, and on the US West Coast it is 8 hours

A version of `ftp`, known as NcFTP (command `ncftp`), may be available on your system, which will automatically connect you to a remote FTP site as an anonymous user, without the necessity of typing in the username FTP and your username as password. NcFTP has extra commands not available with ordinary FTP, and provides a superior user interface. Most Web browers are also able to connect to anonymous FTP sites. If you use a local network to which non-UNIX machines, such as PCs, are connected, it will probably be possible to use FTP to transfer files between the UNIX and non-UNIX machines.

`ncftp` was developed at the University of Nebraska-Lincoln by Mick Gleason

Web browsers

The availability and choice of Web browsers, and the facilities offered, are changing frequently. At present, there are three principal browsers which are widely used.

NCSA Mosaic was the first Web browser to become popular. It was written at the National Center for Supercomputing Applications at the University of Illinois in Urbana-Champaign. It has remained a good browser, however since it is written and maintained by a small number of volunteers the facilities it supports are now much more basic than some other browsers.

Netscape is a product of Netscape Communications Corporation, a company whose founders were at one time involved with NCSA Mosaic. The company is developing the browser rapidly, and introducing innovative features such as **frames** (enabling a browser window to be subdivided into smaller windows) and **plug-ins** (so that third-party software vendors can develop utilities which will integrate seamlessly into the browser).

Both Mosaic and Netscape are currently available free to individuals (for personal use) and to educational institutions, but a licence fee is required for commercial use. Both are available for several platforms, including UNIX machines and PCs running the Windows operating system.

Including Windows 3.1, Windows NT and Windows 95

Internet Explorer is the browser written by **Microsoft Corporation**, and the competition between Microsoft and Netscape for domination of the market for browsers is intense. It too is packaged with extra features, but is only available for PCs and not for UNIX machines. It is distributed together with the **Windows 95** operating system.

These three browsers enable the user to do far more than just view documents on the Web. They are news readers, they will manage your email, and will download files from FTP sites. Be careful – it is very easy to send and receive mail using a Web browser, but the facilities it offers are unsuitable for a sophisticated user, and it does not replace a purpose-designed mail program.

WARNING!

Also called 'hotlists'

Web browsers can use encryption for communicating with sites on the Internet, if this is required. Using **bookmarks** you can note interesting documents you have seen so that you can return to them later. Other facilities may be available – all these browsers have excellent on-line help and it is easy for you to find out for yourself.

There are other browsers, mainly distributed by Internet service providers, but few if any seem likely to survive. There is one exception - the browser called **Lynx** is the only browser specifically designed for use with dumb terminals. Originally developed at the University of Kansas it is now maintained at the Worcester Foundation for Biological Research.

Some sites will install them under different names

UNIX commands for running the Mosaic, Netscape and Lynx Web browsers are usually `mosaic`, `netscape` and `lynx`.

HTML

It is likely you will have the opportunity of writing your own documents (**pages**) for the Web. The acronym **HTML** stands for **Hypertext Markup Language** – the important word here is **markup**. A Web page consists of a file, containing text, and extra information which is the markup, and takes the form of **tags** which specify *how* the text is to appear and

Tag names are not case sensitive

links to other Web pages. The appearance of a page can include **tables**, **forms**, images, frames and Java applets. Each tag is enclosed in angle brackets, and has a **name** followed by optional **options**. For instance, `<IMG SRC="tree.gif">` is a tag specifying that an image contained in source code file `tree.gif` should appear at that point on the page.

SRC='source code'

Some tags come in pairs, such as `<TABLE>` which with its end tag `</TABLE>` *encloses* a table. For some such pairs of tags, such as `<P>` which starts a new paragraph, the end tag is optional; for most it is compulsory.

The smallest HTML file looks like the following:

```
<HTML> <HEAD> <TITLE>My first HTML file</TITLE> </HEAD>
<BODY>
<H1>Header</H1>
</BODY> </HTML>
```

HTML tags do not have to start on separate lines

Note the document is enclosed in `<HTML>...</HTML>` tags, and is then subdivided into a **head** and a **body**.

A link to another document is denoted using the `<A href="`*link*`">` tag; the link is either a filename on your machine, or the name of a document somewhere elso on the Web, known as a URL.

A = 'anchor'

URL = 'Uniform Resource Locator'

Your browser will have help facilities which will explain in more detail what other HTML tags are available, and what options can be used with them. Figure 10.2 lists the most commonly encountered tags; those described as *enclosing* text *require* both the start and end tags (with the exception of the optional `</P>`). The others have no end tag.

Tag	Description
`<P>`	Enclose paragraph
` `	Insert line break
`<HR>`	Insert horizontal dividing line
`<IMG SRC="`*image*`">`	Insert image
`<H`*n*`>`	Header (*n*=1 for large size, *n*=6 for very small size)
`<UL>`	Enclose unordered list (bulletmarked)
`<OL>`	Enclosed ordered list (numbered)
`<LI>`	Enclose list element
`<PRE>`	Enclose preformatted text
`<EM>`	Enclose emphasized text (usually italicised)
`<STRONG>`	Enclose strong text (usually presented as bold face)
`<CODE>`	Enclose text representing code fragments
`<I>`	Enclose italicised text
`<B>`	Enclose bold face text
`<TT>`	Enclose text to be dispayed in fixed-width font
`<FORM>`	Enclose a fill-out form
`<TABLE>`	Enclose a table
`<APPLET CODE="`*program*`">`	Java applet

Figure 10.2   *HTML tags.*

Java

One development which, at the time of writing, has the potential to revolutionise the Web, is the programming language **Java**, designed and developed by Sun Microsystems. Programs written in Java can be copied by a Web browser *and run by the browser*.

Only Java-compatible browsers can run Java programs

Java has been created with security as a high priority, and its authors are confident that viruses will not be transmitted by running Java programs on browsers. For instance, a Java program running on a browser *cannot* access the host machine's file system, so cannot read from or write to files. The actual mechanism used is that a Java program is compiled to a low-level code called **bytecode**, and it is this code which is copied and run by a browser. Bytecode is machine-independent, and so it does not matter what machine a browser is running on. As a result, useful programs can be run without the computer user needing to be familiar with the machine which they are using.

A Java program can also be compiled and run on a machine as an *application* program, just as any other compiled language can, in which case the security mechanisms are *not* used.

Superficially Java resembles the language **C++**; it has a similar syntax and it is **object-oriented**. There are fundamental differences, however, and it would be unwise to think of Java as a dialect of C++. Java is supplied with substantial libraries of pre-written modules (**classes**), enabling a Java programmer to create programs with sophisticated user interfaces quickly and easily. Many of the classes are tailored for use in a Web-based context, and cater for multimedia and for Internet communication.

A Java program is run by a browser by use of the HTML `<APPLET>` tag with option `CODE` specifying the URL containing the compiled bytecode.

Other information services

The Internet serves to transmit data between computer systems. That data may relate to interactive sessions (`telnet`), transfer of files (`ftp`), transmission of hypertext (`http`), or any other information which has established protocols. Some sites have set up servers which will provide information in a manner which superficially resembles FTP, except rather than expecting the user to know the files which are required, will provide the data in a format which can be 'browsed through'. Utilities which allow you access to this 'information universe' include `archie`, which automatically searches for documentation and software at FTP sites, and `gopher`, now seldom used, but which resembles rudimentary hypertext. This is an active development area, and both the utilities which sites make available and the networked information which can be accessed, are rapidly changing. Many – if not all – will eventually be subsumed by improvements in Web browsers, as has already happened with `gopher`.

X and GUIs

GUI = 'Graphical User Interface'

At the time of writing, several windowing systems, or **GUIs**, are available. Of these, the most common one which runs with UNIX is known as **X**. This developed from a project undertaken jointly by MIT, IBM and DEC in the mid-1980s, and known as **Project Athena**. The present system is sometimes referred to as **X11** since it is version 11.

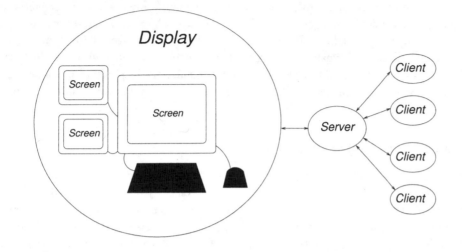

Figure 10.3   *A typical X display.*

In order to understand X some concepts must first of all be explained. These have very specific meanings to X, and not the more general meanings which they would have in other contexts. Central to X is a **display**, which means the terminal or workstation at which you are working. A display includes the keyboard, mouse, etc., together with one or more **screens**, as pictured in Figure 10.3. Normally a display – such as a typical workstation – will only have one screen, but one can conceive of systems where a user has several screens controlled from a single keyboard. Each display is controlled by a program called an **X server**. The X server manages all the data sent between the UNIX system and the display, controls the mouse and keyboard, and displays text and graphics on the screen.

Each program you then run which needs input from or output to the display is known as a **client**. The server and its clients communicate by exchanging messages – those from client to server are known as **requests** and a message from the server to a client is an **event**. Thus requests involve clients telling the server to write something on a screen, and events inform clients of happenings elsewhere on the system. Some systems require you to start X by typing in a command to your terminal (often this command is `startx`); on others X is started automatically when you login. The type of terminal known as an **Xterm** or **X terminal** is a graphics terminal which has within it a processor which runs one program and one only, namely an X server.

When you have started X, a program will be run called a **window manager** or a **desktop manager**, whose function is to control the layout of the graphical objects on the screen, to convert input (key presses, mouse movement, etc.) to specific X requests, and to interpret X events which affect the look and state of the screen. Thus X defines the *messages* which are transmitted between server and client, and the window or desktop manager generates and interprets the messages.

The difference between a window manager and a desktop manager is that a desktop manager will have extra functionality built-in. As standard on UNIX systems will be a manager called **CDE**, which includes an editor and a file manager. If you wished to examine

CDE = 'Common Desktop Environment'

your collection of files (and perhaps move or delete some), using a window manager you would need a window running a copy of the shell into which you would type suitable commands such as ls and mv. If you were using the CDE, this would not be necessary as the file manager would enable you to perform the same tasks with a 'user-friendly' user interface, obviating the need to learn the shell commands. At the present time, a desktop would not *replace* a shell, but for very simple use of a UNIX system would mean that knowledge of the shell would not be necessary.

Locales and extended character sets

In previous chapters the concept of **locale** has been mentioned briefly. A locale defines the character set available to the user, and may include such symbols as accented letters or letters from other alphabets. A locale can be defined by the user, or can be chosen from a standard set of locales, although the availability of these may be limited. Complementary to locales is a family of standards, known as **LATIN-1**, **LATIN-2**, etc., which supplement the ASCII character set by defining extra characters (which locales may use). In Figures 10.4 and 10.5 the non-ASCII characters from the LATIN-1 character set are presented. It is thus possible to write programs, and to produce documents, which use these characters in addition to ASCII characters, and for keyboards to be made with keys for the extra characters. At the time of writing, however, it is not easy to use the LATIN-1 character set, since these character set standards are fairly recent and most utilities are set up for ASCII only. Wordprocessors and text formatting programs may have their own methods for including non-ASCII characters. If you need to prepare documents which require use of these other characters, you should consult your System Administrator.

There are currently 9 'LA-TIN' character sets

ÀÁÂÃÄÅÆÇÈÉÊËÌÍÎÏÐÑÒÓÔÕÖØÙÚÛÜÝÞß
àáâãäåæçèéêëìíîïðñòóôõöøùúûüýÿþ

Figure 10.4   *LATIN-1 letters.*

Text formatting and wordprocessing

It is very likely that you will wish to produce some documents while using your UNIX system. You could create text files using vi, and then send them to the printer using lp, but you would then have little control over how they were formatted – in fact, no more than if you were using a typewriter. There exist utilities which will format text (and possibly simple pictures as well) according to your specifications; these include aligning paragraphs and tables, counting page numbers, changing fonts, highlighting sections of text, and so on.

These utilities are of two main types. Firstly there are **wordprocessors**, sometimes described as **WYSIWYG**. These are used on graphics terminals, and will allow you to create on the screen an exact copy of the document you wish to print. Such a processor will be menu-driven, and further discussion of how to use one would be inappropriate here.

WYSIWYG = 'What You See Is What You Get'

¦	broken bar	±	plus-minus
¤	currency sign	¥	yen sign
£	pound sterling	¢	cent sign
ª	feminine ordinal	¼	one quarter
¬	not sign	½	one half
§	section sign	¾	three quarters
®	registered trade mark	©	copyright
–	soft hyphen	¨	diaeresis
µ	micro sign	¹	superscript one
¶	pilcrow sign	²	superscript two
¯	macron	³	superscript three
º	masculine ordinal	·	middle dot
´	acute accent	÷	division sign
¸	cedilla	×	multiplication sign
°	degree sign	¿	inverted question mark
«	left angle quotation mark	¡	inverted exclamation mark
»	right angle quotation mark		

Figure 10.5   *Other LATIN-1 symbols.*

Such processors are more common on PCs than on UNIX machines, although one called **FrameMaker** is in common use, and it is likely others will follow.

> FrameMaker is a registered trademark of Frame Technology Corporation

The second type is known as a **text formatter**. This requires you to create a file which contains the text you wish to be formatted together with special instructions describing *how* the formatting is to be performed. These include such commands as 'start a new paragraph here', 'begin a table' or 'italicise the following text'. The processor will then read in that file and output the text formatted according to those instructions. Two main text formatters of this variety are likely to be available to you. One is called **troff**, and was the first one available under UNIX. The other is called T$_E$X. This is similar to the paradigm employed by HTML, with one crucial difference. A text formatter has markup which will allow the author to design a page of text *accurately*, whereas HTML does not permit that precision. The markup for a text processor is generally richer than HTML, and more complex.

> Known as 'markup'

> Pronounced 'tee-roff'
> T$_E$X, originally developed by Donald Knuth, is usually pronounced 'tek'

Neither troff nor T$_E$X is user-friendly in its 'raw' form, and both come equipped with **macros**, which allow them to be used more easily. Unless you need to do some very complex work you would only use them with those macros. The macro package commonly used with troff is known as ms, and that with T$_E$X is known as L^{A}T$_E$X. The command to run L^{A}T$_E$X is `latex`. Figure 10.6 is the L^{A}T$_E$X source for the first few lines of this chapter.

> The most recent version is L^{A}T$_E$X2$_\epsilon$

```
\chapter{Internet and multimedia}
\objectivesstart{In this chapter you will learn about:}
\boxitem networks and graphical user interfaces;
\boxitem wordprocessing and text formatting utilities;
\boxitem legal requirements incumbent on using a computer
system;
\boxitem the Internet and the World-Wide Web.
\objectivesend
\noindent
The first nine chapters of this book have concentrated on
those aspects of UNIX, specified in the POSIX standard,
which are relevant to someone meeting UNIX for the first
time.   POSIX.1 and POSIX.2 do not attempt to cover aspects
of a computer system beyond those basic utilities which
a shell and kernel might be expected to include. Further
discussion of UNIX systems, and how they fit into the more
general scheme of things, is therefore essential if you
are to get the most benefit from use of your UNIX system.

\hdr{Networks}
Most general-purpose computers are parts of {\textbf
networks}\index{\textrm network}, that is, they are linked
to other computers in some manner which allows them
to communicate with each other. In an office, desk-top
computers may be able to access a common filestore and
exchange electronic mail. A company might use hand-held
computers which use radio signals to talk to each other and
to computers in the company's offices.  Larger computers
may be linked by high-capacity telephone lines.
Some or all of those computers may also be connected to the
Internet.

It is becoming increasingly difficult for a computer user
to be aware of exactly where the physical communication
links between the system they are using and 'the rest of
the world' are situated, and what form they take. We can,
however, broadly categorise the types of network which
exist, and indicate their function from the user's point
of view.
```

Figure 10.6   *The LATEX source for the start of this chapter.*

Troff, although now seldom used, and not as powerful as TEX, has one very specific and widespread application. The source for manual pages is written using troff and the macro package `man`. Markup for troff is either a two-letter **request** preceded by a dot in column 1, or an in-line request, usually two or three alphanumeric characters preceded by a backslash. The source for the manual page for *topic* is typically held in files such as `/usr/man/mann/topic.n` where *n* is the volume, if you wish to see some examples.

Images

A graphics terminal can display images, where an image might be a colour landscape, a geometric diagram, or even just a block of text. The word **image** is used for any such picture that can be displayed on a graphics terminal. How can we describe, store and display images in a UNIX environment? The problem is that they are two-dimensional, and there is no obvious method of describing their contents (unlike ordinary text, which can be stored character-by-character). This even holds true for blocks of text, if there is a selection of fonts, since the fonts must be represented somehow. There is the added problem of the accuracy of the description – most methods of storing images only do so approximately. An everyday example would be a television picture, where if you look closely at the screen you can see the 'granularity' of the image.

We can assume that, if we wish to represent an image that we are to store on UNIX, then we will create a file containing data representing that image. That file will be manipulated using any standard UNIX utilities. There are two questions that must be answered:

- In what format is the data contained in such a file?

- What utilities exist to decode such data and display it?

There are a number of methods of coding image data, each having a variety of programs which are able to use the data. A format which is useful for images containing text is **dvi** although it does not take the form of a human-readable programming language, so cannot be edited by hand. A dvi file can be viewed on a terminal running X using `xdvi`. Alternatively, a dvi file can be converted to PostScript using the command `dvips` and then viewed using `gs` or `ghostview`. Wordprocessors and text formatters, which were discussed in the previous section, often use either PostScript or dvi as an 'intermediate' code which can be sent to a printer. [dvi = 'device independent', and pronounced 'dee-vee-eye'. gs = 'ghostscript']

'Irregular' images, such as fine art, are more efficiently coded using formats such as **GIF** and **JPEG**, and many viewers will display images coded with these formats. Commonly available is `xv`, which is able to handle both of these formats, together with other less frequently encountered ones. [GIF = 'Graphic Interchange Format'. JPEG = 'Joint Photographic Experts Group']

It is possible to store sequences of images, which can be considered as part of a 'movie'. Various different formats have been used to store these in the past, but a family of industry standards collectively known as **MPEG** have recently been evolving. MPEG.1 and MPEG.2 have become formal standards, whilst MPEG.4 is being drafted. Utilities for viewing MPEG files include `mpeg_play` and `xanim`. [MPEG = 'Motion Picture Expert Group']

A very widely used format which you are likely to encounter is **PostScript** which is also a general-purpose computer language. The language specifies the placement of objects within a defined viewing space. PostScript works best where those objects are words or [PostScript is a trademark of Adobe Systems Inc.]

geometric objects, but is able to handle images defined as 'bitmap' patterns. PostScript is a language, not just a notation, and it can perform calculations, and an image coded using PostScript can be scaled with ease. Since it uses only printable characters, a PostScript file can be edited by a PostScript programmer.

Actually, most PostScript files are generated automatically. Many printers, especially laser printers, have within them processors which control what they print, and use PostScript as the language which instructs them. Utilities which send data to such a printer will typically produce an intermediate PostScript file which the printer will then read.

PostScript files can represent both black-and-white and colour images, and can be viewed on a terminal using utilities such as `gs` and `ghostview`. The PostScript file in Figure 10.7 can be used to draw the European flag (in colour, though it's shown here in greyscale).

Audio

Some terminals are equipped with a speaker and a microphone, and are capable of recording and playing sounds. This is usually achieved by sending data to device `/dev/audio`, if sounds are to be played on the speaker, or receiving data from the same device, if it is to be stored. There is a device `/dev/audioctl` which is used to control such characteristics as speaker volume and sample rate.

Typically you would interact with these devices using programs such as `soundtool`, `gaintool` or `play`. Since audio is a relatively recent feature of UNIX systems, we may expect more sophisticated software for processing such data to become available in the near future.

WARNING!

If your system is capable of supporting audio, be sensitive to other users. Do not disturb other users in the same terminal room with noise from your terminal – use headphones.

MIME

MIME = 'Multipurpose Internet Mail Extension'

Electronic mail has, until recently, only been capable of sending text messages. Improvements in network technology, together with a new mail standard known as **MIME**, mean that messages can also include images (in various formats), audio files, and other non-textual data. MIME works by including within a text file instructions to a mailer. These instructions can indicate various properties of the message.

In a similar fashion to FTP

For example, MIME can indicate that the next few lines of the mail message are an encoded version of an image file – a mailer reading such a message would automatically decode those lines and display the image. MIME also allows a mail message to refer to documents not actually present in the message, but stored on some system connected to the Internet. Such an instruction would cause a mail program to connect to that remote system and retrieve the document automatically.

When a document is transmitted using HTTP, MIME is used to specify what type of data is contained within the document. The use of MIME extends well beyond just mail.

Legal issues

As a computer user, certain duties and restrictions are placed upon you by law. Your institution will also issue rules and regulations relating to use of the institution's computer

```
%!PS-Adobe-3.0 EPSF-3.0
%%Title: European Flag
%%Date: January 28th 1993
%%Creator: Nick Holloway
%%BoundingBox: 25 400 565 760
%%EndComments

295 580 translate        % drawing relative to the centre
0.0 0.2 1.0 setrgbcolor  % draw the blue background
newpath
-270 -180 moveto 0   360 rlineto
540     0 rlineto 0 -360 rlineto
closepath fill

1.0 0.7 0.0 setrgbcolor  % draw the 12 golden stars
0 30 330 {
    gsave
        dup rotate        % rotate flag so star position up
        0 120 translate   % move to centre of star
        neg rotate        % and realign with the page
        0 20 translate    % move to top point of star
        0 0 moveto
        162 rotate        % point in direction for first side
        5 {               % for each of the 5 sides...
            0 38 rlineto  % ...draw a side...
            144 rotate    % ...and position for next
        } repeat
        fill              % colour it in!
    grestore
} for
showpage
%%EOF
```

Figure 10.7   *The European flag.*

system. You are required to obey these regulations, and provided you do, you are unlikely to be in breach of the law. In the context of United Kingdom legislation, three Acts of Parliament relate specifically to using computer systems: the **Data Protection Act 1984**, the **Copyright Designs and Patents Act 1988** and the **Computer Misuse Act 1990**. The European Union in November 1995 issued a directive on Data Protection and related legislation, and UK law will be amended to follow the directive in due course.

Directive 95/46/EC

In the US, the **Communications Decency Amendment** of the **Telecommunications Reform Act 1996** has recently placed restrictions on material which can be placed on the Web, and is being challenged in the US courts on the grounds that it is in breach of the first amendment to the US constitution.

The first amendment guarantees freedom of speech

In the rest of this section some major issues which you should be aware of are mentioned. If you think that you may be affected by any of them, you should in the first instance seek further advice from your System Administrator.

- *You must not access any computer system which you know that you do not have authorisation to use.* This is relevant given that you may have access to computer networks such as the Internet.

Authorisation may be implicit, such as advertised documents on the Web

- *You must not deliberately damage other users' data.* This is common sense, really.

- *You must not deliberately access any data which you know that you do not have authorisation to access.* 'Hacking' is illegal.

- *You must be aware of copyright legislation.* Data and programs held on computers can be subject to copyright just as the printed word can be.

- *Strict regulations apply if you wish to store data relating to living individuals.* The Data Protection Act requires under most circumstances that personal data be 'registered', and lays down restrictions about what can be done with personal data.

- *You must not store pornographic, obscene, or otherwise offensive material.* Don't be tempted.

- *You must not divulge official secrets (or other classified information).* Legislation protecting sensitive confidential government or military information is rigorously enforced in most countries.

- *You must not disseminate defamatory material.* Libel/slander is as illegal on computers or computer networks as it is on paper.

Such as health and safety legislation

Computer law is relatively new, and many of the provisions of United Kingdom legislation which relate to computers are as yet untested in the courts, but the penalties for breach of the law can be severe. There are many other laws which to a greater or lesser extent govern our relationship with and use of computers. Make an effort to be aware of the law – it *does* affect you – and remember that ignorance of the law cannot be used as a defence in court.

Answers to problems

Chapter 2

2.1 Whenever you need to find out information about a command, you should use `man`. With option `-k` followed by a keyword, `man` will display commands related to that keyword. In this case, a suitable keyword would be `login`, and the dialogue would look like:

```
$ man -k login
...
logname (1) - print user's login name
...
```

The correct answer is therefore `logname`. Try it:

```
$ logname
chris
```

2.3 As in problem 2.1, you should use `man` to find out more information on `date`. In this case, however, you need specific information on `date`, so the command you use is

```
$ man date
```

The manual page for `date` is likely to be big, but this is not a problem. Remember that the manual page is divided into sections. First of all, notice that under section `SYNOPSIS` the possible format for arguments to `date` is given:

```
SYNOPSIS
        date [-u] [+format]
```

This indicates that date may have up to two arguments, both of which are optional (to show this, they are enclosed in square brackets). The second one is preceded by a + symbol, and if you read further down, in the `DESCRIPTION` section it describes what **format** can contain. This is a string (so enclose it in quotes) which includes **field descriptors** to specify exactly what the output of `date` should look like. The field descriptors which are relevant are: `%r` (12-hour clock time), `%A` (weekday name), `%d` (day of week), `%B` (month name) and `%Y` (year). The argument you would give to `date` would therefore be:

The POSIX standard specifies only two arguments to `date` — some systems may in addition allow others

```
+"%r on %A %d %B %Y"
```

so that the command you would type would be

```
date +"%r on %A %d %B %Y"
```

2.5 The first decision to be made is which command to use to display the machine's users. Use man with a suitable keyword:

```
$ man -k logged
...
who (1) - show who is logged on
...
```

The script should therefore echo the one-line message and then run who:

```
echo "The following are logged in:"
who
```

Chapter 3

By this stage, you should be getting used to using man to decide which commands to use, and to decide which options to give to commands.

'1' is digit one

3.1 Use ls with options -a (to include listing 'dot' files), -1 (to list filename on each line of output) and -t (to list in order of modification time). Pipe this output to head, with option -n 3 (to select the first three lines in the list):

```
ls -1at | head -n 3
```

3.3 Use ls with option -i (to list inodes as well as filenames), and pipe the output to sort with option -n (to indicate numerical rather than lexical order):

```
$ ls -i | sort -n
```

'1' is lower-case letter l

3.5 Running ls with options -l and -d followed by a dot (the current directory) will display details about the current directory. The owner of the file begins in character column 16 and may continue until column 23, so use cut with option -c to select columns 16 to 23:

```
ls -ld . | cut -c 16-23
```

3.7 Use ls with option -l, and pipe the output to sort. Since the fifth field is the field which is to be used for sorting comparisons, argument +4 should be given to sort (the fields are counted starting from 0). The sort should be according to numerical order rather than lexical, so sort requires option -n also:

```
ls -l | sort -n +4
```

Chapter 4

4.1 Use `crontab` `-e` to edit the `crontab` file, adding the following line to that file:

```
0 8 * * 1 echo "Good Morning"
```

This instructs `crontab` to run

```
echo "Good Morning"
```

(whose output will be mailed to you) at 0 minutes past 8 o'clock every first day (i.e. Monday) of every week regardless of the month or the date.

4.3 Use `at` to schedule the alarm call by giving it argument `now + 1 hour`. Remember that `at` will **mail** you the standard output from the commands you give it, so you must send the message directly to the device which is your terminal. You can find out the device name using `tty`:

```
$ tty
/dev/ttypf
$ at now + 1 hour
at> echo "Your alarm" >/dev/ttypf
at> ctrl-D
```

4.5 This is an exercise in knowing the names of the environment variables which store the relevant information. These were presented in figure 4.1.

```
echo "Your username is $LOGNAME"
echo "Home directory is $HOME"
echo "You are using a terminal which is a $TERM"
echo "The default lineprinter is $PRINTER"
```

4.7 Set `MY_NAME` to be the string containing your first and family names, and enclose that string in quotes so that the blank space between the two names is part of that string:

```
$ MY_NAME="Chris Cringle"
```

Chapter 5

5.1 Use `find` followed by a dot (the current directory) to select files from the current directory, and argument `-print` to list them. Other arguments are needed to perform the selection, and as there are many possible arguments you should read the manual page. Argument `-type` `f` selects regular files. To check on the file size, argument `-size` followed by an integer **n** selects all files whose size is between (**n**-1) and **n** blocks of 512 bytes. The command thus becomes:

```
$ find .  -type f -size 1 -print
```

5.3 The script must initially check that all the arguments are readable, then it can simply
pass them all to cat:

```
for i in "$@"          # For each argument
do
    if [ ! -r "$i" ]   # if it is not (!) readable (-r)
    then exit 1         # then bomb out
    fi
done


cat "$@"               # cat the files
```

5.5 Use printf to format and who to find the users. With option -q two lines will be
displayed by who, the first contains the users, the second the number of them. Use
head to select the first line of the output of who -q, then a for loop to print out
each of them in turn. A count must also be made so as to know when to finish a line
of output.

```
COUNT=""                        # Use to count to 4
ALLUSERS=$(who -q | head -1)    # Get the list of users
for i in $ALLUSERS              # Loop through in turn
do
    printf "%10s" $i           # Print each in width 10
    COUNT=$COUNT"x"            # Add an "x" to COUNT
    if   [ "$COUNT" = "xxxx" ] # If 4 "x"s in COUNT
    then printf "\n"            #   terminate the line
         COUNT=""              #   and reset COUNT
    fi
done


# At the end, if the final line contains less than
# four columns, that line must be terminated
if   [ "$COUNT" != "" ]
then printf "\n"
fi
```

5.7 You need to keep a count of the number of the line, which can be incremented with
the aid of bc. Use read to read in the standard input line-by-line, and printf to
ensure that the format is the same as cat -n (i.e. six character columns for the line
number, followed by two blank spaces, followed by the line).

```
LINENUMBER=1          # To store the line number
while read LINE       # 'read' returns false at end
do                    #              of input
    # Print the line number and the line
    printf "%6d  %s\n" $LINENUMBER $LINE
```

```
      # Add one to the line number
      LINENUMBER=$( echo "$LINENUMBER + 1" | bc )
done
```

Chapter 6

6.1 This is an exercise in arithmetic expansion only.

```
printf "Enter cm: "          # Prompt
read CM                      # Read number of cm
FEET=$(( $CM / 30 ))         # Feet is easy to calculate
CM=$(( $CM % 30 ))           # Replace CM by residual cm
                             #   above the previous feet
INCHES=$(( $CM * 12 / 30 ))  # Convert residual cm
                             #   to inches


printf "%d cm is %d foot %d inches\n" $CM $FEET $INCHES
```

6.3 This exercise requires the use of the test command at the start to perform the
checks on the filename given as argument to the script, followed by a miscellany of
UNIX utilities.

```
# Check number of arguments
if      [ $# -ne 1 ]
then    echo "Requires one argument"
        exit 1
# If a single argument, check it's readable
elif [ ! -r $1 ]
then    echo "File is unreadable"
        exit 1
fi


LINES=0              # To count number of lines
COL=0                # To count number of characters
while read LINE      # read returns false at end of input
do
    # Characters on line (including NEWLINE)
    COLONLINE=$( echo "$LINE" | wc -c )
    # Add to COL and subtract 1 for the NEWLINE
    COL=$(( $COL + $COLONLINE - 1 )
    # Increment line count
    LINES=$(( $LINES + 1 )
done <$1             # Input from the file

# Since 2 decimal places needed, must use bc to
#    calculate the average, not arithmetic expansion
```

```
AVERAGE=$( echo "scale=2; $COL / $LINES" | bc )

# Finally, display the average
printf "Average is %s\n" $AVERAGE
```

6.5 Use date to display the hour, then pattern match on the output:

```
# Format %H gives the hour as 2 digits, 00-23
case $( date "+%H" ) in

    # Any hour 00 to 09, also 10 or 11
    0?|1[01]) echo Good Morning ;;

    # Any hour 12 to 17
    1[2-7])    echo Good afternoon ;;

    # Any other time is evening
    *)         echo Good evening ;;
esac
```

6.7 This solution involves a moderately complex while loop.

```
# Check number of arguments
if   [ $# -ne 1 ]
then echo "Requires 1 argument"
     exit 1
fi

# Check the argument is between 1 and 15
case $1 in
    [1-9]|1[0-5])  ;;
    *)             echo "Require number 1-15"
                   exit 1
esac

LINE=1      # Use to count through the lines
while [ $LINE -le $1 ]
do
    # For the top and bottom lines of the square
    if [ $LINE -eq 1 ] || [ $LINE -eq $1 ]
    then    printf "+"      # First column
            COL=2           # Column to print in next
            while [ $COL -lt $1 ]
            do    printf "-"
                  COL=$(( $COL + 1 )
            done
```

```
                printf "+\n"    # Last column, and end line
        # The middle lines
        else    printf "|"       # First column
                COL=2            # Column to print in next
                while [ $COL -lt $1 ]
                do     printf " "
                       COL=$(( $COL + 1 )
                done
                printf "|\n"    # Last column, and end line
        fi
        LINE=$(( $LINE + 1 )
done
```

6.9 This could be solved using pattern matching on the arguments, but since there are many possibilities for running eurhello with options, the clean way to solve the problem is with getopts.

```
# Set the string GREETING to the usual greeting
GREETING="Hello"

# Use getopts to go through the possible options
# These can be f or g, or G followed by an argument
# An option is stored in OPTIONNAME when encountered
while getopts fgG: OPTIONNAME
do
    # Check the three possibilities
    case "$OPTIONNAME" in
            # French
        f) GREETING="Bonjour";;
            # German
        g) GREETING="Guten Tag";;
            # Argument to -G held in OPTARGS
        G) GREETING="$OPTARG";;
    esac
done

# If the script is called with invalid options,
# getopts will discard them and display an error
# message

# Now get rid of the options which have been processed
shift $(( $OPTIND - 1 )

# Check a name string is an argument to the script
if [ $# -eq 0 ]
then echo "usage: $0 [-f] [-g] [-G greeting] name"
```

```
        exit 1
fi

# Finally, produce the output
echo "$GREETING $*"
```

Chapter 7

7.1 This is a straightforward function, just requiring two commands between the braces.

```
thisyear() {
   printf "This year is "
   date "+%Y"
   }
```

Alternatively, this could be done using echo:

```
thisyear() {
   echo "This year is $( date +%Y )"
   }
```

Note that the argument to date does not **need** to be enclosed in quotes, as in this case it contains no characters with special meaning to the shell. In the first solution they are included for clarity, in the second one they were omitted to avoid clashing with the quotes enclosing the argument to echo.

7.3 The body of this function is the same as a script, if you had written it as a script instead. It must be written as a function in order that the value of PATH in the current shell can be altered — you cannot export from a child process to its parent.

```
addtopath() {
   printf "Enter directory name: "    # Prompt
   read NEW                           # Read name
   if [ -d "$NEW" ] &&                # Check directory
      [ -r "$NEW" ]                   # Check readable
   then PATH="$PATH":"$NEW"           # Update PATH
   fi
   }
```

7.5 The only complication with this example is that you must remember to enclose the sh -x in quotes, since there is a blank which is part of the alias:

```
$ alias debugsh='sh -x'
```

7.7 This is simple use of eval.

```
printf "Type in a variable name: "
read VARIABLE

# Construct the name of the variable
#    and echo its value
eval echo \$$VARIABLE
```

Chapter 8

8.1 We require a `grep` pattern which matches the five vowels, either upper- or lower-case, separated by zero or more other characters. The pattern [Aa] matches an upper- or lower-case 'a', and the pattern .* (dot followed by an asterisk) any sequence of other characters:

```
$ grep '[Aa].*[Ee].*[Ii].*[Oo].*[Uu]' /usr/dict/words
```

8.3 Use `grep` with option -l:

```
$ grep -l program *
```

8.5 Begin by replacing all characters which are not digits by blanks, then translate each blank to a newline, remove all empty lines, and finally sort the result to be in numerical (rather than lexical) order, removing duplicates:

```
sed 's/[^0-9]/ /g' |     # Pattern [^0-9] matches
                         #        any non-digit
    tr " " "\n"   |       # Replace blanks by newlines
    grep -v '^$' |       # Select all lines NOT
                         #        matching ^$
    sort -u -n           # Sort, remode duplicated lines
                         #        into numerical order
```

8.7 Use `csplit` to split the file at the position denoted by the BRE ^middle$ – we have to 'anchor' the m and the e to be at the start and end of a line so that it does not split the file earlier if there is another word **containing** middle.

```
$ csplit /usr/dict/words '/^middle$/'
```

Chapter 9

For these problems, the solutions are in no way unique. See if you can devise different answers.

9.1a The number of trains run is simply the number of lines in the file, which is the value of NR at the end of processing the data.

```
END { print NR }
```

9.1b Use a variable count (say) to count the lines where the seventh field is 5:

```
$7 == 5 { count++ }
END { print count }
```

9.1c Similar to the previous problem, but the count is incremented when field 7 is 5 and field 5 is fast:

```
$7 == 5 && $5 == "fast" { count++ }
END { print count }
```

9.1d Rather than incrementing count by one each time a line of input relates to May (field 7 is 5), sum all the values of field 4:

```
{ passengers += $4 }
END { print passengers }
```

9.1e As the previous example, but the incremented fare total depends on the value of field 5. The solution presented here does the calculation in pence, and converts to pounds only at the end.

```
$5 == "local" { fares += 10*$3*$4 }
$5 == "fast" { fares += 12*$3*$4 }
$5 == "express" { fares += 15*$3*$4 }
END { printf "%.2f\n", fares / 100 }
```

9.1f In this case we have three variables for the different fare categories.

```
$5 == "local" { localfares += 10*$3*$4 }
$5 == "fast" { fastfares += 12*$3*$4 }
$5 == "express" { expressfares += 15*$3*$4 }
END { printf "%.2f\n", localfares*100/ \
                (localfares+fastfares+expressfares) }
```

9.1g In this solution, floating-point arithmetic is used throughout, all the calculations being performed in pounds.

```
BEGIN { rate["local"] = 0.10
        rate["fast"] = 0.12
        rate["express"] = 0.15 }
{ cost = 100 + 5*$3
  revenue = $3*$4*rate[$5]
  profit = revenue - cost
  printf "%d/%d %s-%s: ", $6, $7, $1, $2
  if (profit > 0)
      printf "profit %.2f\n", profit
  else
      printf "loss %.2f\n", -profit
}
```

Appendix — summary of utilities

The utilities defined in POSIX.2 are summarised here in alphabetical order. To discover which commands your system has available which are *not* covered by the standard, you should use man.

Utility	Description	Chapter
alias	define or display aliases	7
ar	maintain a library archive	7
at	execute commands at a specified time	4
awk	pattern scanning and processing language	9
basename	display non-directory part of filename	3
batch	execute commands when system load permits	4
bc	calculator	5
bg	run a job to the background	4
break	exit from for, while or until loop	5
cat	concatenate and print files to standard output	2
cd	change working directory	3
chgrp	change file group ownership	3
chmod	change file access privileges	3
chown	change file ownership	3
cksum	file checksum utility	7
cmp	compare two files	3
comm	select/reject lines common to two files	7
command	execute a simple command	7
continue	continue for, while or until loop	5
cp	copy files	3
crontab	schedule periodic background work	4
csplit	split a file according to context	8
ctags	create a 'tags' file	7
cut	select columns or fields from each line of a file	3

date	display current time and date	2
dd	convert file format	7
df	display free disk space	3
diff	show differences between two files	3
dirname	display directory part of a pathname	3
du	display file space usage	3
echo	write arguments to standard output	2
ed	basic text editor	2
env	set environment for a command	4
eval	construct command by concatenating arguments	7
exec	execute command by replacing shell process	7
exit	cause the shell to exit	6
expand	replace tabs by spaces	7
export	set export attribute for a variable	4
expr	evaluate an arithmetic expression	6
ex	text editor (see vi)	2
false	returns 'false' value, exit status 1	5
fc	process command history list	4
fg	run a job to the foreground	4
file	describe file contents	3
find	find files	5
fold	fold lines	3
getconf	get configuration variables	7
getopts	parse options for a utility	6
grep	select lines matching regular expression	8
head	show the first few lines of a file	3
id	display information about a user's identity	3
jobs	list the jobs in the current session	4
join	relational database operator	7
kill	send a signal to a process	4

`ln`	link files	3
`locale`	display information about the 'locale'	7
`localedef`	define the 'locale'	7
`logger`	log message for the System Administrator	7
`logname`	display your login user name	2
`lp`	send files to a printer	3
`ls`	list files (directory contents)	2
`mailx`	process electronic mail messages	2
`make`	maintain and update groups of programs	7
`man`	display manual pages	2
`mesg`	allow or deny messages on your terminal	2
`mkdir`	create new directories	3
`mkfifo`	create a FIFO file	7
`more`	'pager'	2
`mv`	move files	3
`newgrp`	change your current group-id	3
`nice`	run a command with changed priority	4
`nm`	display name list of an object file	7
`nohup`	run a command immune to hangups	4
`od`	dump files in various formats	3
`paste`	merge corresponding lines of text files	3
`patch`	apply changes to files	3
`pathchk`	check pathname is valid	7
`pax`	file archiver and format translator	3
`pr`	a very basic formatter for text files	3
`printf`	write formatted output	5
`ps`	display information about processes	4
`pwd`	display working directory	3
`read`	read a line from standard input	4
`readonly`	set read-only attribute for variables	4
`renice`	change the priority of a running process	4
`return`	return from a function	7
`rm`	remove a file	2
`rmdir`	remove empty directories	3

sed	stream editor	8
set	set options and positional parameters	6
sh	the shell	2
shift	shift positional parameters	5
sleep	suspend execution for a time interval	4
sort	sort or merge text files	3
split	split a file into pieces	7
strings	display printable strings in a file	3
strip	remove unnecessary data from executable files	7
stty	set terminal options	7
tabs	reset the tab positions	6
tail	show the last few lines of a file	3
talk	talk to another user	2
tee	duplicate standard input	2
test	evaluate expression	5
time	display execution time for a command	4
touch	change last modification time of a file	3
tput	change terminal characteristics	6
tr	translate characters	8
trap	intercept a signal	7
true	returns 'true' value, exit status 0	5
tty	display the terminal name	2
umask	change access privileges when files are created	3
unalias	remove alias definition	7
uname	display the system name	2
unexpand	replace spaces by tabs	7
uniq	filter out repeated lines	3
unset	unset options and positional parameters	6
uudecode	decode a file which was coded with uuencode	7
uuencode	encode a binary file	7
vi	full-screen text editor	2
wait	suspend process until completion of another process	4
wc	word, line and byte count	3
who	list who is using the system	2
write	write a message on another user's terminal	2
xargs	construct argument list and execute command	7

Index

! 123
!= (arithmetic expansion) 119
!= (awk) 179
" 83
\ 83
\\ (backslash) 109
\a (alert) 109
\b (backspace) 109
\f (formfeed) 109
\n (newline) 109
\r (carriage return) 109
\t (tab) 109
\v (vertical tab) 109
' 77, 83
((ASCII character) 7
((command grouping) 95
() 140
) (ASCII character) 7
) (case) 124
)) 118
* (arithmetic expansion) 119
* (ASCII character) 7
* (awk) 179
* (bc) 96
* (BRE) 162
* (pattern matching) 122
* (tr) 160
+ (arithmetic expansion) 119
+ (ASCII character) 7
+ (awk) 179
+ (bc) 96
+ (ERE) 163
+= (awk) 188
- (ASCII character) 7
- (awk) 179
- (bc) 96
- (BRE) 162
- (filename) 6
- (option) 16

- (pattern matching) 123
- (standard input) 25
-empty (find) 108
-eq (test) 100
-exec (find) 108
-ge (test) 100
-gid (find) 108
-group (find) 108
-gt (test) 100
-inum (find) 108
-le (test) 100
-links (find) 108
-lt (test) 100
-name (find) 108
-ne (test) 100
-perm (find) 108
-print (find) 107
-printf (find) 108
-size (find) 108
-type (find) 108
-user (find) 108
. (ASCII character) 7
. (BRE) 162
. (command) 82
. (directory) 40
. (filename) 6, 40
. (vi address) 172
.. (directory) 40
.a (filename suffix) 123, 152
.c (filename suffix) 123
.f (filename suffix) 125
.o (filename suffix) 123
.p (filename suffix) 125
/ (arithmetic expansion) 119
/ (ASCII character) 7
/ (awk) 179
/ (bc) 96
/ (root directory) 40
/ (vi) 20, 22

/dev 85
/dev/audio 85, 214
/dev/audioctl 214
/dev/console 85
/dev/null 86
/dev/rst8 85
/dev/tty 85
/etc/passwd 190
/tmp 135
/usr/dict/words 28
0 (vi) 22
0< 27
1> 27
2> 27
: 95
: (vi) 19
:+ 116
:- 114
:0 (vi) 21
:= 115
:? 115
:q (vi) 22
:q! (vi) 22
:w (vi) 22
:wq (vi) 22
:$ (vi) 21
:n (vi) 21
:] 158
;; 124
< (arithmetic expansion) 119
< (ASCII character) 7
< (awk) 179
< (input redirection) 24
<< 33
<= (arithmetic expansion) 119
<= (awk) 179
= (alias) 142
= (ASCII character) 7
= (test) 100
= (variable assignment) 77
== (arithmetic expansion) 119
== (awk) 179
> (arithmetic expansion) 119
> (ASCII character) 7
> (awk) 179

> (output redirection) 24
> (prompt) 84
>= (arithmetic expansion) 119
>= (awk) 179
>> 27
? (ERE) 163
? (more) 29
? (pattern matching) 122
? (vi) 20, 22
@ (ASCII character) 7
[(ASCII character) 7
[(BRE) 161
[(pattern matching) 122
[(test) 98
[: 158
90
(string length) 116
$ (ASCII character) 7
$ (BRE) 162
$ (prompt) 15
$ (variable) 76
$ (vi) 20, 22
$(86
$((command substitution) 86
$((118
$* 111
$0 111
$0 (awk) 177
$1, $2, etc. 111
$1, $2, etc. (awk) 177
$? 93
$@ 112
$[118
$# 111
${ 114
% 69
% (arithmetic expansion) 119
% (ASCII character) 7
% (awk) 179
% (bc) 96
% (conversion specification) 109
% (prompt) 15
%% 69
& 66
& (sed) 167

&& 94
&& (awk) 179, 182
{ (ASCII character) 7
{ (csplit) 169
{} (find) 108
} (ASCII character) 7
~ 29
~ (directory) 41
~v (vi) 29
^ (awk) 179
^ (bc) 96
^ (BRE) 162
^ (vi) 20, 22
_ 6
] (arithmetic expansion) 118
] (ASCII character) 7
] (test) 98
` 86
| 31, 92
| (ASCII character) 7
| (ERE) 163
|| 94
|| (awk) 179, 182
a (bc arctan function) 97
a (vi) 19, 22
absolute filename 40
access privileges 47
ACK (ASCII character) 9
action (awk) 176
Ada 4
alias 142
alias 142
ampersand (ASCII character) 7
and-list 94
anonymous FTP 205
API 12
apostrophe (ASCII character) 7
append 27
Application Programming Interface 12
ar 149
archie 208
archive 59
argument 16
arithmetic expansion 118
array (awk) 187

array index (awk) 187
article (news) 202
ASCII 6, 154
associative array (awk) 187
asynchronous list 91
Asynchronous Transfer Mode 199
at 71
at queue 72
atan2 (awk arctan function) 193
ATM 199
audio 214
awk 175
axe 21
b (more) 29
b (vi) 20, 22
background 66
backquote 86
backslash 83
backslash (troff) 213
backup 59
bandwidth 199
base 60
basename 61
bash 5, 15
BASIC 4
basic regular expression 161
batch 72
batch queue 72
baud 151
bc 95
BEL (ASCII character) 9
bell 8
bg 69
bit 6
block 154
body (HTML document) 207
bookmark 206
border 3
Bourne shell 5
bracket expression 161
BRE 161
break 106
BS (ASCII character) 9
BSD 11
buffer 23

buffered input 21
button 3
byte 6
bytecode 208
c (bc cosine function) 97
C (language) 4, 11
C shell 5
C++ (language) 4, 208
c89 147
Cambridge Ring 199
CAN (ASCII character) 9
caret (ASCII character) 7
case 124
cat 24
cc 147
cd 41
cd (ftp) 204
CD-ROM 6
CDE 4, 209
character 6
character class 158
character special file 85
checkdigit 6
checksum 147
chgrp 48
child process 67
chmod 49
chown 49
circumflex (ASCII character) 7
cksum 147
class (Java) 208
client (X) 209
close (telnet) 201
cmp 53
collating sequence 158
colon 95
colon character (ASCII character) 7
colon-mode (vi) 19
comm 152
comma (ASCII character) 7
command 141
command 91
command argument 16
command grouping 102
command history list 70

command option 16
command substitution 86
command-mode (vi) 19
comment 90
Common API Specification 12
Common Desktop Environment 4, 209
Communications Decency Amendment 216
compilation 64
compiler 4
compound command 92
compress 60
compression 60
Computer Misuse Act 1990 216
continuation prompt 84
continue 106
control character 8
controlling terminal 65
conversion specification 109
Copyright Designs and Patents Act 216
core 106, 139
coredump 139
cos (awk cosine function) 193
cp 44
cpio 59
CPU 8
CR (ASCII character) 9
crontab 73
csh 5
csplit 169
ctags 152
ctrl-\ 139
ctrl-C 28, 151
ctrl-D 16, 23
ctrl-D (vi) 20, 22
ctrl-G 8
ctrl-U (vi) 20, 22
ctrl-] 201
current directory 39
current message (mailx) 30
cursor 2
cut 55
cw (vi) 22
D (vi) 19, 22
data 5

Data Protection Act 1984 216
date 15
dbx 139
DC1 (ASCII character) 9
DC2 (ASCII character) 9
DC3 (ASCII character) 9
DC4 (ASCII character) 9
dd 154
dd (vi) 19, 22
debugging shell scripts 127
decoration 3
default job 69
definition 140
DEL (ASCII character) 9
DEL key 23
delimiter 55
DESCRIPTION (manual page) 36
desktop manager 3, 209
device 3, 84
df 42
DIAGNOSTICS (manual page) 36
diff 53, 61, 152
directory 39
directory hierarchy 39
dirname 61
disk 6
display (X) 209
DLE (ASCII character) 9
domain 200
dot (filename) 6
dotdot 40
double quote 83
double quote (ASCII character) 7
du 61
dumb terminal 2
dvi 213
dvips 213
dw (vi) 22
e (bc exponential function) 97
e (vi) 20, 22
EBCDIC 7
echo 32, 109
echoing 7
ed 21
EDITOR 77

egrep 163
elapsed time 74
electronic mail 29
elm 30
EM (ASCII character) 9
emacs 21
email 29, 144
emergencies 28
ENQ (ASCII character) 9
env 78, 81
ENVIRON (awk) 188
environment 76
EOT (ASCII character) 9
ERE 161, 163, 186
esac 124
ESC (ASCII character) 9
ESC (vi) 19
ESC key 8
escape character 8, 109
escape character (telnet) 201
ESCAPE key 8
ETB (ASCII character) 9
Ethernet 199
ETX (ASCII character) 9
eval 143
event (X) 209
ex 21
exclamation mark (ASCII character) 7
exec 142
executable shell script 81
execute permission (file) 47
executing 16
EXIT 139
exit 16, 126
exit status 93
exp (awk exponential function) 193
expand 152
expiry date 203
export 79
expr 120
extended regular expression 161, 163, 186
false 95
fc 70
FDDI 199

`fg` 69
`fgrep` 163
Fiber Distributed Data Interface 199
field 55, 176
field delimiter 55
field separator (`awk`) 189
field width 110
FIFO 151
FIFO file 99
`file` 51
file 6
file access control 47
file group 47
file owner 47
`FILENAME` 184
filename 6, 42
`FILENAME` (`awk`) 184
filename suffix 123
`FILES` (manual page) 36
filesystem 42
filter 157
`find` 107, 154
floating point number 179
`FNR` (`awk`) 184
`fold` 56
`for` 104
foreground 66
form (HTML) 206
FORTRAN 4
frame 206
FrameMaker 211
FS (ASCII character) 9
`FS` (`awk`) 184, 189
FTP 204
`ftp` 204
function 140
function (`awk`) 192
function (`bc`) 96
function definition 92, 140
Fvwm (window manager) 3
`gaintool` 214
`get` (`ftp`) 205
`getconf` 150
`getline` (`awk`) 193
`getopts` 129

`ghostview` 214
GID 46
GIF 213
gigabyte 39
global cursor 2
global variable 79
`gopher` 208
graphics character 6
graphics terminal 2
grave accent (ASCII character) 7
`grep` 163
group 46
group (file) 47
group-id 46
`gs` 214
GS (ASCII character) 9
GUI 208
`h` (`vi`) 19
hangup 74
hard link 45
hardware 3
hash (ASCII character) 7
`head` 52
head (HTML document) 207
help 35
`help` (`ftp`) 205
here-document 33
high-level language 4
`HOME` 77
home directory 41
hotlist 206
HT (ASCII character) 9
HTML 206
HTTP 202
hypertext 202
Hypertext Markup Language 206
hyphen (standard input) 25
`i` (`vi`) 19, 22
icon 3
`id` 46
idle time 18
IEEE 1
`if` 103
image 213
`include` (directory) 134

index (array) 187
inode 42
input 1, 23
input mode (vi) 19
int (awk truncation function) 193
Internet 200
Internet Explorer 206
Internet number 200
interpreter 4, 64
IP address 200
ISO 3166 200
ISO C 12
j (vi) 19
J (vi) 20, 22
Java 4, 208
job 67
job control 67
jobnumber 66
jobs 68
join 152
JPEG 213
k (vi) 19
kernel 4
key 204
key escrow 204
keyboard 1
kill 67, 139
killed process 65
Korn shell 5
ksh 5
l (bc logarithm function) 97
l (vi) 19
LAN 198
LATEX 211
latex 211
LATEX2ε 211
LATIN-1 7, 210
LATIN-2 210
length (of a string) 116
length (awk) 193
length (bc) 97
less 28
lib (directory) 134
lines 52
link 45, 48, 132

link (hypertext) 206
linking (object files) 147
Linux 13
list command 92, 94
list command grouping 95
ln 45
local area network 198
local variable 79
locale 154, 158, 210
locale 154
localedef 154
log (awk logarithm function) 193
logger 154
logging in 15
logging out 16
login 15
login shell 32, 65
logname 37
LOGNAME 76, 77
logout 16
low-level language 3
lp 58
lpr 58
ls 18, 41
ls (ftp) 204
Lynx 206
lynx 206
machine code 3
macro 211
magnetic disk 6
magnetic tape 6
mail 30
mailbox 134
mailx 29
make 148
makefile 148
Makefile 148
makefile 148
man 35
manual page 35
manual volume 35
markup 206, 211
match (awk) 193
matching list 161
mesg 30

Microsoft 206
MIME 214
minus sign 6
mkdir 43
mkfifo 151
more 28
Mosaic 206
mosaic 206
mouse 2
MPEG 213
mpeg_play 213
ms (troff) 211
mush 30
mv 44, 61
NAK (ASCII character) 9
NAME 113
name (array) 187
name (HTML tag) 206
NAME (manual page) 36
named pipe 151
NcFTP 205
ncftp 205
NCSA 206
NCSA Mosaic 206
Netscape 206
netscape 206
network 8, 198
Network Information Service 190
Network News Transfer Protocol 202
newgrp 46
NEWLINE 52
newline character 8
news 202
newsreader 203
NF 185
NF (awk) 184
nice 74
NIS 190
NL (ASCII character) 9
nm 152
nn 203
NNTP 202
nohup 74
non-printing characters 7
nonmatching list 161

NOTES (manual page) 36
NP (ASCII character) 9
NR (awk) 184
NUL (ASCII character) 9
o (vi) 22
object-oriented language 208
octal dump 57
od 57
OFS (awk) 184, 192
Open Group 12
Open Software Foundation 12
open system 12
operating system 4
OPTARG 130
OPTIND 130
option (HTML tag) 207
options 16, 129
OPTIONS (manual page) 36
or-list 94
ORS (awk) 184, 192
OSF 12
other (file) 47
output 1, 23
output field separator 192
output record separator 192
owner (file) 47
packet 199
packet switching 199
page 206
pager 28
parameter expansion 113
parent (directory) 40
parent process 67
parity bit 7
parity check 7
PASC 12
Pascal 4
passwd 16
password 14
paste 55, 153
patch 61
PATH 77, 82
pathchk 149
pathname component 77
pattern (awk) 176

pattern matching 121
pattern space (sed) 165
pax 59
PC 2
period 6
perl 195
perm symbol 49
pg 28
PGP 204
PID 65
pipe 31
pipeline 92
play 214
plug-in 206
positional parameters 111
POSIX 1, 11
POSIX compliance 10
POSIX.1 4
POSIX.2 1
PostScript 59, 213
pr 58
precedence 97
prefix (csplit) 169
Pretty Good Privacy 204
print (awk) 177
PRINTER 77
printf 109
printf (awk) 178
printing character 6, 8
prioritise 74
private key 204
process 64
process-id 65
processing time 74
processor 64
program 4
Project Athena 208
prompt 15
protocol 202
ps 65
PS1 77
PS2 77, 84
public key 204
public key encryption 204
put (ftp) 205

pwd 41
q (more) 29
Q (vi) 21
q (vi) 22
q! (vi) 22
question mark (ASCII character) 7
queue 72
quit (telnet) 201
rand (awk random number) 193
range 158
RE 161
read 79
read permission (file) 47
readonly 84
real time 74
record 176
record separator 191
redirection 24
regular expression 161
regular file 99
relative filename 40
release 17
renice 74
repetitive strain injury 15
request 213
request (HTTP) 202
request (X) 209
return 142
RETURN (more) 29
RETURN key 8
reverse slant (ASCII character) 7
rm 27
rmdir 43
rn 203
root 40
RS 191
RS (ASCII character) 9
RSA Data Security 204
RSI 15
running process 65
running program 16
s (bc sine function) 97
scale (bc) 96, 97
scheduling 67
screen 1

screen (X) 209
screendump 3
script 32, 126
script (awk) 176
script (grep) 163
script (sed) 165
secret key 204
sed 165
SEE ALSO (manual page) 36
semicolon (ASCII character) 7
sequential list 91
server (X) 209
service provider 201
set 128
sh 5, 32
shell 4
SHELL 77
shell options 127
shift 113
SI (ASCII character) 9
SIGALRM 140
SIGEXIT 139, 140
SIGHUP 74, 139, 140
SIGINT 139, 140
SIGKILL 67, 139, 140
signals 67
SIGQUIT 139, 140
SIGTERM 140
SIGTTIN 69
simple command 92
sin (awk sine function) 193
single quote 77, 83
Single UNIX Specification 12
slash 40
sleep 66
SO (ASCII character) 9
soft link 132
software 3
SOH (ASCII character) 9
solidus 40
sort 56
soundtool 214
SPACE (more) 29
space character (ASCII character) 7
SPEC 1170 12

split 146, 168
split (awk) 193
spool (directory) 134
sqrt (awk square root) 193
sqrt (bc) 97
standard error 23
standard input 23
standard output 23
startx 209
stderr 23
stdin 23
stdout 23
stopped (process) 64
stopped job 68
stopped process 65
stream 23
strings 58
strip 149
strong encryption 204
stty 150
STX (ASCII character) 9
SUB (ASCII character) 9
sub (awk) 193
sub-domain 200
subdirectory 45
substr (awk) 193
suffix 60, 123
sum 147
SuperUser 10
surfing the Internet 202
suspended (process) 64
symbol 152
symbolic link 132
SYN (ASCII character) 9
SYNOPSIS (manual page) 36
syntax 90
system 10
system (awk) 193
System Administrator 10
system time 74
System V 11
T shell 5
tab character 8
TAB key 8, 133, 152
tab position 8, 133

table (HTML) 206
tabs 133, 152
tag (HTML) 206
tail 52
talk 31
tape 6
tar 59
target 148
tcsh 5
tee 34
Telecommunications Reform Act 1996 216
telnet protocol 202
temporary files 134
TERM 77, 78
terminal 1, 17
test 98
TEX 211
text files 52
text formatter 211
tilde (ASCII character) 7
tilde (directory) 41
time 74
time-sharing 65
tmp (directory) 134
token ring 199
tolower (awk) 193
touch 58
toupper (awk) 193
tput 132, 150
tr 158
trap 138
trapping signals 138
trees 40
trn 203
troff 211
true 95
tty 17
UID 46
UIUC 206
umask 50
unalias 142
uname 17, 36
uncompress 60
underline (ASCII character) 7

underscore 6
unexpand 152
Unicode 7
uniq 54, 152
Universal Time Coordinates 16
unset 114
unset variable 114
until 105
US (ASCII character) 9
Usenet news 202
USER 76
user-id 46
username 14, 18
UTC 16
utility 91
uudecode 144
uuencode 144
value 76
var (directory) 134
variable 76
VDU 2
version 17
vi 18, 172
vilearn 21
VISUAL 77
VT (ASCII character) 9
w (vi) 20, 22
wait 75
WAN 198
wc 53
weak encryption 204
Web browser 202
Web client 202
Web server 202
while 105
whitespace 133
who 18, 35
who symbol 49
wide area network 198
window 2, 17
window manager 3, 209
Windows (operating system) 206
word 6
wordprocessor 210
workstation 2

World-Wide Web 202
wq (vi) 22
write 30
write permission (file) 47
WWW 202
WYSIWYG 210
X 2, 208
x (vi) 19, 22
X server 209
X terminal 2, 209
X/Open 12
X11 208
xanim 213
xargs 154
xdvi 213
xedit 21
xmail 30
xv 213
ypcat 190
zsh 5
ZZ (vi) 19, 22